herod

PROFILE OF A TYRANT

Also by Samuel Sandmel

THE HEBREW SCRIPTURES
WE JEWS AND JESUS
THE GENIUS OF PAUL
PHILO'S PLACE IN JUDAISM
A JEWISH UNDERSTANDING OF THE NEW TESTAMENT

herod

PROFILE OF A TYRANT

by Samuel Sandmel

J. B. LIPPINCOTT COMPANY

Philadelphia & New York

PRINTED IN THE UNITED STATES OF AMERICA

Library of Congress Catalog Card Number 67-16920

In warm appreciation to many associates
(the "Fourth Floor")
for innumerable acts of kindness, and especially to

Miriam K. November
Maxwell Lyons
Rabbi Joseph Karasick

Contents

Genealogical Table[1]

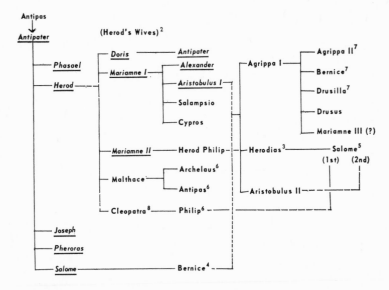

1. The underscored names figure prominently in our account. The broken lines indicate marriages. Solid lines indicate descent.

2. Of the ten wives, two are unnamed. Three additional named wives are Pallas, Phaedra, and Elpis.

3. She was married first to Herod Philip and later to Antipas. She bore Salome to Herod Philip.

4. Wife of Aristobulus.

5. Stepdaughter of Antipas; married in turn to Herod's son Philip and then to his grandson Aristobulus, one of the children of the executed Aristobulus.

6. Three sons among whom Herod's throne was divided at his death. Antipas, often known simply as Herod, executed John the Baptist. Herodias, after being divorced from Herod Philip and having borne Salome, married Antipas.

7. Mentioned in Acts of the Apostles. Paul speaks before Agrippa (25:13-27 and 26:27-32), in the presence of Bernice. She was the mistress of Titus, Roman general and then emperor. Drusilla married Felix, procurator of Judea, 52-60; he is mentioned in 23:24-24:27.

8. Not to be confused with Cleopatra of Egypt.

Part I

卍卍卍卍卍卍卍卍卍卍卍

Background: Herod's Father

168-63 B.C. 63-47 B.C.

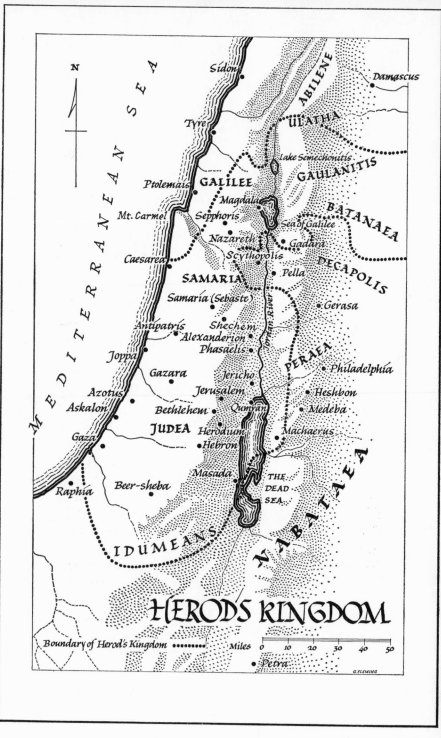

HEROD'S KINGDOM

Boundary of Herod's Kingdom ••••••••   Miles   0   10   20   30   40   50

G. FLEMING

1

"Herod" is one of those names which are known to many but usually in either a vague or even a confused kind of way. Herod is mentioned in the New Testament but so are some of his children, and they are there also called Herod, so that people often mix them up. The subject of this book is usually known as Herod the Great, probably not so much to confer an accolade on him for his achievements, which were mingled with his misdeeds, but simply to separate him from his children. In a sense he merits being called "the Great," especially when we limit the word to his eminence as a ruler and dissociate it from any broader acclaim. He was not born to the office of king, but he aspired to it, and he gained the throne, and he held it despite inordinate difficulties, and his will divided it for three of his children.

If the life of Herod were fiction, something dreamed up by a novelist, we should be inclined to wonder about some excesses. We would probably say that the novel was filled with too much violence, too much passion, too much despair, too much cruelty, too much plot. Moreover, since Herod lived in times and situations which merit the word "turbulent," the imperishable names of conquering emperors, who were also celebrated lovers, enter directly into the account, as if to strain our credulity through a pretentious name-dropping.

But it is fact, not fiction, which makes Herod a fascinating man to study. He was guilty of unusual inhumanity, yet his human traits, when they are perceived, enable us to understand better some of the many facets which are actually or potentially part of the make-up of every human being. Even in the repulsive deeds which Herod did, his humanness is always present.

This profile is principally an inquiry into what Herod was, and why. Although his particular qualities are in their essence independent of time and place, we can understand him the more clearly by an acquaintance with the world in which he lived. The international alliances and wars and conquests and rebellions are secondary to the study of the man himself. There is, however, the added significance for our day about that era in that Herod lived immediately prior to the time when Christianity was born within Judaism, and in the time when Judaism, nurturing a new inner vigor, was in the early stages of the profound transition from biblical to rabbinic religion.

While there is a sense in which Herod illumines his age, there is a deeper sense in which the age illumines Herod. We begin, therefore, as we must, with the matters of the background. The proper beginning is an event of little consequence when it took place, but without that event, the sequels which will come to concern us could not have happened. Specifically, at some time during the reign of the Judean monarch John Hyrcanus (135–104 B.C.), national and royal policy brought it about that the conquered Idumeans were forced to convert to Judaism, and among the converts were the forebears of Herod. That policy, extremely distasteful to our own age, was a relatively mild one, stemming, as such policies often did, from considerations of national interest—that is, internal unity—rather than from religious zeal.

John Hyrcanus was the second of the line of a Jewish dynasty, known sometimes as the Hasmonean, and sometimes as the Maccabean. The Hasmonean family, the chief hero of whom was Judah the Maccabee, had risen from insignificance into prominence through its dedicated military leadership after 165, more than a quarter century before John Hyrcanus had come to the throne. Palestinian Jewry before the Maccabees was a kingless people, and subject to the imperial power to the north, the Syrian Greeks, the Seleucids. These were the heirs of the conquest of Palestine by Alexander the Great in 331; their king was Antiochus IV Epiphanes. To the southwest lay another remainder of Alexander's empire, the Grecian kingdom of the Ptolemies of Egypt. The two Grecian kingdoms had alternated in their sway over Palestine; it lay between the two rivals, and any conquest by the one of the other necessitated the prior neutralization or acquisition of the Holy Land. Within Judea, especially within its capital, Jerusalem, there were to be found both the customary divisions among people (as well as some particular ones we shall notice, including partisans who saw personal advantage in subjection to the Seleucids and those who saw it in subjection to the Ptolemies). External conquest and internal machinations of these partisans prompted the Seleucids and the Ptolemies each to wish for and in fact try to gain a total allegiance of Judea to the one against the other. Antiochus IV Epiphanes came to the throne of Syria in 175, when Judea was that kingdom's vassal. To safeguard his southern border against the prospect of an Egyptian invasion, which he learned was in the process of development, he determined to move against the Egyptians. He made two campaigns, the first of which took place in 169/168.

Judea, though subject to Antiochus, was ruled internally by a succession of high priests, including some who acted in the way that history has demonstrated is the usual manner of the cleric with political power: self-service, chicanery, ruthlessness, and cruelty. The high priest in those times was one Menelaus, who was able to maintain his advantageous, indeed lucrative, office by resorting to

· 1 3

briberies of the Seleucid officials, and also by the repression of the Jews who opposed him, especially the surviving adherents of a certain Jason from whom Menelaus had seized the high priesthood in 176

In 169, after his first campaign in Egypt, Antiochus Epiphanes set out to return to Antioch, his capital. He paused to visit his subject city Jerusalem. He had Menelaus escort him into the sacred Temple, and there he helped himself to a sizable portion of the vast Temple treasuries. A year later, in 168, Antiochus embarked on a second expedition against the Ptolemies, and, though he defeated the Egyptians, he ran directly athwart the power of Rome then rising in the east. The Romans ordered Antiochus out of Egypt, and Antiochus felt compelled to comply with the menacing demand. It chanced at this juncture—in that age rumors of all kinds circulated in abundance—that the report got about that Antiochus had died. Jason, who had been in exile, seized the occasion to return to Judea, to muster a small army, and to set out against Menelaus with the intention of regaining the high priesthood. When he arrived at Jerusalem to besiege it, Menelaus took refuge in the fortress there, to withstand Jason's attack. Antiochus, however, was very much alive, and, having been humiliated by the Romans, he had no intention of allowing the indignity of an ousted Jason supplanting his appointed vassal Menelaus. So his generals laid siege to the city, which was already under siege, and Jason found it necessary to flee. The Antiochenes proceeded to raze the walls of Jerusalem, butcher its inhabitants, and desecrate the Temple by rededicating it to Jupiter. Moreover, an imperial degree prescribed that the subjects of Antiochus, all of them, were to be fused into a single people and were to accept the Greek religion, with the implication clear that the practice of Judaism was prohibited even in Judea. The plans of Antiochus called not only for the extirpation of Judaism but also for the offering of pagan sacrifices at Jerusalem and for the erection of pagan altars throughout the land.

The names "Menelaus" and "Jason" are Greek, not Hebrew, and they can be regarded as indicative of the broad Hellenization that had penetrated Palestine in various degrees and depths. For more than a century and a half since Alexander the Great had conquered the country, the Greek language had been current in Palestine, and it there vied with the native Aramaic and Hebrew, particularly among the upper classes, and especially in Jerusalem. Among these upper classes were those who were warmly receptive to the Grecian ways, seeking to blend these with their Judaism, and such people were known as "Hellenizers." Among the populace, as is natural, there were those who were aghast at the Grecian ways, and who considered them inconsistent with Judaism, and, indeed, its very antithesis; we know them as Hasidim, "pietists." Hence the clash at arms which shortly broke out between the pietist nationalists and the Greek overlords was both ethnic and religious, for those alien Greeks were seeking to destroy Judaism, and the resistance to them, in the Maccabean revolt, implied not only the need to do battle against aliens, but also to do battle against Jewish Hellenizers on behalf of preserving the Jewish religion from paganism.

The outcome of the Maccabean revolt was in part related to the peculiar geography of Palestine. The influence of the Holy Land on western history is so great that its relative tininess is a recurrent surprise to the modern reader and the modern visitor. This is the case even when the present-day division of Palestine into the states of Israel and Jordan is overlooked. The distance from Dan to Beer-Sheba, the traditional northern and southern points, is about 150 miles; the east-west dimension is about one hundred miles. (Portions of the modern state of Israel are measured, from east to west, in terms of about fifteen miles.) What is also surprising is the geographical distinctions within this small territory, for the regions are quite diverse.

The coast of Palestine is quite regular. It is broken by the mouths of many tiny streams, but by no single river of any importance. Devoid of cliffs and of estuaries, Palestine did not, and does not, possess natural harbors. The coast itself is sandy. Immediately to the east of the coast lies the coastal plain; north of the Carmel Mountains (where Haifa stands) this coastal plain is rather narrow; south of the Carmel the plain widens considerably, especially as one moves southward from the Plain of Sharon (today this former swampland has been transformed into productive orange groves), and then it broadens to the fertile agricultural plain which was shared, or fought over, with the Philistines.

Directly east of the irregular coastal plain lies what some have called the "western highlands." This is a line of ridges and plateaus. Its northern, or rather northeastern, extremity is beyond the usual boundary of Palestine, and is usually anchored in lofty Mount Hermon, within the territory we may call Syria. Indeed to outsiders, especially conquerors, Judea was deemed to be within Syria and as constituting its southern portion. Immediately to the south of that high ridge lies Upper Galilee, a plateau land which in places is three thousand feet above sea level; more southerly lies Lower Galilee, an area of fertile high hills, more or less bounded by Mount Carmel on the west and by the Sea of Galilee on the east. Upper Galilee was never dotted with as many towns as was Lower Galilee. To the south, the very fertile Plain of Esdraelon separated Lower Galilee from the highlands southward, which were called the "hill country of Israel," the capital of which, Samaria, accounts for its alternate name, the "hill country of Samaria." A rather broad valley, running from Joppa to Jericho, separates these hills from the "hill country of Judea," farther to the south, where lay such famous cities as Jerusalem, Bethlehem, and Hebron. South of Hebron the Judean hills taper down toward Beer-Sheba; south of Beer-Sheba lies the barren wilderness known as the Negeb.

The Jordan River is a deep cleft which divides the hill country west of it from the hill country and the plateau east of it. The eastern hills and plateau are known as the Arabah, and the Jordan rift as the Wadi Arabah. The northern part of the Arabah was known as Bashan; south of Bashan lay the fertile hills of Gilead, and still farther south the plateaus of Moab and Ammon, and beyond them the craggy desert lands of the Nabateans. The Jordan rift begins even farther north than Bashan; it follows the Jordan southward to the Dead Sea, and extends southward from the Dead Sea to the Gulf of Aqaba—and even farther south into Ethiopia.

The consequence of the distinctive geographical regions was the emergence throughout biblical history of regional political entities, whether of petty states or of independent cities. Since Palestine, the "land bridge" between Egypt on the west and Assyria or Babylonia or Persia to the east, participated in the great international commerce of the ancient world, certain cities flourished on the coastal plain, where travel was relatively easy, but towns in the hill-country often languished. Moreover, no matter how centrally the government might be established in Jerusalem, it could be difficult to maintain full control over the cities and towns that were at some distance. Just as cities in the past two hundred years have passed back and forth from German to French control, so too those cities which lay near the borders could veer from being Judean or Phoenician, or Judean or Syrian, or Judean or Nabatean.

When we speak of Judea, we are often trapped into vagueness and indefiniteness. Basically Judea is only that area encompassing Jerusalem and the surrounding regions. By extension, however, it can come to mean the territory controlled by the Judeans, whether on the coast or in Galilee, or east of the Jordan, or even southward into the Negeb. Geographically, Galilee is quite distant from Judea, but at those intervals when Galilee was fully under Judean control, Galilee was politically part of Judea. The word "Palestine," derived from *Philistia*, is not used in any surviving documents prior to the fourth Christian century. While today we ordinarily use the word "Palestine" in allusion to the territory comprised by modern Israel and Jordan, the word was unknown in the age of the Herods. We shall, accordingly, use instead the word "Judea," and this will ordinarily mean the extended political state, though occasionally it will mean the narrow geographical entity.

The absence of that full political unity in the Judean lands must lead us to face another consequence, which we shall soon encounter. It was the frequent capacity of certain Judean leaders, defeated by opponents in Jerusalem, to muster men and money from the countryside either to continue their fight or even, after another defeat, to renew and reinstitute it. We must not let the word "Judean" ring in our ears as if it implied the relative unity and stability that we ordinarily associate with countries and states in our time. The aspirant for hegemony, on being defeated in Jerusalem, might readily arouse patriotic Judeans to join him in an assault on the capital city, pitting Judean against Judean. The corollary was that the more remote the city was from Jerusalem, the less was it likely to be blindly loyal to the authority in Jerusalem, and the more was it likely to embrace whatever opportunity it thought it saw in rival leadership. Indeed, Judean patriotism was at its highest when there was an external foe to contend with, such as the Syrians, and patriotism and unity were at the highest point when independence, self-rule, was at stake, and religious freedom an issue. The hills of Galilee and Judea made it a difficult region to conquer and to keep conquered, for rebellion and guerrilla warfare were abetted by geography, and the residents had the confidence that their knowledge of the geography was a military asset denied to any outsider or invader.

The resistance by pietist nationalists to the Seleucids broke into the open in 168 in the town of Modin, and was led by the sons of what we may call a lay priest, that is, a priest not of the Temple at Jerusalem. The priest was Mattathias the Hasmonean (which latter word we cannot explain; perhaps it was simply a family name); chief among his five sons was Judah the Maccabee (often Maccabee is rendered as "hammer" but its meaning is uncertain). The Maccabean revolt was the abrupt emergence of a well-organized guerrilla warfare against the Syrian Greeks, a cause which aroused and attracted an increasing number of patriotic Jews and which spread in intensity throughout Judea. Antiochus was beset at that time on his eastern border by the growing power of the Parthians.

This eastern kingdom lay in what is today the northeastern part of Iran. Parthia threw off the yoke of the Seleucids about 248 B.C., and began to grow into a spreading and conquering empire. The Parthians turned westward to harass the Seleucids at the border, and later they intermittently made deep incursions into Seleucid territory. Antiochus regarded the Parthians as a more significant threat, so he entrusted the crushing of the rebellion in Judea to incompetent and unenthusiastic commanders. These proved to be no match for the highly motivated and highly skilled Judeans, and, guilty of underestimating the guerrillas, they were roundly defeated. The Maccabeans moved on to try to retake Jerusalem, still in Syrian hands. In an initial success they regained not the whole city but the sacred Temple, whose cleaning and rededication Jews still celebrate in the winter festival, Hanukkah. The Syrian Greeks and their Jewish sympathizers still occupied their fortress in Jerusalem; they proposed to the Maccabees a kind of truce which apparently the Romans favored, the terms of which were, on the one hand, the freedom to practice Judaism, and, on the other hand, a renewed political loyalty to the Syrian Greek state.

In view of their successes, the Maccabeans found it unnecessary to accept terms that they regarded as unsatisfactory, and, moreover, their increasing military might spurred them on to further goals. Communities of Jews resident in pagan cities, within tiny Judea and also beyond its borders, both to the south and across the Jordan to the east, were undergoing pressures and restrictions or persecutions from resident Greeks or from native populaces, as in Ammon and Idumea. The larger goals, then, became the relief of these communities by the reconquest first of all of Judea, and then of the neighboring lands. The fortress in Jerusalem remained still in Greek hands: the effort by the Maccabees there to dislodge them proved unsuccessful, and the new Syrian armies dispatched southward were only held off, not defeated. But negotiation became congenial to the Greeks, for in 163 Antiochus Epiphanes had died, and a pretender seized the throne of his son (Antiochus V Eupator). The new Syrian king was ready to offer religious freedom; he arranged for a new high priest, Alcimus, to replace Menelaus. But Alcimus appeared to the Jews to be a tool of the Greeks, as he was, especially after he executed some sixty men of good reputation who were leaders among the unquestionably pious Jews. The Maccabees wanted to oust Alcimus, since he was the symbol of the odious Hellenization condoned or espoused in some segments of Judea, and hence he was vigorously opposed by the nationalistic Maccabees and their followers. In a sense, internal Judean civil war tended to vie for a while with the continuing Maccabean rebellion against Syria. The warfare between the Maccabees and the Syrians was renewed, and another large Syrian army was sent into Judea in 161. Again Judah defeated the foe, led by Nicanor, a Syrian general.[1]*

Mere religious toleration by the Seleucids was, of course, no longer sufficient, for now national independence itself was the objective. To the Maccabean leader, Judah, it was clear that such independence needed the confirmation of Rome, so he dispatched an embassy there, with the result that the Senate concluded a treaty of amity with the Judean state about 161.

The Syrian Greeks, nevertheless, maintained their pressure and sent additional troops. Judah himself died in battle, and the revolt was all but crushed. Resistance to Syria persisted, however, and the tide turned first one way and then the other from 160 to 153. Then internal difficulties in Antioch, and attempted usurpations of the throne there, presaged the end of direct hostilities. In 152, Jonathan, one of the sons of Mattathias, was designated high priest by the new Antiochene king, Alexander Balas; by this act, the Syrian king virtually conceded Judean independence, especially since thereafter the Syrians did nothing to impede it. By this title of high priest Jonathan was the equivalent of the king. Disorders continued only on a lesser scale, as when warfare was again imminent between the Egyptians and the Seleucids (and Jonathan seized the opportunity to retake a number of Palestinian cities). Jonathan died in these continuing disorders, and his place as high priest was taken by another brother, Simon. From the Syrian monarch this Simon succeeded in wresting an acknowledgment of the tacitly conceded independence, in 142, and it is from this time that Jews began to date their legal docu-

* Superior numbers refer to Notes at end of the section.

ments, and that we can date the beginning of the Maccabean dynasty and of full Judean independence.

Simon recaptured even more Judean cities, from native pagan hands rather than from the Syrians. It was his policy to expel the pagan inhabitants from these cities. In 141 Simon was designated a "prince" as well as high priest; despite disorders he succeeded in consolidating much of the territory he controlled and in fostering relative tranquillity and prosperity. Simon died in 135, murdered by his son-in-law, so that Simon's son, John Hyrcanus, came to the throne. The latter, too, found himself in frequent difficulty with the Syrian Greeks, but he achieved an ultimate and enduring independence from them. Like his father, he proceeded to recapture Palestinian cities and areas. Hence, he entered into Idumea, subdued it, and forced the Idumeans to accept Judaism, reminding one of the effort of Antiochus Epiphanes to achieve religious conformity in his domain. This was the forced conversion that brought the forebears of Herod into the Jewish fold.

The Idumeans are the biblical Edomites, *Idumea* being the Grecian form of the word "Edom." A people kindred to the Judeans, they were descended, according to the biblical account, from that son of Isaac who bore two names, Esau and Edom, and who was the older brother of Jacob, who was renamed Israel. The habitation of the Edomites in early biblical times was in the area south of the Dead Sea, and their capital was the city known in Hebrew as Sela and in its Greek translation as Petra, "the rock." Unquestionably a people kindred to the Hebrews, the passage in Amos 1:11 denounces them for pursuing "their brothers"; Psalm 137:7–9 speaks vindictively of the misdeeds of Edom and commends the casting of Edomite children onto the rocks of the craggy mountain region. On the other hand, Deuteronomy 23:8 [23:7] reads, "Do not abominate the Edomite, for he is your brother." In this context the sense of *abominate* is "exclude"—that is to say, an Edomite, according to this sentiment, must not be excluded from the Jewish community. There are scholars who, despite the ascription of Deuteronomy to Moses as tradition has it, or to the year 621 as Higher Critics have often suggested, regard this verse, Deuteronomy 23:8 [23:7], as representing a very late period when the border between Judea and Idumea had become vague and the mixing of population an ordinary event.

The Edomites did not retain their original territory south of the Dead Sea. They filtered into southern Judea and, perhaps in the fourth pre-Christian century, abandoned their land and Petra to the Nabateans. The Nabateans were a desert people, who are often and ordinarily called by our sources simply Arabians. Possibly the Nabateans abetted the Edomite migration by pushing them northward. When we speak of Idumea, therefore, we have in mind southern Judea, and the region west, rather than south, of the Dead Sea. The new Idumean capital was the old Judean city of Hebron.

We do not know precisely what this forced conversion by King John Hyrcanus of the Idumeans meant, either with respect to the coercion or to the conversion itself. As to the conversion, in the ages long, long before the Maccabean period—indeed, in the very early times—a man living in a land sacred to a particular god, who moved to a land sacred to another, simply exchanged his old god for the new. In a sense this amounted to conversion, though it was bereft of both depth and choice. Such superficial conversion obtained in that part of the world, even for the Hebrews, as long as the primary connection was deity and land. The Babylonian exile, in the sixth pre-Christian century, had wrought a great change in Hebrew thinking, for it ruptured the primacy of the connection of deity and land, replacing it with the conception of the deity and the people; the exiled Jewish community in Babylon regarded itself as still an entity, and as still the special property and concern of its deity. Conversion in this latter situation was not the bare matter of geographical movement, but instead the matter of a deliberate and conscious choice of a new allegiance and a new worship, and without reference to geography. That is to say, before the sixth century, the Babylonian pagan who became a Jew did so by moving to Judea; in the sixth century the option was available for a Babylonian pagan to remain a Babylonian "national" and nevertheless to become a Jew by what we may describe as joining the Jewish community of Babylon. The obverse side of the passive admission of such a pagan to the Jewish community was the rise of a missionary impulse which actively counseled, urged, invited, or importuned the pagan to join. Indeed, after Jews left Babylon and returned to Judea, there arose the hope that innumerable people would convert; such is the import of Zechariah 8:20–23, written in the latter part of the same sixth century:

Thus says the Lord of Hosts: "Peoples shall yet come, even the inhabitants of many cities; the inhabitants of one city shall go to another, saying, 'Let us go at once to entreat the favor of the Lord, and to seek the Lord of hosts; I am going.' Many peoples and strong nations shall come to seek the Lord of hosts in Jerusalem, and to entreat the favor of the Lord. Thus says the Lord of hosts: "In those days ten men from the nations of every tongue shall take hold of the robe of a Jew, saying, 'Let us go with you, for we have heard that God is with you.' "

Conversion to Judaism, accompanied by acceptance into the Jewish people, became operative after the sixth century, even though we are not informed as to what it was precisely that a convert did to mark his conversion; probably the only formal rite in early times was the circumcision of the male convert. The Book of Ruth, which most modern scholars believe reached its present literary form in the fifth pre-Christian century, seems to be satisfied with a declaration, such as Ruth, a Moabite, made to her Jewish mother-in-law, Naomi, "Your people shall be my people, and your God my God. . . ."

Barred as we are from specific information, we confront an additional problem, again a product of our lack of knowledge. It is the question of the particular form, version, or emphasis in Judaism that a convert in the days of John Hyrcanus would be embracing. Here we may sketch in the outlines of the question of inner Jewish religious diversity which later we shall look at in more detail.

At the end of the second pre-Christian century Judaism was far from unified or monolithic. Were a conversion such as that of the Idumeans to have taken place either two centuries earlier or two centuries later, we could be reasonably sure of its external form. Earlier, it would have been conversion to the Judaism of the Temple and its sacrificial cult; later, to the Judaism of the synagogue and its prayer. At some point in the Maccabean period, synagogue-rabbinic Judaism began to arise, but the biblical, sacrificial system persisted, lasting until A.D. 70, when the Romans under Titus destroyed the Temple. We do not know whether the Judaism of the synagogue was sufficiently developed in the age of John Hyrcanus to suppose that it was in the synagogue that converted Idumeans found the focus of their new religion, or whether it was by allegiance only to the Temple cultus of Jerusalem. Possibly it was both, for there was a period between the unknown time of the origin of the synagogue, and that of the destruction of the Temple, in which synagogue and Temple abided side by side.

Connected with the rise of the synagogue was a partisanship that developed among the Jews, which was the consequence, just before the age of Alexander, of the rise to unparalleled eminence of the Five Books of Moses. While this partisanship was unconscious, it was nevertheless real. It took the form of an implicit rivalry between the Temple in Jerusalem with its array of priests descended in theory from Aaron, the brother of Moses, and Scripture itself. Though the pages of Scripture presented the charter for the Temple and its priests, it was able to become a surrogate, a substitute for the Temple. For example, the Temple was located in Jerusalem, and could, of course, not be moved from there, but Scripture could accompany Jews wherever they wandered and wherever they settled. The Temple rites, however faithfully they conformed with the prescription of the Sacred Books, were fixed and settled rites, and a man could be ignorant of the scriptural injunctions about the rites, through relying on the priests to execute the rites in the proper fashion; ignorance could become the handmaiden of dispensability, in the sense that one could, as it were, do without Scripture, provided he conformed to the rites. On the other hand, a dedication to Scripture ruled out ignorance; for, at the minimum, literacy and some comprehension were inescapably necessary.

Beyond this elementary contrast, which is here only illustrative and not historically based, there developed among Jews a historically significant set of antithetical positions regarding Scripture, rotating around the questions of literalism and of interpretation. The literalist maintained that the bare word of Scripture, shielded from all interpretive addition, was the authentic Scripture. The earnest student of Scripture, on the other hand, maintained that there was an array of inferences and corollaries which necessarily attached themselves to Scripture. The advocacy of scriptural literalism was found among the Sadducees, and that of interpretation, and of inferences and corollaries, among the Pharisees. Unhappily, we are not informed about the extent of the development of these conflicting viewpoints in the age of John Hyrcanus, and we are equally unin-formed to what extent the viewpoints were at that time crystallized into well-marked social groupings. More than one scholar has stubbed his toe through attributing to the Maccabean age the substance of the distinctions, and of the quarrels, between the Sadducees and the Pharisees which can be confirmed for later decades. Josephus (*The Jewish War* I, 110) allocates the rise to eminence of the Pharisees to the reign of Alexandra, the queen (76–67 B.C.) who suc-ceeded Hyrcanus' son Alexander Jannaeus (reigned 103–76 B.C.) to the throne; in his *Antiquities* (XIII, 398), Josephus implies that the Pharisees had by this time already achieved eminence; earlier in *Antiquities* (XIII, 171), he attributes to the age of Jonathan (who died in 142 B.C.) the existence of three parties: Pharisees, Sadducees, and Es-senes. We must confess that we are poorly informed re-garding the extent of the influence of these (and possibly other idiosyncratic movements) in the period we are dis-cussing, and we are necessarily imprecise when we asso-ciate economic and social attributes to them, as is done conventionally. It is quite reasonable that the Sadducees represented the upper classes economically and socially in Jerusalem, and the Pharisees the middle classes, and the Essenes a quasi-monastic group. It is also reasonable to attribute to the Pharisees a punctilious regard for the re-quirements of Scripture, and to the Sadducees only a gen-eral mechanical adherence, with the consequence that the Pharisees were strict in matters of custom and law, and the literalist Sadducees lax, or careless, and possibly even dis-dainful. Granted, however, that we are in the realm of some uncertainty, we can nevertheless be sure that the Judaism of the age of John Hyrcanus was already well divided, and we can suppose that the beginnings of the synagogue, of proto-rabbinism, had already appeared. It is quite likely that the conversion of the Idumeans had no relationship at all to these parties, and that it was a matter only of social controls allied to religious belief, rather than religious beliefs as such—that is to say, the conversion can have taken such form as moving from the use of pork to its abstinence, as adopting the circumcision of male children at the age of eight days, and as participation in the tax in the amount of a half shekel for the support of the Temple in Jerusalem. This could mean a nominal rather than a profound conversion.

But it was at a time of some turbulence within Jewry that the forced conversion of the Idumeans took place, and in all likelihood it was marked by confusions and inconsistencies. Undoubtedly it was a peculiar conversion, but it was a conversion nevertheless.

Our chief source of information about Herod is the Jewish historian, Flavius Josephus, who was born in A.D. 37. He commanded Jewish troops in Galilee about 66, in good loyalty, but turned to espouse the Roman side in the Judean rebellion against Rome which erupted that year and was crushed in 70. Josephus then settled in Rome, and proceeded to write an account of the war of rebellion, naming it, curiously enough, *The Jewish War against the Romans* rather than, as he might have, *The Roman War against the Jews.* Josephus devotes the bulk of the first of the seven books to a brief review of the Maccabean age and a rather detailed account of Herod. We do not know exactly when he wrote *The Jewish War.* In another, and later, work, *The Antiquities of the Jews,* in twenty books, Josephus devotes most of XIV, all XV and XVI, and a large part of XVII to Herod. The latter account runs, in translation, to about 365 pages, and the former to about 115.

Unhappily, the parallel accounts contain difficulties, inconsistencies, contradictions, and problems. These have been investigated with great patience and acumen by generations of scholars. Moreover, since the age of Herod overlaps that of Pompey, Julius Caesar, Mark Antony, and Octavius Augustus Caesar, the scholars have searched the Greek and Roman historians diligently for the relevant data in a thorough and admirable manner. Issues of fact, chronology, and geography, unclear in Josephus, have been clarified by such research.

As to Josephus himself, the circumstance that he lived later than Herod implies his reliance on sources, and about at least one such source we have good data, since Josephus himself supplies it. A Gentile, Nicholas[2] of Damascus, became attached to the court of Herod, in part as tutor in philosophy and in part as a councilor, or even counselor, and wrote an account of Herod which Josephus both used and disparaged, charging Nicholas with presenting only the favorable aspects of Herod and with suppressing the unfavorable. An issue for the modern scholar is the question, first, of the reliability of the sources, such as Nicholas, which Josephus used, and second, Josephus' own reliability in his use of the sources. In general, one can normally trust the direct quotations which Josephus makes, even in the case of certain overfavorable Roman documents that he cites. The speeches which he quotes are not verbatim transcripts, but belong to a normal procedure in Greek historical writing in which a later historian indulged himself in the luxury of composing for his ancient character that speech which the historian deemed appropriate for the given occasion. Yet beyond such harmless rhetoric, Josephus was susceptible to both bias and error, and one must always read him with great caution. Without him, we should possess virtually nothing; possessing him, we are in need of restraint and of prudence. The modern historian is often called upon to declare his judgment in certain matters in which hunch rather than evidence is the decisive element. From time to time I shall find it necessary to mention Josephus, especially where a conclusion seems in order that is out of keeping with what Josephus tells us.

It was the grandfather of Herod who was the first in his family to rise to some notice, for King Alexander Jannaeus designated him "general over all Idumea." The prerogatives of this office are uncertain, but it is likely that the grandfather was something akin to a military governor. Josephus adds that the grandfather made friends of the neighboring Arabs—that is, the Nabateans—and of the inhabitants of the two Philistine cities, famous even in early times, Gaza and Ascalon.

This grandfather bore the name of Antipas, and, rather significantly, two false legends have circulated about him. The earlier legend comes to us via Josephus, informing us that Nicholas of Damascus, the court biographer of Herod, provided this Antipas with the noble heritage of supposedly being of one of the leading Jewish families which had returned to Judea from Babylon in the sixth century. The later legend, found in the church father Justin Martyr, describes Antipas as an Ascalonite; a still later church father, Julius Africanus, makes Antipas a temple slave to Apollo at Ascalon. If the court biographer was interested in aggrandizing Herod's grandfather, the legend of his origin in Ascalon is the result of the wish completely to disparage him.

There is no reason to doubt that this Antipas was a man of some genuine significance and of some wealth, for otherwise we would be hard pressed to understand the role of Antipas' son, Antipater, who was to father Herod. When we first encounter Antipater, he is a resident of Jerusalem. He moves in high circles, and is already a trusted adviser in the Maccabean court. We shall presently need to see his position in fuller clarity, in order to understand

Herod. But even at this point we should attribute to Antipater some modicum of wealth and position, inherited in Idumea from Antipas, in turn transported to Jerusalem, and thereafter enhanced in the capital city.

John Hyrcanus, as we have said, died in 104 B.C. Though he was king in fact, at that time the ruling title was still unspecified, normally being the office of high priest. He left a will which bequeathed the government to his wife, but his son Aristobulus I seized the governing authority and assumed the title of king. According to Josephus, this assumption of kingship, especially by title, is the first instance of a king of the Jews since the middle of the sixth century when the last previous king died in Babylon. Strabo (*Geography* XVI. 2. 40), however, attributes the title of king only later—that is, to Aristobulus' successor. Aristobulus imprisoned his mother and let her starve to death in prison. When Aristobulus died without issue, his widow, Salome Alexandra, married Alexander Jannaeus, the oldest of three brothers who survived Aristobulus. Alexander Jannaeus became both king and high priest. His long reign of twenty-seven years was marked by warfare, civil war, and by acquisition of more territory—and by a dangerous crisis with the Ptolemies of Egypt, who wanted to regain Judea. During his reign a bitter quarrel arose between him and the Pharisees, who felt Jannaeus ineligible for the high priesthood, for he had shed much blood. The quarrel came to a head on a festival day and culminated in Jannaeus' slaughter of six thousand people. (Most of us who work in Josephus are inclined to distrust his numbers, and we would understand that by six thousand he means only a great many.) Civil war then arose in the land, and Jannaeus utilized foreign mercenaries to put down the rebellion; the rebels appealed to the Seleucids for help, and received it. The disorders were constant, the military situation often confused, and the foe numerous, at one time including even the Nabateans. The hatred of Jannaeus by his subjects in time gave way to their preference to be subject to a Hasmonean tyrant rather than to some alien; and Jannaeus, from his side, repented of his cruelties and his opposition to the Pharisees. We can take the measure of the man from this, that during the last three years of his life he suffered the aftereffects of excessive drinking. Yet after his death, so Josephus tells us, the Pharisees went to the people and made public speeches in which they said of Jannaeus "that a righteous king had been lost to them, and by their praise they so greatly stirred the populace to mourning and lament over him that they provided him an even more glorious funeral than any for the kings before him" (*Antiquities* XIII, 406).

Antipater, the father of Herod, may well have moved to Jerusalem even before the death of Alexander Jannaeus; on the other hand, his removal there may have awaited the reign of the widow, Salome Alexandra, 76–67 B.C. At any rate, Herod was born about 73 B.C., during the reign of this queen, usually known simply as Alexandra. The hallmark of the age in which he was born was violence, murderous intrigue, fratricide, civil upheavals, international plots and counterplots, an age marked by the absence of security. Men in his time and milieu, when they were ambitious, were ruthless and devoid of mercy, and we must expect Herod to be a child of his age.

It is in connection with the death of Salome Alexandra, who left two sons begotten by Jannaeus, that Antipater makes his first appearance in the pages of Josephus. Well before her death, Salome Alexandra gave the older son, Hyrcanus II, the office of high priest (to which women were ineligible and therefore the queen needed to bestow it on someone); she designated the younger son, Aristobulus II, commander of the army. When she fell ill and her death was awaited, Hyrcanus was, of course, in line for the throne in addition to the high priesthood. Aristobulus initiated a rebellion, in 68, so as to seize the throne for himself. Hyrcanus assumed the leadership of the loyalists, and the queen meantime passed away. The outcome of the civil war of the next years was destined often to be shaped by Antipater, and ultimately largely to be determined by him, for he it was who spearheaded the resistance to Aristobulus' domestic revolt, which came to have international complications.

Our supposition must be this, that Antipater, by 67 B.C., was already established in some high situation of influence and prestige in Jerusalem.

Antipater's wife, Cypros, was a Nabatean. Josephus speaks of her illustrious family, but he gives us none of the data which we would welcome in order to understand most clearly the relationship of Antipater to Judaism. Cypros may have been a convert or she may not have been; we do not know. Herod is attacked in a number of instances as a half-Jew—that is, the son of a Jewish father and a Gentile mother. The practice among Jews of much later ages was to reckon Jewishness in the case of a mixed marriage according to the faith of the mother, not the father (for one can be sure about maternity but not nearly so sure about paternity); by this later test, the children of Antipater would have been classified as Jews only if Cypros was Jewish by birth or conversion.

These obscurities are beyond our penetration, and it is for this reason that we must begin with only the bare fact that when the fratricidal war broke out between Hyrcanus and Aristobulus, Antipater was already important enough to be able to volunteer acceptable suggestions to Hyrcanus. To this datum we must add a fact, which will soon become relevant, that Antipater had close relations with the Nabatean royal house. Yet nothing in the account about Antipater obstructs our taking his proclaimed Jewish loyalty at face value.

As to the civil war between Hyrcanus and Aristobulus, which our sources describe confusingly, a prompt development was the defeat of Hyrcanus' forces by Aristobulus in a battle which took place near Jericho; Hyrcanus was forced to flee. He took refuge in Jerusalem in a citadel known at that time as Baris; later it was renamed Antonia in honor of Mark Antony. In this same citadel, however, Queen Salome Alexandra had imprisoned Aristobulus' wife and children at the time when Aristobulus had first embarked on his design to seize the sovereignty; these prisoners now became hostages for Hyrcanus' safety.

Josephus, in his account, furnishes us with quick and contrasting characterizations of the brothers: Aristobulus was braver and possessed of greater capacity than Hyrcanus; Aristobulus was quick and aggressive, while Hyrcanus was quiet, retiring, and passive.

With Hyrcanus virtually a prisoner in the citadel, and with fortress after fortress falling into Aristobulus' hands, the younger brother proceeded to the step of besieging the citadel. In some way, however, anonymous peacemakers found a formula for resolving the acute difficulties, with the terms of the agreement implying that Aristobulus was to desist from conquering his brother in the citadel in return for the safety of his family. Also, Hyrcanus agreed to abandon the throne (and possibly the high priesthood) to Aristobulus, and he received in return "all the honors as the king's brother," these contingent on his retiring from public life. The settlement seemed mutually agreeable, and so the brothers became reconciled with each other, embracing cordially in the presence of many onlookers. This took place in the Temple; the reconciliation was marked by oaths and pledges that both took in order to give credibility to the assurance that each would observe the agreement. It seemed that a permanent settlement had been reached.

But Aristobulus had his foes in Jerusalem and Judea, and the settlement that had been made alarmed them. Among these foes of Aristobulus was Antipater. We have no inkling of the background of the basis of the animosity which Antipater bore to Aristobulus. Antipater's course of action was quite simple. Able somehow to gain the ear of Hyrcanus, he repeatedly told the deposed ruler how unjustly he had been deprived of the right which was his by primogeniture ("first born"), and he repeatedly warned Hyrcanus that Aristobulus would put him out of the way. So decent and trusting was Hyrcanus that he long resisted believing these menacing words. But finally Antipater managed to persuade Hyrcanus that his life was in danger, and he urged him to flee southward to Petra, the capital of Nabatea, where King Aretas III would give him refuge. Hyrcanus was prudent enough to look for safeguards; he dispatched Antipater to Aretas to ascertain that the Nabatean monarch would actually provide him with refuge, and would even assist him in recovering his throne, as Antipater had said. Antipater returned to Jerusalem with the very assurances which Hyrcanus wanted, and so the two slipped out of Jerusalem one night and made the hundred-mile journey to Petra. The next step was for Hyrcanus and Antipater to persuade Aretas to take that military action necessary to restore Hyrcanus to the Judean throne. Antipater was able to bring about the persuasion of Aretas by cajolery and bribery, and also by the promise to restore to Aretas twelve cities which Alexander Jannaeus had seized from the Nabateans.

Accordingly, the next development in the machinations typical of the times was that Aretas raised a large army—Josephus gives the number of the troops as fifty thousand!—and he set out to encounter Aristobulus. First occurred a battle at an unnamed place, and there Aristobulus was defeated and many of his troops deserted to Hyrcanus. But Aristobulus made his way to Jerusalem, to the Temple compound. Except for the priests, whose fate was bound up with the Temple, the citizens of Jerusalem had become partisans of Hyrcanus, and the defeat of Aristobulus seemed certain, so certain, in fact, that the Jews of best repute left the country and fled to Egypt.[3]

So all was in readiness for Hyrcanus to destroy his brother.[4] It was at this point that the offstage character, Rome, entered. Throughout the careers of both Antipater and Herod, Rome was present, often directly, but at all times at least indirectly; and however much Antipater and Herod would seem to act as though in their own right and freedom, it was always in the limited freedom that Rome would allow.

The interest of Rome, and its conquests, had been primarily westward prior to the end of the third pre-Christian century. But during the Second Punic War (218–201), Hannibal of Carthage succeeded in attracting Macedonia into a compact against Rome, and as a consequence Rome's attention was drawn eastward, especially to the lands on the eastern side of the Adriatic Sea, the region called Illyria, which separated Rome from Macedonia. At that time some Greek states became united in a so-called Aetolian League in order to resist Macedonia's encroachments upon them, and thereupon Rome made an alliance with that League. Warfare by Rome against Macedonia, from 215–205, was sporadic, desultory, and indecisive, and it terminated in 205, largely because the Aetolian League made a separate peace with the Macedonians. Rome conceded to Macedonia their claims in Illyria. Again in the ensuing years, Roman conquest, and consolidation of its expansion, was primarily westward as in Spain, or southward as in North Africa (where Carthage was finally conquered in 146 B.C.).

This consolidation included the absorption of the Grecianized portions of southern Italy and Sicily, which had previously been conquered; the culture of the Greeks began to penetrate Rome itself.

But the Macedonians embarked on a new conquest of Asia Minor, around 200, and thereupon appeals from that region to Rome elicited first Roman interest, and next partial intervention, and thereafter the proclamation of a second war against the Macedonians. In 197 the Romans defeated the Macedonians, with the result that the latter retired into a restricted territory, and Roman garrisons were established in various Greek lands, to replace the Macedonian garrisons. But now the Seleucids began to spread northwestward from Syria into Asia Minor, and even into the Greek peninsula, Thrace for example, and again the insecure Greek states appealed to Rome. Some Greek states were partisan to Syria and some partisan to Rome, so that Rome and Syria were destined to fight a war. A decisive battle ending with a Roman victory took place at Thermopylae in 191, virtually terminating the sway of Syria on the Greek mainland. Two years later the Romans invaded Asia Minor and again defeated the Syrians; a peace treaty at Apamea provided that the Syrians were to retire to the territory east of the Taurus Mountains. Rome was meanwhile contented merely with asserting an influence in the former Syrian lands, for she as yet abstained from annexing any Grecian territory.

In the ensuing decades the tiny Greek states were in almost constant upheaval, both against each other and against Roman influence, and a third Macedonian war erupted in 171; the Romans won a notable victory at Pydna in 168, bringing an end to the rule of the Macedonian royal dynasty. In 148 Macedonia lost the vestiges of independence and became a Roman province. Elsewhere in the Grecian lands and Grecian islands, disorders continued; Rome put these down, destroyed various leagues and states, and replaced the governments here and there, but still without annexing territory. Yet Roman influence in the east was now such that a mere warning by a Roman commissioner was sufficient to occasion the withdrawal, mentioned above, of Antiochus Epiphanes from Egypt in 169. A Roman protectorate was then established over Egypt. Similarly, the independence of Judea from Syria was recognized by a Judean treaty with Rome in 142.

Protectorates and influences, however, led gradually to direct Roman control. States far to the east, such as Parthia, emerged to challenge and conquer portions of the Syrian empire, and to expand westward, and an ultimate head-on clash between Rome and the eastern monarchs was impending. A particular threat arose from the kingdom of Pontus, on the south shore of the Black Sea. Its able monarch Mithradates conquered Asia Minor, and crossed into Europe to take Athens, which city became the base of his operations against Rome. But the Romans defeated the forces of Mithradates, first in 86 B.C. and again in 85, and now Rome virtually annexed Greece and Asia Minor. The Roman commander in the east, Sulla, returned to Rome to face a civil war that had arisen there, and he subdued his foes. Sulla established a dictatorship, introduced a new constitution, and then abdicated in 79 B.C.

The lieutenant of Sulla, Gnaeus Pompey, had distinguished himself in military leadership, especially in Spain, and as a consequence, he became a leading contender for the high dual office of consul, this in the year 70. Pompey shared the office with Marcus Licinius Crassus. When Pompey's term was up, disorders again arose in the east, this time from pirates operating in the eastern Mediterranean. Rome itself began to suffer from a food shortage to the point of near famine because of the pirates, so that Pompey was given the mandate of restoring peace in the east. To that end he received unlimited power to requisition ships, men, and money from all the cities and states under Roman possession; thereby Pompey became virtually an absolute monarch in all the eastern portion of the Roman empire. The real focus of Pompey's attention was Pontus, and other more eastern territories. But Pompey had had to traverse Syria, and he was in the general vicinity of Judea when Hyrcanus and Aristobulus first became locked in civil war. Just as in Greece and Asia such local rivalries had led to Roman intervention, so it was now in order for Pompey to divert Roman attention southward to Judea.

Pompey himself had moved on to Armenia. He sent orders to a general of his, Scaurus, to march from the Roman headquarters in Damascus, Syria, into Judea. Hyrcanus was engaged in besieging Aristobulus at Jerusalem. Promptly envoys from both Hyrcanus and Aristobulus visited Scaurus, each seeking assistance from the Romans against his brother. The vehicle of persuasion was not so much eloquence as money, and each brother offered his bribe. Aristobulus was wealthier than Hyrcanus, so that Scaurus preferred the offer from Aristobulus, especially since Aristobulus offered cash, while Hyrcanus proffered a promissory note. Scaurus then ordered Aretas, the ally of Hyrcanus, to lift the siege of Jerusalem, threatening that otherwise the Romans under Pompey himself would invade Nabatea. Aretas withdrew his forces and moved southward, so Scaurus supposed that hostilities were ended, as he wished them to be. But Aristobulus mustered all his forces and he set out after the retreating Hyrcanus and Aretas and overtook them, and then inflicted heavy losses —Josephus says six thousand men—in a battle fought at a place called Papyron, the location of which is unknown. In this battle a brother of Antipater was among the soldiers of Hyrcanus who were slain. Whatever was the previous motive of Antipater's animosity toward Aristobulus, there was now added the strong motive of personal revenge.

Since Aretas had proved of no real assistance to Antipater and Hyrcanus, Antipater naturally needed to look elsewhere. With perceptive realism, as it obtained in those days, he determined to turn to Pompey himself. Certain confusions in the account of Josephus obscure the precise sequence of events relating to this approach by Antipater to the Roman commander, especially just where Pompey was, though probably in Syria. What is clear, however, is that the determination of Antipater to appeal to Pompey was matched by a similar desire on the part of certain esteemed Judeans and also of Aristobulus. The purpose of these Judean leaders was to urge the Romans to espouse neither of the brothers, and to propose, instead, that kingship be terminated and replaced with a high priesthood.

Aristobulus injured his case before Pompey by tactlessly alluding to his bribery of Scaurus, and also by being accompanied by some young swaggerers, who offensively displayed their purple robes, long hair, metal ornaments, and other finery, as if they were marching in a festive procession, instead of being petitioners.

Antipater was himself the envoy to Pompey on behalf of Hyrcanus, of course, and he cannily brought with him a deputation of Jews—Josephus counts the deputation as numbering a thousand—highly reputable men. Antipater ignored the "esteemed Judeans." He made the accusation that Aristobulus was a usurper, and, more germanely to Pompey, that Aristobulus had participated in that piracy a few years earlier which had been the occasion for Pompey's first excursion into the eastern Mediterranean. Pompey took under advisement the various arguments made before him. Aristobulus was impatient for Pompey's verdict, and he departed from Pompey's presence, thereby

offending the Roman. Pompey thereupon set out to punish
Aristobulus, who had retired to a superb fortress, Alexandreion.[5] Pompey pursued him, and, encamped at the foot
of the mountain on which this fortress was located, he demanded that Aristobulus descend to see him. Aristobulus,
importuned by some followers not to try to wage war
with Pompey, went through a number of humiliating con-
ferences with Pompey, the upshot of which was his sur-
render of Alexandreion to the Romans. Having surrendered
the fortress, Aristobulus then withdrew to Jerusalem, ostensibly reconciled to his defeat, but in reality intending
to prepare there for a further and more decisive war with
Pompey. Pompey, however, was a relentless pursuer, so
that he proceeded to encamp outside Jerusalem, with the
result that Aristobulus, in terror of Pompey, now came to
him with promises of money and the offer of a peaceful,
unresisted Roman entry into the Holy City. Pompey accepted the proposals and sent his general Gabinius to take
over the city and to receive the promised money. But Aristobulus had not reckoned with the mind and will of the
inhabitants of Jerusalem; not only did Gabinius fail to receive the money, but the Jerusalemites would not admit
Gabinius into the city. So Pompey arrested Aristobulus,
and himself proceeded to move his troops against the city.

Within the capital, dissension had divided the populace
into those who preferred the peaceful capitulation to Pompey, and those, partisans of the now arrested Aristobulus,
who preferred war with the Romans. The latter group had
occupied the Temple area, and they prepared for a siege;
the other faction admitted Pompey's army into the city
and allowed it to take over the royal palace. Pompey then
moved against the Temple, with all the ingenuity and all
the military paraphernalia of the Romans, and he was
abetted by Hyrcanus himself. The Romans needed to erect
earthworks and towers toward this siege of the Temple,

and they might well have been prevented from accomplishing this preliminary to the actual siege were it not that the Jews desisted from harassing the Romans on the Sabbath; the Romans took advantage of the respites from opposition to bring their task of construction to completion, this over a period of three months. The Romans were finally able to break into the Temple, to inflict an impressive slaughter on the defenders—Josephus enumerates the Jewish dead as twelve thousand—and to proceed to the ultimate humiliation of the Jews by entering the sacred precincts of the Temple itself, and even the Holy of Holies, where the high priest alone was allowed by Jewish law and practice to enter, and he only once a year, on the Day of Atonement.

Yet except for this horrendous act of improper entry, Pompey desisted from further desecration of the Temple. Rather, he gave orders for the Temple to be cleansed, and for the regular sacrificial rituals to be resumed. As to the partisans of Aristobulus, these he punished with ample beheadings. He made Judea, through its capital Jerusalem, a tributary of Rome; he took away from Judea certain cities located in Coele-Syria[6] and on the coast, thereby reducing Judea to a small area to be administered under Syria. He imposed on Judea a huge fine of ten thousand talents.[7] He then set off for Rome, carrying with him as a prisoner in chains Aristobulus and two daughters and two sons, Antigonus and Alexander. Alexander managed to escape from Pompey and to flee.

Before Pompey left Judea, however, he appointed his general Scaurus as administrator of the province, and he designated Hyrcanus as the high priest. By this double appointment the independent kingship terminated in Judea, the result of the enmity and rivalry of the royal brothers.

We must confess that we do not know the precise role of Antipater in the events of the Roman invasion, siege, and conquest. We last saw him directly on the occasion of the embassy to Pompey; he now comes into clear view again in connection with Scaurus. The latter marched southward against the Nabateans in 62, hoping to take their capital Petra, which was difficult of access since it lay high on a craggy cliff, amidst mountains. Scaurus laid waste the Nabatean countryside, but in the arid country he was brought to a lack of food, so that he turned to Hyrcanus for provisions; it was Antipater whom Hyrcanus sent southward to bring to Scaurus the needed supplies. Given an opportunity to help the Romans, Antipater went on to become a trucemaker between Scaurus and Aretas. The Nabatean was willing to accept the Roman offer to be bought off from attacking Petra, a purchase which could bring pleasure both to Scaurus and to Aretas. So Antipater supplied Scaurus and Aretas with what each of them wanted.

Apparently the situation in Judea, with Scaurus as administrator and Hyrcanus as high priest, remained relatively stable for five years or so. In 57 the general Gabinius was named governor. At that same time Aristobulus' son Alexander, who, we recall, had escaped from Pompey in 63, returned to Judea. First he made a raid on a number of cities; then he came to Jerusalem, and, despite the Roman garrison there, began the attempt to rebuild the wall which Pompey had destroyed. Although Alexander was driven away from Jerusalem, he gathered a large army of patriots from the countryside, and he managed to go on to fortify a number of strongholds, principally the fortresses of Alexandreion and Machaerus. This challenge by Alexander was formidable not alone to Hyrcanus, but to the Romans also, and Gabinius felt the acute need to subdue Alexander. He himself marched against Alexander, and in the course of his strategy he sent a force ahead of him under the command of Mark Antony. The latter was at that time a young man of twenty-five; there still lay before Mark Antony notable future events, the campaign in Gaul, in which he assisted Julius Caesar, against whom even later he conspired, and still later his liaison with Cleopatra of Egypt.

But it was not Roman troops alone who marched against Alexander. Along with these there went some troops described as belonging to Antipater—Antipater, not Hyrcanus. Antipater was thereby allied or at least associated with the Romans. Alexander was defeated in a battle, and fled to his fortress, Alexandreion. Here in due time Gabinius pressed his siege, with the result that Alexander was ultimately forced to capitulate, and his fortress was destroyed by the Romans. It appeared then as if the side represented by Hyrcanus, Antipater, and the Romans had fully triumphed. Yet scarcely a year later, Aristobulus escaped from his confinement in Rome, returned to Judea, assembled new troops, and began to rebuild Alexandreion. When the Romans gathered against him there, Aristobulus retreated southward to the fortress Machaerus, but he was again defeated and again taken to Rome in chains.

Shortly thereafter, imperial policy necessitated a Roman march on Egypt, for Gabinius needed to restore to the throne there a certain deposed king, Ptolemy XI Auletes, the father of Cleopatra. Not only did Antipater supply Gabinius with food, he also rendered him another service. Slightly to the east of the mouth of the Nile there lay a city, Pelusium, which served as a kind of frontier outpost on the highway from Palestine into Egypt. Also, on a westward journey into Egypt, Pelusium was the first place for fording the Nile. This city, a military stronghold, was peopled largely by Jews. Pelusium could well have barred the way to Gabinius, and seemed inclined to do so, but Antipater appealed to the Jewish residents and won them over, and thereby gained unopposed access into Egypt for the Roman general. His appeal to the residents of Pelusium was based only on their common Jewishness. Perhaps Antipater couched his appeal as if it came from Hyrcanus, but if so, our accounts do not say so. We must conclude that it was on the basis of his Jewishness, and theirs, that Antipater made his appeal. We shall presently encounter Pelusium again.

This sojourn of Gabinius in Egypt provided Alexander, the son of Aristobulus, with still another opportunity to raise troops in Judea and to challenge Roman authority. Alexander was proving successful in winning Palestinian Jews to his army, or, perhaps, in coercing them; Gabinius therefore dispatched Antipater from Egypt with the mission of wooing Alexander's troops away from him. Josephus speaks of Antipater's success in this effort, and he comments that Antipater was a man of good sense. Despite Antipater's efforts, Alexander nevertheless retained an army of some thirty thousand troops. A little later, a battle took place between Alexander and Gabinius, and it brought still another defeat to the Maccabee.

Gabinius now prepared to return to Rome. He needed to settle affairs at Jerusalem before he turned over the governorship to the man named his successor, Marcus Licinius Crassus; it was Antipater whose wishes he sought out and he made his arrangements in accordance with these. Slowly but steadily, then, the tacit alliance was fashioned, and it bound Antipater and Rome to each other; almost continually the Maccabeans, Aristobulus or his children, were at war with Rome, and with Antipater. Inasmuch as Hyrcanus was by now known as a weakling and inefficient, the Romans were ready to see in Antipater a person who could serve their need for peace, and also for money. Antipater saw that his own power depended not on Hyrcanus but exclusively on Rome.

The new Roman governor, Crassus, needing to mount an expedition against the Parthians, plundered the Temple in Jerusalem of its gold to help finance it. He then set off for the east, and there he perished in battle, in 53. A subordinate of his returned to the west, where Syria now needed some subduing, for apparently the campaign against the Parthians gave opportunity for revolt throughout the area. That subordinate was Caius Cassius Longinus, the Cassius to whom Shakespeare attributed the "lean and hungry look." Cassius became the governor of Syria in 53.

Revolt was aflame in Judea too, in continuation of the movements constantly spurred on by Aristobulus. The immediate leader of the Jewish forces of revolt was a certain Peitholaus, who had been a trusted general under Antipater when Mark Antony had come into Palestine, but who had thereafter joined forces with Aristobulus. Cassius marched into Judea and, at Tarichaea on the Sea of Galilee, defeated a large Jewish force and captured Peitholaus. Once this revolt was crushed, Antipater emerged to even greater overt power than before. He was especially influential with Cassius, and he persuaded the Roman to execute Peitholaus. Mercy was a rare quality in those days.

The several factions at the time in Judea are susceptible of those various descriptions found among the scholars who have interpreted the foregoing events. Certainly there was an alignment of Hyrcanus with the Roman forces, and certainly Aristobulus and his son Alexander and the general Peitholaus represented a sturdy, almost relentless effort against the Romans on behalf of independence and freedom. Some historians, accordingly, equate Aristobulus with commendable patriotism, Hyrcanus and Antipater with detestable subservience to Rome. Perhaps a contrast of this sort is partially admissible, but only when it is accompanied by the recognition that Aristobulus and his son Alexander were quite as much self-seekers as patriots, and to scorn the patriotism of Hyrcanus is to do him an injustice, for he was beholden to Rome, which had recognized the legitimacy of his claims over those of his brother, and had sustained them.

After the defeat and execution of Peitholaus, Hyrcanus receded all the more from notice, and the power of authority and decision in Judea was now increasingly the prerogative of Antipater. He did not hold any specific office at this stage; one can speak, however, of his tremendous influence, both over Hyrcanus and with the Romans. Had there been a throne in Judea, Antipater would have been the power behind it. Some two years later, in 49, Antipater's power became indirectly confirmed. This came as a consequence of upheavals in Rome. The conflict there, between Pompey and Julius Caesar, broke into civil war, with Caesar marching with his army across the Rubicon, and taking Rome. Pompey had to flee. Caesar set out in pursuit, and he defeated Pompey in battle at Pharsala in Thessaly. Aristobulus was then a prisoner in Rome; apparently on the principle that "an enemy of my enemy is automatically my friend," and possibly on the basis of extravagant promises from the Maccabean, Caesar not only freed Aristobulus from prison, but even provided him with two legions to take with him to Syria to fight there against the remaining adherents of Pompey. Abruptly as Aristobulus was raised, that abruptly he met misfortune; partisans of Pompey in Rome poisoned him even before he could depart from the city, and his son Alexander, a prisoner of adherents of Pompey in Antioch, was there executed by beheading. The other son of Aristobulus, Antigonus, still survived.

Judea became relatively tranquil, for the deaths of Aristobulus and Alexander weakened the challenge to Hyrcanus and thus to Antipater.

The task before Antipater internally was to consolidate

the peace, and externally to cement relations with Rome. This latter involved some delicacy, for Antipater was faced with the prospect of having to transfer his old allegiance from Pompey to Pompey's enemy, Julius Caesar. After the defeat at Pharsala, Pompey fled to Egypt, and there he was immediately assassinated. For Antipater the prospect changed into an urgent necessity.

Caesar now turned his attention to the direct conquest of Egypt. For this enterprise he required both additional troops and also supplies. Here, then, arose opportunity for Antipater, and he seized it. He raised support for Caesar, through the recruitment of Jewish troops, which Antipater himself commanded, and also through the promptings of monarchs friendly to him, such as the Nabatean king, and other rulers, to send supporting troops.

This pro-Roman army of Antipater's marched against Egypt from the east; Pelusium was therefore its first objective. Here the troops encountered resistance, and the city had to be taken by force. Antipater was able to make a breach in the walls and to take the lead in entering the city at the head of his forces. Beyond Pelusium the way was further barred by settlements of Egyptian Jews in an area between Pelusium and Memphis called the "district of Onias." This Onias had been by birth the proper heir to the high priesthood, from which his father had been deposed. Onias went to Egypt in 154; there he built a temple at a place known as Leontopolis.[8] It comes as something of a surprise, for we know so little about Onias and his temple, to read that a district was known a century later by his name; it is even more of a surprise to read that the Jews in that district were able to be a barrier to the troops moving westward to join up with Julius Caesar. The choice before the Jewish invaders under Antipater was either to attempt conquest or to persuade the Egyptian Jews to desist from barring the way. Antipater chose to try the latter course. He repeated his experience of the march with Gabinius. By personal appeal, as from one Jew to other Jews, and by exhibiting letters from Hyrcanus supporting his own proposals, he won the support of these Egyptian Jews. They not only did not bar the way, but they even contributed supplies to him. A battle shaped up between the invading forces and the resisting native Egyptians; it took place in a locality known as "the Jews' camp." For a time it appeared that the invaders might be defeated; Antipater, however, even after being wounded, managed a strategic maneuver which not only relieved the hard-pressed invading troops but also routed the Egyptian forces. The report of Antipater's exploits came to the ears of Julius Caesar, and the Roman rewarded Antipater by granting him Roman citizenship, and by confirming Hyrcanus as the high priest. This latter gesture by Julius Caesar meant a confirmation of the power of Antipater.

At about this time, Antigonus, the surviving son of Aristobulus, appeared before Julius Caesar to press his dwindling claim to the throne of Judea. Antigonus could argue for the alleged legitimacy of his claims through his father; and he could, moreover, try to disparage the claims of Hyrcanus and Antipater, and to undermine their influence on Caesar, by reminding the Roman of their erstwhile partisanship for Caesar's enemy, Pompey. Antigonus could go on to allege that the support of Caesar's effort to subdue Egypt was less a matter of loyalty than the need to expunge the memory of their relationship to Pompey. Antigonus would need, of course, to play down the theme, precious to his father and himself, of the complete independence of Judea from Rome. But however strong a case Antigonus could manage to concoct, he chose to present his claim to Caesar, at Antioch, in the very moment when Caesar was indebted to Antipater for the favors received so recently.

Antigonus made the accusation before Julius Caesar that Hyrcanus and Antipater had banished the family of Aristobulus from Judea, an accusation for which the account in Josephus provides no direct basis, and that Hyrcanus and Antipater had repeatedly acted lawlessly and arrogantly toward the Jewish nation.

Antigonus could scarcely have selected a less opportune time. Antipater was himself in Antioch, and either present to hear Antigonus' words or nearby so as promptly to receive the report of them. To these allegations which were made before Julius Caesar, Antipater might have chosen to make a detailed refutation, and to meet the charges with countercharges; that is, he might have elected the lawyer's way of logical rebuttal and verbal eloquence. Antipater, however, was too canny to rest his refutation on mere words. The battles in Egypt were recent, and his body bore numerous scars from the wounds that he had received. He began his reply, then, in a dramatic way. He stripped off his clothes and exhibited his numerous scars, saying at the same time that his loyalty to Caesar needed no words from him, for even were he to remain silent, his body would proclaim that loyalty. He then turned to counterattack: Antigonus was an enemy of the Romans, the son of an enemy of the Romans, whose legacy from his father, Aristobulus, was a passion for revolt and sedition. It would have been more becoming to Antigonus, Antipater said, to be grateful to Caesar merely for being alive, and not to go on presumptuously to demand favors. Moreover, were Caesar to show pity for Antigonus' poverty and were he to provide him with resources, these gifts Antigonus would employ to sow sedition against the very person who would have provided them.

Caesar, after listening to both men, dismissed the claims of Antigonus and proclaimed Hyrcanus high priest. Possibly he also proclaimed him "ethnarch," ruler of the

Herod: Profile of a Tyrant

1. he was not born to the office of King, but he aspired to it & he gained the throne & he held it despite inordinate difficulties, & his will divided it for 3 of his children

2. chief source of info about Herod is the Jewish historian, Flavius Josephus, which he gained from a Gentile, Nicholas of Damascus

ethnos, "the people," a title much less glorious than that of king. The confusion about Hyrcanus' title, whether only high priest, or both high priest and "king," is deeply embedded in Josephus, and as a consequence allusions will appear in subsequent pages to Hyrcanus as king. Perhaps Hyrcanus never again truly possessed that title; or perhaps he possessed it at random intervals. Yet if Hyrcanus received a supreme title, as befitting his royal blood, it was to Antipater that Caesar gave the privilege of the power to rule, and the right to choose the form of office Antipater preferred. Wisely Antipater declined to make a choice of title, for he might have selected one that Caesar considered too grand. He asked Caesar to make the choice. Thereupon Caesar named him *epitropos*, a term not completely clear to us, but roughly the equivalent of "governor." As for Antigonus, he disappeared from notice for a while, but to return again.

The grateful Caesar conferred two more favors on Antipater. He gave him permission to rebuild the walls of Jerusalem, and he then took steps to have all of the favorable actions entered into the records at the Capitol at Rome.

As the new governor, Antipater faced the inevitable and almost constant task of restoring tranquillity to the country. The impulse to independence, associated with Aristobulus and his sons, still animated much of the population. Antipater undertook the burden of traveling and speaking, setting before the populace the alternatives of loyalty to the docile Hyrcanus and quiet compliance with the Roman mandate or of a Hyrcanus turned tyrannical and a benevolent conqueror turned cruel. Antipater found himself in this endeavor bereft of any active support from the almost inert Hyrcanus. Since Antipater needed to get the job done, and he needed help, and had the power to appoint high officials, he turned to two of his sons.

Notes

1. The defeat of Nicanor resulted in a Jewish sacred occasion, "Nicanor's Day," observed by Jews and forgotten many centuries ago; it celebrated the triumph over the Syrian general.

2. His name is to be found in several other spellings, Nicolaus and Nicolas.

3. Josephus digresses to tell how a certain saintly man, Onias (whom the rabbinic tradition calls Honi "the Circle-maker," for he could cause rain to fall within a circle, and not fall outside it) was killed by a mob for refusing to become a partisan of either wicked side. He is not the Onias who had a temple at Leontopolis.

4. A rather quaint story is told in the rabbinic literature (Ta'anit III, 8 and 23a) but only alluded to by Josephus. The priestly adherents of Aristobulus, in need of animals for the sacrificial offerings, purchased them from the adherents of Hyrcanus, dropping money in a basket over the wall and raising the purchased animals over the wall and into the Temple compound. Thereupon an old man made the comment that so long as the partisans of Aristobulus could maintain the cult practices, they would evade capture. The next day the money was dropped and a pig was set in place for lifting over the wall. When the pig was raised halfway up, the land of Israel was shaken by an earthquake (Menahot 69b; Sotah 49b; Baba Qama 82b). Dio Cassius, a Roman historian, speaks (II, XXXVII) of a great and destructive earthquake in Asia Minor in 64. To the warring brothers, the sanctity of the Temple was of no great moment.

5. It was located about three miles west of the point where the Jabbok River flowed into the Jordan, near the modern Jordanian village of Qam Sartabeh.

6. By Coele-Syria is ordinarily meant the area around Damascus.

7. The talent, sometimes gold but usually silver, weighed from 88 to 95 pounds. One writer in 1890 gave its monetary value then as about $1,700 to $2,000. In the past seventy years, various writers have tried to estimate in current coin what the ancient values represented. In view of the many inflations, each effort has quickly become out of date; I have found no way of communicably translating talents into the devaluated money of our time. Perhaps it might suggest something to reckon a talent as roughly equivalent to $5,000 or $10,000 today. I have elsewhere usually avoided

copying Josephus' financial figures, simply because they are rather meaningless.

8. Much is obscure about this Onias, and also about his short-lived temple. On the one hand, Scripture asserted the legitimacy only of the Temple in Jerusalem; on the other hand, Onias may have been motivated to build this rival temple not alone because he was deprived of the high priesthood, but possibly also because he wanted a temple without the record of desecrations undergone by the Temple in Jerusalem. Only at Leontopolis did Jews in the many lands of their far-flung dispersions ever build a temple.

The use in modern times of the word "temple" as the name of a Jewish place of worship may occasion some confusion; these modern temples are synagogues. The Temple and the synagogue, were quite different. The nub of worship at the Temple was animal sacrifice, at the synagogues it was prayer. The Temple was presided over by hereditary priests, the synagogues by "commoners." Unlike the Temple, the synagogues, since they were totally different, could legitimately exist anywhere.

Part II

瓦瓦瓦瓦瓦瓦瓦瓦瓦瓦瓦

The Ascent to the Throne

47-37 B.C.

2

Antipater had begotten four sons and a daughter.

Their names are given in a list which probably designates the order of their birth: Phasael, Herod, Joseph, Pheroras, Salome. We can estimate the year of Herod's birth; we do not know the ages of the others. We may put the year of Herod's birth with some confidence in 74 or 73, by counting back from the year of his death, which we know to be 4 B.C., for Josephus tells us that Herod at the time was seventy. There is a well-known difficulty, however: Josephus, at the point in his accounts when Antipater turned to his sons to help him in restoring tranquillity in the land, in one version gives the age of Herod as fifteen and states that Herod was quite young, and in the other version relates that Herod "was a mere lad." This second version prevents our supposing that fifteen was an accidental slip of Josephus' pen, but must be an error of substance. Through the fullness of information which we possess about Julius Caesar, we can fix the date of Herod's appointment by Antipater as the year 47; if the age of Herod at his death in 4 B.C. was seventy, then it is ruled out that in 47 Herod was in the middle teens, and his age in that year was twenty-six or twenty-seven. How, then, can the error be explained? Possibly that Josephus, or some source which he utilized, sought to suggest that mere youthfulness and immaturity were the cause of an action which very shortly was to plunge Herod into great difficulties.

No account has come to us of Herod's youth or his education. An unimportant legend we shall see later. One

bit of information that we have is that in 67, when Aristobulus and Hyrcanus were first pitted against each other,
Antipater seems to have sent his wife Cypros and the
children to Petra, the capital of her native Nabatea, so that
they would be out of the way of the dangers inherent in
the disorders. Since Herod was the child of parents both
of whom came from families of some distinction, it is
understandable that his youth at Petra meant the possibility
of association with royalty, and that Herod felt himself
both at home in, and essentially a sharer in, that royalty.
Perhaps there were lulls and quiet months or isolated years
during which he visited Jerusalem; there too, in view of
his father's position, Herod would have associated with
royalty, and would have assumed himself to be properly at
home in such circles. The children of Antipater were
Judeans in Nabatea, and in Jerusalem half-Jews, and we
may conjecture that these anomalies developed in them the
intense family solidarity which we shall later witness. It
was, however, perhaps more than mere solidarity, for it
included boundless affection, and unending solicitude, and
even the toleration of bitter interference.

Stray passages in Josephus suggest that Herod was ath-
letic, agile, tall of stature, and possessed of great physical
strength, and we can infer that the boyish pastimes of the
upper classes, such as riding horses, hunting, and playing at
being a soldier, were his.

Where we are completely at a loss is the matter of his
formal education, for we know all too little about education in that time in general, and nothing about Herod's
education in particular. His speech was in all probability
the Aramaic which was the spoken language of the time,
and it is quite likely that this Aramaic, whether of Judea,
Idumea, or Nabatea, was so much a part of a common
linguistic entity as to be free of separation into different
dialects, so that Herod was quite at home in the spoken

language of the Judeans, despite his years at Petra. He appears to have known some Greek. More to the point, however, is the question, which cannot be answered, did he or did he not know Hebrew? Though Hebrew had largely given way to Aramaic as the spoken tongue, it was by no means unknown among Judeans, and its strong survival as a literary language is beyond question; there are on record disputes among modern scholars as to the extent to which Hebrew abided in those days in some quarters as a spoken language. The significance of raising the question of Herod's knowledge of Hebrew is not at all the language question but the tremendously more significant question, how much Jewish education did Herod have? Did he know enough Hebrew to read the Pentateuch in the original Hebrew? Was he ever trained in Scripture, ever trained in the basis of the Jewish faith, ever systematically indoctrinated into the observance and meaning of the sacred days of the annual calendar? Was his Jewishness merely that which he caught from the Jewish environment, or was he deeply instructed in it? Did he understand the religious issues which separated Pharisees from Sadducees, or was he aware only of the social, economic, and political configurations? Was he a Jew by training and conviction, or only by the accident of his birth into a family the father of whom was a convert, or the son of one, and the mother possibly no convert at all? Did he feel himself, in his early years, fully identified both with Judaism and with the Jewish people, or did his years at the court of Aretas preserve or strengthen a certain gap which he may have felt between him and the religion and people adopted by his forebears? Was he exposed, in whatever youthful visits he made to Jerusalem, to the sneers of the Judeans about the Idumean ancestry of his father, and the Nabatean ancestry of his mother? And did his pride in his family's importance lead him to resent all the more the snubs he may have received? We are completely without knowledge of these things, for when we encounter him the first time in the pages of Josephus, he is already mature, and already married. This wife, Doris, was the first of many; Josephus numbers them much later as ten, but he provides the names of only eight. We know nothing about Doris or her family, and those historians who, like Josephus, term her a "commoner" are probably right; those who designate her a Nabatean do so out of pure conjecture, for she may well have been a Judean.

The sons whom Antipater called on to assist him in his duties were, we said, two. He designated his oldest son, Phasael, as governor of Jerusalem and of the surrounding region, and Herod as governor of Galilee.

The wooded hills and gullies of Galilee rendered them ideal for guerrillas, determined to resist any political authority which they had come to despise. Indeed, the very word "guerrilla" carries with it a particular connotation, implying a defiance of law and officials. When such defiance is on behalf of a cause to which one is partial, the guerrillas are supreme patriots, men who risk their lives on behalf of a cause to which one attributes high value. When, on the other hand, one is antagonistic to the cause, then the guerrilla appears to be an outlaw, a brigand. We shall persistently understand as guerrillas men whom Josephus invariably calls brigands. When Herod became the governor of Galilee, it was a place of widespread guerrilla activity, directed against the power of Rome and therefore against those Judeans who held power through the grace of Rome. One such guerrilla was a certain Hezekiah (called, in Greek style by Josephus, Ezechias), whom Josephus labels a "bandit." The activity of Hezekiah centered in the northern part of Galilee, and included forays against cities in southern Syria. As part of Herod's duty to keep the peace, he set out against Hezekiah, captured him, and promptly executed him. He treated an unknown number of Hezekiah's followers similarly. For this achievement, Herod won the praises of the Syrians. They in turn praised him to the Roman governor, Sextus Caesar, a relative of Julius Caesar, so that very early in his career Herod won the approving notice of Rome.

In Jerusalem, in the meantime, Phasael was using great tact in winning the good will of the inhabitants. The father Antipater also increased in his personal power. While Antipater was able to keep the aging Hyrcanus II content and relatively free from jealousy, nevertheless it was inevitable that Antipater alienated influential citizens of Jerusalem through his acquisition of authority. When it was time to send on to the Romans the tribute money due them, Antipater first appropriated the money to himself, and then sent it as if coming from him rather than from Hyrcanus. While Hyrcanus seems to have been either indifferent to this action of Antipater's or even pleased to have escaped the administrative burden, the foes of Antipater in Jerusalem approached Hyrcanus with a compound set of complaints. Antipater, so they alleged, had seized the prerogative of Hyrcanus, and had done so as part of an urge for power which marked his whole family. Moreover, Antipater's family were acting not as stewards on behalf of Hyrcanus but, rather, were clearly motivated by self-interest. As for Herod, his execution of Hezekiah, so they alleged, represented a serious usurpation of judicial power, for the authority to sentence a person to death was vested in the Sanhedrin even under Roman overlordship, and Herod had violated the Jewish law in proceeding on his own to a summary execution without due process. The Sanhedrin was an "assembly"; the word is Greek, *synhedrion*, but Aramaized into the more familiar form. Precise information about it is lacking, especially respecting specific periods of time, particularly for the period when it was a relatively young institution. Our knowledge is better for later times, when its character had perhaps changed. But assuming that there was some continuity, its chief functions would have been both legislative and judicial. It consisted of seventy-one persons, presided over by the high priest. We are uninformed about its constituency and the mode of their selection; the tendency of scholars to see the Sanhedrin as an aristocratic rather than a democratic body is probably correct, especially for the early period. Perhaps at a later time it became more democratized, and perhaps its Sadducean character in early times had gradually given way by this time to a Pharisaic character. The Sanhedrin seems to have had authority over internal affairs, which had been delegated to it by the Romans; to say this in another way, Rome ruled Judea largely indirectly, allowing the Sanhedrin to enjoy a limited direct authority. The rabbinic book, the Mishnah, informs us, though possibly for a period later than that of Herod, that the Sanhedrin customarily met in the Temple, in the "Hall of the Hewn Stones." The members sat in a semicircle, so as to be able to see each other. Certain clerks were stationed in front of the Sanhedrin, and back of them were seated three rows of young men deemed to have legislative or judicial promise. Some rules of procedure were in force; for example, a member of the Sanhedrin who spoke in favor of an accused person was debarred from later speaking against him. Again, a person who was on trial could be acquitted by a simple majority, and the decision had to be announced immediately. A conviction, on the other hand, required a majority, but the later rabbis insisted on more than a bare majority of 36–35; the announcement of the decision needed to be deferred until the next day. Beyond its legal power, however, the Sanhedrin was the symbol of the corporate Jewish authority.

In the matter of the unlawful execution of Hezekiah, Herod was in theory answerable to the Sanhedrin on the charge of murder. The choice of intervening in the matter may well have lain with the disposition of the high priest, that is, with Hyrcanus.

Yet Hyrcanus appears to have had little interest initially in making any to-do over Herod's action. The foes whom Antipater had made saw an opportunity to injure him by occasioning difficulties for Herod. They accordingly made representation to Hyrcanus that Herod, in sentencing the guerrillas to death and thus usurping the prerogative of the Sanhedrin, was thereby a lawbreaker himself, guilty of a capital crime, and that he should stand trial before it. Moreover, these enemies of Antipater provided Hyrcanus with an interpretation of Herod's action; it was, they asserted, a calculated seizure of the power of Hyrcanus, as if Hyrcanus were the servant of Herod rather than his master.

It is uncertain how much Hyrcanus was initially moved by these contentions, but they were accompanied and climaxed by the almost daily appearance before the Temple of the mothers of the men whom Herod had slain, and these women pleaded with Hyrcanus to bring Herod to trial. So Hyrcanus ordered Herod to return to Jerusalem to stand trial for his life. We must notice that we have scarcely come to know Herod when we find him in a most serious situation, with the concomitant complexity of a powerful father possessed of formidable enemies, a high priest of passive disposition, and Rome in the background.

For Herod to disobey the summons of Hyrcanus was out of the question. He took a precaution, however; he prevailed on Sextus Caesar to write to Hyrcanus, urging the acquittal of Herod, and also threatening dire consequences in case he were to be convicted.

Though direct disobedience of the Sanhedrin was not possible, a restrained haughtiness was by no means ruled out. Accordingly, Herod, on the advice of his father, went from Galilee to Jerusalem accompanied by a bodyguard. Herod entered the city in the company of enough troops to assure his personal safety, but still few enough not to seem to be challenging the authority of Hyrcanus.

While Herod was the person on trial, his handsome appearance and his unconcerned manner completely overawed those who were trying him. Indeed, Herod's posture was exactly the reverse of that of a man before whom lay the possibility of the sentence of death. A crucial procedural necessity, the appearance of witnesses to testify against Herod, was not met, for no witnesses appeared to stand up and speak against him. Also, it was known in the Sanhedrin that Hyrcanus wanted an acquittal. The appearance of Herod before the Sanhedrin, under these circumstances, would have been a complete fiasco, were it not that there arose a member of the Sanhedrin named Samaias,[1] who spoke with some fearlessness. Whether the eloquence is that of Samaias, or of Josephus, or whether one of his secretaries composed the speech which, in the custom of Greek historians, would have been appropriate for the occasion, we do not know:

"My fellow members of the Sanhedrin, and my King, I myself do not know of anyone ever summoned for trial, nor do I believe you can name anyone, who has come before us in such a manner. Everyone else who has come before this Sanhedrin for trial has appeared humble, has seemed fearful, and has sought mercy; everyone has let his hair grow long and has dressed in a black garment. This splendid Herod, accused of murder and now summoned before us on that charge, stands arrayed in purple, with his hair carefully adorned, and he has his soldiers around him, either that he might slay us if in accordance with the law we should condemn him, or else that he may save himself by our doing violence to our justice. But I do not blame Herod for putting his own concern above the law. Rather

I blame you, and I blame our king, for giving him such great licence. You must know that our God is great; this man, whom for the sake of Hyrcanus you wish to release, will some day damage you, and then the king himself."

Yet despite the eloquence of Samaias, Hyrcanus adjourned the trial, and he secretly advised Herod to flee from Jerusalem so as to escape danger.[2]

On the face of it, the account of Herod before the Sanhedrin reads like a well-planned act of defiance, successfully carried off. Yet certain matters which here lie below the surface were destined to appear in full clarity later on. There can be no question but that Herod was frightened by the summons of Hyrcanus to stand trial before the Sanhedrin, and that he obeyed through being afraid to disobey. Since Sextus Caesar had intervened with Hyrcanus on his behalf, that meant that Sextus was to some extent united with Hyrcanus, and to defy Hyrcanus was for the moment equivalent to defying Sextus. The bravado of the accompanying bodyguard should not obscure the genuine fear that Herod felt, and if he indeed appeared before the Sanhedrin in the insolent manner which the speech of Samaias attributes to him, this was not so much due to Herod's intrepid character as to bluff and bluster. Herod, as we shall see, was an insecure man, and quite cognizant of the forces arrayed against his father, Antipater; and he was acutely aware that his Idumean origin made him uncongenial to the Judeans, just as the authenticity of their being Judeans made them distasteful to him. He went to Jerusalem to stand trial only because he saw no alternative. Once there and subjected to direct humiliation, and probably to countless indirect ones, Herod turned his fear and his insecurity into hatred and into the wish for a satisfying vengeance. He could forget that Hyrcanus, the Maccabean, had graciously let him flee to Damascus; he was never to forget that Hyrcanus made him come to stand trial. In fleeing to Damascus, Herod associated himself there with the Roman authorities to whom he was already congenial. Back in Jerusalem, the agitation by the enemies of Antipater continued, so that Hyrcanus was counseled and implored to summon Herod home to face a real trial. But Hyrcanus seemed aware that Herod would defy him; moreover, Hyrcanus reasoned that now Herod was with the Roman governor, he was too strong for Hyrcanus to challenge. Hyrcanus found it convenient to retire into his accustomed combination of inactivity, cowardice, and folly. He did not summon Herod, with the result that the latter had no need to scorn a demand to return.

At Damascus, Herod's fortunes rather quickly took a turn of considerable significance. Sextus Caesar, after accepting the appropriate and customary bribe, appointed him the governor of Coele-Syria and of Samaria. This was in 46 B.C. Promptly Herod marshaled his troops, not for his assigned area, but instead he set out for Jerusalem with the intention of taking the city and of deposing Hyrcanus.

On learning of this intention, Antipater and Phasael went forth to intercept Herod, and to set before him the reasons, which they considered cogent, why Herod should desist from his anger and from attacking Jerusalem. It would be sufficient, they argued, if he frightened and intimidated Hyrcanus; it was unnecessary to depose that very person who had acquiesced in the appointment which Herod had received as governor of Galilee. Moreover, so they argued, Herod could consider that he had been acquitted at the trial and had escaped being punished by death. Furthermore, the cause on which Herod now embarked was unjust, and therefore God would not support it, and without God's support even Herod's military strength might not suffice. (We shall encounter further examples of piety as a forceful argument.)

Satisfied by these appeals to him that he now possessed

genuine and decisive strength, Herod let himself be persuaded not to launch an attack, at least not at that time.

But as an aftermath of the civil war in 49, between Julius Caesar and Pompey, the Romans in Syria had come to be divided into the two camps of Pompeyites and Caesarites, and an imitative civil war persisted between the factions. Shortly after Sextus Caesar had named Herod governor of Coele-Syria, Sextus was assassinated by a follower of Pompey, Caecilius Bassus. Generals loyal to Sextus Caesar thereupon attacked Bassus. Antipater moved promptly to send assistance to the Caesarites, dispatching troops under the command of his sons to assist the loyal general Antistius Vetus in a siege of Apamea in northern Syria; this was in the fall of 45. In early 44, a new general, L. Statius Murcus, arrived in Syria to replace Antistius; and at the same time the Pompeyites sought and received assistance from the Parthians to the east. Syria, then, was caught in indecisive war. In March of 44, Julius Caesar, the friend and benefactor of the Judeans, was assassinated, and Cassius, one of the conspirators, arrived in Syria. Cassius raised the Caesarite siege of Apamea, and he then managed to consolidate the erstwhile warring Roman forces into a unity, under him.

Cassius required funds, and the Judeans had been friends of his foe Julius Caesar; Cassius thereupon levied a tribute on the Judeans. The sources disagree as to whether it was seven hundred or one hundred talents, in either case an enormous sum. The obligation fell nominally on Hyrcanus to raise the money, but in actuality on Antipater. The latter delegated the responsibility for imposing tax levies both on his sons and also on others, including a certain Malichus, a shadowy figure who may have had some officer's commission in the militia of Jerusalem. Cassius not only wanted the money, but he wanted it promptly; and when four cities in Judea were either slow or recalcitrant, he reduced them to servitude and sold all the men into slavery. Malichus was in some way guilty of dilatoriness, or at least suspect, and thereby he earned the hostile attention of Cassius; he was spared the wrath of Cassius only through the intervention of Antipater, who prevailed on Hyrcanus to furnish the money which Malichus was failing to supply. It seems probable that Malichus was not only dilatory but also on the point of rebellion against Cassius and Rome, and Antipater's intervention, although on behalf of Malichus, actually was designed to prevent the rise of disorders against himself, because of his connection with Rome. If Malichus was grateful to Antipater, he nevertheless continued to resent the Roman imposition of tribute, and he soon began to include Antipater and his sons as the objects of his hatred.

From the standpoint of Herod, and of whatever ambitions for personal power he may or may not have had at that moment, his situation at that juncture was one of complexity and of some perplexity. Toward Hyrcanus, Herod felt a hostility as a result of the order to stand trial before the Sanhedrin; on the other hand, there still existed in Judea, and in Galilee, some warmth of sentiment for the family of Hyrcanus' brother and erstwhile rival Aristobulus, whose surviving son Antigonus might some time return to Judea, and undoubtedly Antigonus could rally much of the populace to his cause. Antigonus, then, was clearly a potential enemy, as Hyrcanus did not need to be. The ultimate power, as Herod saw matters, was with either Antigonus or Hyrcanus—and as yet not with himself. Herod knew that he could not reasonably expect Judea to rally to him or support any endeavor of his own, for his strength in Judea was only the residual power of Antipater —and Antipater had enemies in abundance. As for Rome, the assassination of Sextus Caesar had deprived Herod of his sponsor and patron. Respecting Cassius, it was to his

Caesarite foes that Herod had brought partial relief at Apamea, and hence Cassius was hardly a friend.

It seemed to Herod that there was a greater prospect of winning Cassius to himself than any of the plural factions in Judea. Therefore, in contrast to Malichus who was dilatory in raising the tribute money, Herod, keenly aware that it was politic to please Romans, set out to do so with promptness and efficiency, and with ruthlessness. As soon as the money was in hand, he visited Cassius, and he solicited Cassius' good will, and that of Cassius' underlings, with judicious bribes. For the moment, Herod managed to begin to please Cassius.

Then Malichus raised some troops, and embarked on rebellion against Hyrcanus. Antipater, responsible to Rome for law and order, needed to put down this uprising. Malichus apparently had a following among the Judeans, and Antipater found it necessary to employ Nabatean mercenaries to crush the rebellion. The stage was set, then, for a pitched battle between the forces of Antipater and Malichus, but either the latter feared that his troops were insufficient to match those of Antipater, or else he recognized that Rome stood ready to come to the aid of Antipater. So, instead of a battle, there took place a reconciliation between Malichus and Antipater, with Malichus swearing publicly that at no time had he intended to revolt against Antipater. The Romans, apprised of the incident, proposed that they seize and execute Malichus, but Antipater again intervened on his behalf, less out of trust of Malichus than out of anxiety that such an execution would increase both Antipater's Judean enemies and also the disorders. So Malichus' life was spared.

Herod, in the meantime, consolidated his relationship with Cassius and with Cassius' general Murcus, and again, in 43, he received the governorship of Coele-Syria. His promptness in raising the tribute had paid off; from the standpoint of Cassius, a governor loyal to him was at that moment an urgent necessity. At Rome, Octavius Caesar, the nephew of Julius, had composed some acute difficulties with Mark Antony, and a new triumvirate, Mark Antony, Octavius, and Lepidus, were preparing, among other necessities, to destroy Cassius, who was in Syria, and Brutus, who was in Macedonia. Not only was Herod's courting of Cassius prudent to Herod, but it was also timely to Cassius. Along with Herod's appointment as governor, there came from Cassius the intimation that once Antony and Octavius would be dealt with, and they would be out of the way, Herod could expect to be designated king of Judea.

We have hitherto seen so relatively little of Herod that we have had slight reason to deny him ambition, or sufficient basis on which to specify the objective of the ambition which we have glimpsed; the way in which the connection between Herod and the throne are here intertwined in Josephus is exceedingly abrupt. One almost suspects that, since Herod did become the king, Josephus forgot to tell us when and under what circumstances the wish became clear to him and governed his energies and his purposes. Perhaps, when earlier he set out as if to conquer Jerusalem, he already saw himself as a royal conqueror; it is as likely, however, that that was merely a punitive expedition, especially since Antipater and Phasael so readily diverted him. Again, later on, when the throne was proffered to Herod, the account in Josephus interprets the gesture as striking Herod with some surprise, as if Herod had never contemplated such a thing. The abruptness of the mention of kingship here must appear to us as a product of the unevenness in Josephus' account. We must simply conclude that we do not know when or under what conditions Herod conceived the intention to become the king, but from this point on in our narrative it must be in our minds, even if it was as yet not in Herod's.

In Judea, during that summer, Malichus, the general who was twice saved by Antipater's intervention, expressed his ingratitude in a startling way. Invited along with Antipater to dine with Hyrcanus, he bribed one of the butlers to poison Antipater. On Antipater's death, disorders—probably anti-Roman riots—broke out in Jerusalem, but Malichus, publicly mourning his good friend Antipater, restored order in the capital city. Herod was in Syria; as to Phasael, we do not know his whereabouts at that time; one notes that Phasael receives mention in Josephus only in connection with the acute need which the brothers soon came to feel to take vengeance on Malichus.

Josephus gives two different, brief eulogies of Antipater. In one (*The Jewish War* I, 226), he speaks of Antipater as "a man most energetic in handling affairs, whose crowning merit was that he regained and preserved the royal authority for Hyrcanus." In the other passage (*Antiquities* XIV, 283) he describes Antipater as "outstanding in piety, justice, and devotion to his fatherland." There is no reason to suppose that the practice prevalent today, of concocting eulogies which invent achievement, or exaggerate it, and glide over deficiencies of character, did not exist in those days; hence one cannot take these sentiments as precise description. Indeed, some scholars feel that the account, especially in *Antiquities*, is strongly shaped by the source which Josephus utilized, the court biography of Herod by Nicholas of Damascus, which included the equally favorable appraisal of Antipater. Granted, then, that possibly we cannot accept these assessments at face value, we must weigh them against an opposite assessment which is in the public domain, derived from passages in the New Testament. In the Gospel According to Matthew, the infant Jesus escaped death at the hands of Herod in the "slaughter of the innocents," through the flight of Jesus' father and his family to Egypt; Herod Antipas, Herod's son, beheaded John the Baptist at the behest of his stepdaughter (Mark 6: 14–29; Matthew 14: 1–12). In the New Testament and in the expanding Christian lore the Herodians are all regarded as deep-dyed villains. In this light, it becomes intelligible that in even supposedly scientific summaries, such as are found in standard encyclopedias, Antipater customarily appears as a wily scoundrel, and he is almost universally depicted, not as a Jew of Idumean extraction but, rather, as still an Idumean.

If Josephus errs in overpraising Antipater, the denigration of the man is also an error. Certainly his career reveals his ingenuity and resourcefulness, and one can speak of him as shrewd, but in a quite favorable sense. That Antipater was a self-seeker is unmistakable, but that he was only that is a distortion; moreover, it is not possible to divide the facet of the drive for personal satisfaction in any would-be leader, of any time or any place, from the genuine devotion to a cause, for these are intermingled beyond easy separation. Antipater had prevailed upon Hyrcanus to elect dependency on Rome as the best strategy for assuring the welfare of Judea, while Aristobulus, and the Galilean guerrillas, chose independence, even at the possible cost of a destructive war. One could draw the contrast between servility, on the one hand, and noble patriotism on the other, as if these opposite qualities were necessarily pure and inescapable contrasts, and as if strategy and motive were inevitably interchangeable. But one could readily argue, to the contrary, that those who chose independence were marked by both impulsiveness and irresponsibility, and that the higher loyalty and patriotism lay with those who relied on prudence. In such matters it is quite impossible to probe the hearts of people, even when we know considerably more about them than we do about Antipater, and even when they have lived in situations more nearly comparable to those of the later age which seeks a value judgment. We must, therefore, forgo the dubious pleasure of a meaningless contrast between an Aristobulus and an Antipater on unassessable inner motives, and confine ourselves instead to that which is more demonstrable from the external events.

The facts, then, are these, that Antipater was a Jew, a Jew of Idumean extraction, in his own way dedicated to the welfare of Judea, and in his own way marked by an ambition for personal eminence which reveals a usual combination of laudable and unlaudable aspects. To stress that Antipater was an Idumean seems clearly to emphasize exactly that which Antipater would have resented most deeply, for if anything is implicit in his career it was his wish to be, and to be regarded as, an authentic and fully loyal Jew. Indeed, those aspects in his career in which he labored on behalf of Julius Caesar are intelligible only on the basis of Antipater's Jewishness, as was the case when he appealed to the Jews of Pelusium, on the basis of his and their common Jewishness. In the offspring of a convert, whether then or now, one often finds that the authenticity of his recent affiliation is inevitably suspect in some quarters, and therefore his need to be accepted universally as authentic is acute. Antipater was a Jew, and he needed to be regarded as a Jew, and accepted fully as a Jew, and perhaps his Jewish patriotism, which ought not to be doubted, was the more acute and profound simply because of his need for acceptance.

The effect of the death of Antipater on Herod yielded, we have said, an acute need on the part of both Herod and Phasael for vengeance. Yet the death had still another consequence, of a totally different kind. We saw in Herod's execution of the guerrillas his efficiency and effectiveness, and we saw it again in his quick raising of the tribute money for the Romans. Yet he was not only quick and effective, he was also prone to impulse, as evidenced by his intention to beseige Jerusalem and harm Hyrcanus; in that instance Antipater was able to serve as a deterrent. With the death of Antipater, Herod forever lost the precious tool of restraint. In his subsequent long career Herod was to succumb to frequent impulsiveness, especially when the sense of insecurity was to oppress him. Moreover, in the transition from one generation to the second, there was this significant development, that whereas Antipater's ambition was to have power under Hyrcanus, Herod came to desire the power which was Hyrcanus'.

Malichus, having brought about the death of Antipater, needed the comfort and the public appearance of seeming innocence, for there were enough partisans of Antipater and Phasael in Jerusalem to endanger him. The choice before the survivors of Antipater was that of embarking on immediate reprisal, or of deferring it, so that the reprisal could be achieved with greater smoothness. Herod appears to have preferred immediate reprisal, and to have been prepared to lead troops against Malichus; his older brother, Phasael, persuaded him to resort instead to cunning. As a result, there arose in Jerusalem the broad supposition that Antipater's heirs truly considered Malichus to be as innocent as Malichus had pretended to be. A tranquil, elaborate burial of Antipater took place, and Herod returned to the north, to occupy himself with settling some of the problems of Samaria, where uprisings had taken place. But the time of a festival, probably the fall harvest, Tabernacles, drew near, and it would have been quite ordinary for Herod, like any Jew, to make a pilgrimage to the Temple in Jerusalem, as prescribed in Exodus 23:14; 34:23, and Deuteronomy 16:16. Herod therefore set out for Jerusalem, again accompanied by troops. The knowledge that Herod was approaching Jerusalem alarmed both Malichus and

Hyrcanus, for they suspected that Herod had a motive quite beyond that of religious piety, and it seemed desirable to them to bar Herod from entry into the sacred city. They needed a pretext, however, and this they found in the Gentile mercenary troops who accompanied Herod; they informed Herod that an influx of aliens would destroy the state of ritual purity of the Jews resident or gathered in Jerusalem. Hyrcanus, therefore, at the bidding of Malichus, forbade Herod to enter the city. Herod might have chosen to force his way in at the head of his troops. Instead, he slipped into Jerusalem by night, but made sure that Malichus knew he was there. Malichus, completely terrorized, arranged a meeting with Herod, a step which he took on the basis of information that Herod had left his troops behind him, outside Jerusalem. The two met as if they were friends. Malichus renewed his shedding of tears over the death of Antipater, and Herod pretended to accept the protestations of Malichus' innocence. After this happy meeting, however, Malichus provided himself with an adequate bodyguard. Herod had full clarity about his objective, the killing of Malichus. But he knew that he needed sufficient military strength for what might ensue thereafter, and he needed also the acquiescence of Rome in his objective. So Herod wrote to Cassius for permission to do away with Malichus. At Latakia, Cassius had just defeated the Roman general Dolabella, who had then committed suicide, and Cassius was now preparing to encounter Mark Antony himself. Cassius gladly gave Herod the desired permission, and he instructed his subordinates to provide assistance to Herod in the event that he should require such help.

The setting in which the act of vengeance unfolded was the Phoenician city of Tyre. To that city came both Herod and Malichus; it is probable, though uncertain, that Cassius himself was there to receive the homage, and the bribes, of the grandees of Syria. In some way a son of Malichus had become a hostage, held prisoner by the Romans; Malichus was at Tyre, apparently to effect the release, or else the escape, of his son. Perhaps Malichus may have had in mind a seizure of power from the doddering Hyrcanus, and possibly even a revolt against Rome; in any case, Josephus attributes these several motives to him.

Hyrcanus, a grandee, was also present in Tyre. Herod thereupon invited both Hyrcanus and Malichus to come to him for dinner. When the two guests arrived, they found Roman soldiers waiting for Malichus, and these slew him. Immediately Hyrcanus fainted, shattered by his witnessing the slaying. On reviving, he asked by whose orders Malichus had been slain, and Herod replied that it was by the orders of Cassius. Hyrcanus then prudently expressed his great relief that he and his country had been saved from the wicked conspirator Malichus. So Herod avenged the death of his father, and without any need to fear punishment from or through Hyrcanus.

During the next year, 42, Cassius departed from Syria, and thereupon all Syria became a place of unrest. The forces and partisanships that have only been hinted at up to this point now begin to emerge more clearly in Judea, forces that can now be denominated as pro- and anti-Herod. In Jerusalem, the capital, there was an outbreak of hostilities under circumstances not entirely clear. A certain Helix, or Felix in the Latin usage, had some troops under his command there, possibly under an arrangement made earlier when Hyrcanus had decided to go to Tyre to call on Cassius; Helix and his troops attacked Herod's brother Phasael at the very time that Herod went from Tyre to Damascus to visit the Roman governor. Herod, learning of this attack, wanted to hasten to assist his brother, but he fell ill. Even without Herod's help, Phasael was able to rout Helix, who, significantly, had received some support from Hyrcanus, as if Hyrcanus felt the need to oppose Herod's brother. Phasael moved his troops to the district west[3] of the Dead Sea, where the brother of Malichus was holed up in the famous fortress of Masada; it would seem that this brother of Malichus had gained possession of a good many fortresses, through Hyrcanus' consent. What one begins to perceive in these confusions and partisanships is that with the departure of Cassius from Syria a veritable civil war broke out in Judea, with Phasael and Herod arrayed against Hyrcanus, though by no means openly. When Herod recovered from his illness, he joined Phasael in a successful seige of Masada. But immediately the two factions, the pro-Hyrcanus and the pro-Herod, were increased to three sets by the arrival in Judea of Antigonus, the son of Aristobulus. Whatever attention Herod might have wanted to bestow on the brother of Malichus, apparently Hyrcanus' agent, it was more urgent to meet the challenge from Antigonus. The latter had managed to bribe the Roman governor at Damascus and to persuade Marion, the king of Tyre, so that they were prepared to assist him to regain the throne. Promptly Herod made war against Antigonus and Marion, and defeated them, and again Antigonus fled.

Herod, accordingly, had conquered the troops of the Maccabean Hyrcanus at Masada, and also the forces of the Maccabean Antigonus, and it was therefore appropriate now to return to Jerusalem. He found an unexpected warm welcome at the capital, but we do not know whether this was an earnest greeting bestowed on the triumphant conqueror or only a prudent, calculated acclaim by a frightened populace.

Quite clearly, Herod was the true master of the situation; but the time was not yet ripe for him, in the year 42, to assume the full control of Judea. Unquestionably, Herod did not lack even then the means to assert his control. He did lack, however, a certain semblance of legitimacy, for royal mastery was still broadly deemed to be the prerogative of the Maccabeans, and not of the descendants of Antipater. It will be recalled that Herod was married to a woman named Doris, a commoner, and he already had a son by her, whom he had named Antipater. Now he entered into betrothal—not marriage, but only engagement—with a young woman who was a veritable Maccabean, a woman named Mariamne. Her father was the late Alexander, the son of Aristobulus; her mother was Alexandra, the daughter and only child of Hyrcanus.[4] Mariamne, much younger than the thirty-year-old Herod, is described as a girl of great beauty. This betrothal was a brilliant step on the part of Herod, for it helped to pave the way to his kingship. It might also have paved the way to great personal happiness, for, as we shall see, he loved her deeply. But Herod loved power. Moreover, however important he had already become, and however more eminent he was destined to be, he had married above him. Mariamne knew that this was the case, and Mariamne's mother, Alexandra, who also knew it, was a shrew.

We do not know how Doris responded at that time to her husband's acquisition of a second wife, something in that era perfectly proper, though unusual, among Jews. We can conjecture about her displeasure. Momentarily she disappears from our view; the son Antipater, still only a boy, does not yet enter the scene.

How shall we account for the puzzling attitude of Hyrcanus, in that he allowed and even sanctioned the marriage of Herod and Mariamne? Perhaps his lack of forcefulness, emphasized so often by Josephus, impeded whatever desire he might have felt to block the marriage; yet this is scarcely credible, for if he was anemic, his daughter Alexandra was not; she was able to act with extreme vigor. The answer seems to be that Hyrcanus favored the marriage and welcomed it, for so great was his fear of his nephew Antigonus, and so helpless was he in dealing with the Romans whose support he required to retain his throne, that he found an alliance with Herod an advantage, while to oppose it would be to add to his tribulations. The marriage could well have appealed to Hyrcanus as the best means of ensuring that Herod would become committed to retain Hyrcanus on the throne, rather than determined to seize it. Indeed, insofar as Hyrcanus might have pondered the question of who would succeed him, this marriage could especially have seemed agreeable, for perhaps Herod would desist from the throne, and permit the crown to go to Alexandra, a widow, and thereafter be destined either for Alexandra's only son, the brother of Mariamne, named (how these repeated names tend to confuse!) Aristobulus, or to Mariamne herself. By this impending marriage, then, the Judean throne conceivably could remain in Hyrcanus' family. Or perhaps we raise such questions because of the distaste which we have for machinations and violence and plottings and maneuvers when we are remote from them and can afford to be disdainful; it is quite possible that the marriage appeared to Hyrcanus as a typical arrangement on the part of people in and around high places, and that he saw no ineligibility in Herod and no incongruity such as we ourselves may see. Yet the suspicion defies eradication that, without regard to questions of love and affection between bride and groom, the marriage was Hyrcanus' ultimate bribe of Herod to gain and retain Herod's loyalty.

His betrothal to the Maccabean princess brought Herod to a new pinnacle in his career and ambitions, but the complications of both international and internal Judean politics gradually converted the situation, and Herod's high expectations, into defeat and despair. These complications were tortuous, a matter of indirect and only loosely connected sequels. When Cassius had departed from Syria, it was to join up with Brutus; arrayed against them were Mark Antony and Octavius Caesar. The battle of Philippi was fought in Macedonia in 42. Octavius and Antony were victorious, and Brutus and Cassius committed suicide. Octavius—soon to become known as Augustus—returned to Rome; Antony, who found it convenient to marry a sister of Augustus, for he was a widower, became the master of Roman affairs in the east. The raids and invasions by the Parthians had continued, and one of the chores that lay before Antony was that of reconquering the territory which the Parthians had taken. Arduous military necessities confronted Antony, and, at the same time, so did the diversion of a pleasant and profoundly mutual liaison with Cleopatra of Egypt. That robust woman, it will be recalled, had gained the kingdom of Egypt with the help of Julius Caesar. She had become the mistress of Caesar, even to the point of bearing him a son, and she had followed him to Rome, but had returned to Egypt after the assassination. Later, since Egypt was in the east where Antony commanded, he naturally visited her, with the objective of imposing Roman discipline upon her. Antony had promptly fallen in love with her.

Antony established his headquarters for his expedition against the Parthians in the east, in Bithynia, a province on the Black Sea in Asia Minor. To Bithynia came a host of deputations, from an abundance of petty monarchies, to pay their respects to the new Roman master, and Judea was, of course, represented among the callers. Indeed, a Judean deputation was there, consisting of men whom Josephus calls "leading Jews," whose purpose was to make accusations before Antony against Herod and Phasael. These accusations, according to Josephus, were intended to amount to no more than the illegal grasp of power by Herod and Phasael, who were outwardly retaining Hyrcanus as the monarch. The difficulty is that these allegations were exceedingly mild; moreover, if only the illegal grasp of power was the real substance of the proposed complaint, then the complainant should have been Hyrcanus rather than the leading Jews. Accordingly, some more substantial recriminations might well have been intended by these leading Jews, if only the deputation could obtain an audience with Antony. But Herod too was present in Bithynia; he bribed his own way into an audience with Antony, and he also bribed those Romans in position to prevent the leading Jews from gaining theirs. Since it was the Roman Antony who was being wooed, the contest for attention was unequal, for the leading Jews were personally unknown to Antony, but he remembered the services rendered him by Antipater when Antony was only a general, especially when he was reminded of them. So Herod gained the day at Bithynia.

Antony moved to Ephesus, where again he attracted deputations, and there he acquiesced in a request from unknown petitioners to free some Jews who had been captured and enslaved by Cassius. He moved to Cilicia in 41; an Egyptian delegation came there, led by Cleopatra herself; she had sailed up the Cydnus River in a golden barge to be with her lover. Again at Daphne, near Antioch, rival Jewish delegations appeared before Antony, one to speak against Herod and Phasael, and one for them; indeed, Hyrcanus himself was present. Herod had had the foresight to engage as his spokesman a certain Marcus Valerius Messala, an author and orator of considerable prominence. It was Messala who replied to the accusations which the "Jewish leaders" made against the brothers. With Hyrcanus present, Antony seems to have turned to the latter as if he were an impartial and sagacious adviser; for he asked Hyrcanus to whom the governing of Judea should be entrusted. In his reply Hyrcanus spoke of his prefer-

ence for the brothers Herod and Phasael; thereupon
Antony consented to Hyrcanus' wishes. Herod, then, continued in his ascent. Antony designated the brothers to be
tetrarchs; this term means, literally, "ruler of a fourth," and
might represent the equivalent of a title like duke or baron.
What we do not know about the title is exactly what rights
it ordinarily implied, and we are especially in the dark as
to the division of authority between Hyrcanus and the
brothers. As was the case when Antipater and Hyrcanus
were in close association, we are again left to conjecture
about the specific authority, for if Hyrcanus retained any
prerogative of monarchy, then the authority of his associates was thereby limited; on the other hand, if the associates had the real authority, we do not know what was
left to Hyrcanus. Indeed, we need to remind ourselves of
a vacillation respecting the latter's office between the title
king and the title high priest. Perhaps the answer to the
confusion about the title which Hyrcanus bore may be
resolved by assuming that he was unbrokenly regarded by
the Romans as the high priest, which office carried with it
certain political overtones, but in addition he was at different and uncertain intervals also known, or else regarded, as
king.

As to the Jewish opponents of Herod, Antony rudely
dismissed all but fifteen of them, and these fifteen he prepared to execute. Herod, however, interceded with Antony
on their behalf, not so much out of pity as out of the
awareness that their execution would increase the antagonism to him in Judea.

A little later Antony came to Tyre, and this time the
Jewish deputation to him, if we can trust Josephus, numbered a thousand. Herod appeared before the leaders, accompanied by Hyrcanus, to urge that they disband and
return to Judea. They rejected Herod's appeal; promptly,
then, the Roman soldiers fell upon them, killing a great

many. Enough of them escaped, however, to constitute a group around which the other opponents of Herod would be enabled to rally.

So, despite a succession of delegations whose main purpose was to denounce him, Herod had been winning the support of Rome in general and of Mark Antony in particular. His Judean enemies were increasing.

The Roman control of Syria continued to waver, and the Parthians renewed their westward drive. Antony had gone from Tyre to Egypt, to be with Cleopatra, so that, with Rome indifferent, by the end of 40 the Parthians succeeded in overrunning Syria. Naturally, the Parthians turned next to the invasion of Judea. Antigonus, the son of Aristobulus, now returns to our narrative. The Parthians thought that he would be useful to them in that Judeans would presumably rally to him, and thereby weaken Hyrcanus and Herod; Antigonus thought the Parthians would be useful to him, in that, with Rome against him, they might have the power to bring him to the throne in place of his uncle Hyrcanus.

Antigonus had chosen a propitious moment for his effort, and, if we can believe Josephus, he had offered the Parthians a welcome bribe of money, and five hundred women, including the wives and daughters of Herod and his brothers. Antigonus and the Parthians moved against Jerusalem, and there they won a limited victory. Parthian troops entered the city for a further assault on Herod and Phasael. Despite the assistance which some of the populace gave the invaders, so that Herod had to fight not only against the Parthians but also against the residents of Jerusalem, the brothers were able to withstand the onslaught. If Herod made any appeals to Rome for assistance, these went unanswered. Toward his Jewish foes he was merciless.

In our times warfare seems always total. In the ongoing

contest between the Parthians and Herod at Jerusalem, we appear to deal, at least for a time, with skirmishes, limited in scope. While it seems clear that a great battle was shaping up inside Jerusalem, nevertheless we read that with the approach of Pentecost, one of the three pilgrimage festivals, thousands of visitors were arriving in Jerusalem. Many of these were armed; quite possibly the festival was, for some of the pilgrims, only a pretext for coming to Jerusalem to join Antigonus in his effort.

It would appear that Herod and Phasael at this time had lost all of Jerusalem except the royal palace, but this they controlled with some considerable force. The Parthian general, Pacorus, entered into negotiations with Herod and Phasael. He persuaded Phasael to leave Jerusalem, accompanied by Hyrcanus, to pay a call upon the king of the Parthians, Barzaphranes, who was then in Galilee. Herod was suspicious and advised against the journey, but Phasael insisted on going.

In Galilee the Parthians began with meetings and negotiations with Phasael, as part of a deliberate scheme to immobilize him, and at the propitious moment to assault Herod in Jerusalem. But Phasael began to suspect the Parthians, and he expressed his suspicions to them directly, and to Herod by messenger. The Parthians thereupon made prisoners in chains of Phasael and Hyrcanus, and at the same time sent a deputation to Jerusalem to continue to negotiate with Herod, as if all were well. Word came to Herod that his brother and Hyrcanus were prisoners, and he recognized from that fact that he stood on the threshold of a catastrophe.

Our sources fail to clarify fully this rather abrupt reversal of circumstances, though the inferences seem to be plain enough. Herod was dependent not on Hyrcanus but on Rome, and Antony was more interested in Cleopatra than in fighting the Parthians, and unconcerned about

Herod. Judea had disclosed itself, at least at that juncture, as partial to the line of Aristobulus, and opposed to the coalition of Hyrcanus and Herod. Accordingly, Antigonus and the Parthians were the masters of Judea, while Herod and Hyrcanus, abandoned by the Romans, were bereft of decisive power and of any immediate possibility of regaining it.

Two courses lay before Herod. One was to continue the pretense of negotiation with the Parthians and to use the interval as best he could to strengthen his military position. Yet he felt that he was on the verge of being done in by the Parthians and, in addition his betrothed, Mariamne, kept advising him of their untrustworthiness and treachery. Hence, though negotiation with the Parthians would give him more time to build up his forces, the end result could be a decisive military engagement with the likelihood of a great defeat. The second course, a bitter one, was that of a prompt flight from Jerusalem; it meant abandoning the capital city for the sake of immediate safety, but left the prospect of thereafter mustering forces for a victorious return. Herod chose to flee.

The only direction to go was south, through Idumea, to Nabatea. He took with him on the flight Mariamne and her mother, Alexandra, his own mother, Cypros, his brother Joseph and his sister, Salome, and a body of soldiers to protect him on his journey. He had to move with some swiftness, for the enemy set out in pursuit.

This abandonment of Jerusalem—where apparently Hyrcanus made his way, trusting in his Maccabean lineage —was a total defeat, a great disaster for Herod. Josephus spends a sentence depicting the heartbreak, especially of the women with Herod, at the need to forsake Jerusalem and to undergo the privations of the hasty flight and the unknown dangers that would lie along the way. The danger was not alone that of the pursuit by the Parthians, but in addition hostile Judean guerrillas lay in wait to harass the refugees on the way.

Our source, Josephus, now tells us of two related things of consequence to our understanding of Herod. On the one hand, it was Herod whose bravery and high spirits gave some sense of encouragement to the downhearted refugees; indeed, Herod continually exposed himself to personal danger at the rear in covering the flight of this cumbersome company. On the other hand, there was an incident on the way. The wagon in which his mother, Cypros, was riding overturned. She escaped injury in the mishap, but the delay caused by the accident increased the danger that the foe might overtake them. This double anxiety brought Herod to the very point of taking his own life; indeed, he had pulled his sword out and was on the verge of stabbing himself. His fellow refugees restrained him, and then they reproached him for his readiness to abdicate his leadership and to abandon his near ones to the foe. The attempt at suicide reflects Herod's grasp of the disastrous character of the defeat inflicted by the Parthians. The fugitives managed through a swift journey to reach the safety of the fortress Masada.

Granted that the sudden shift in Herod's circumstances, from the gratifying patronage of the Romans under Mark Antony to his desolation at Roman unconcern at his plight, and the desperate flight for his life, created a mood of despair, the question arises about the significance of this impulse to suicide. Was it commensurate with the drastically and rapidly changed circumstances? Or should we interpret its occasion, the overturning of the wagon, as a despair-laden incident which only chanced, there and then, to prompt a reaction far beyond the incident itself? Was it a moment in which Herod stepped out of character, as it were? Or was it fully consistent with his nature and therefore a typical reaction, the expected response from a highly emotional man? Was this compulsion to inflict injury upon himself only a momentary lapse, during which he felt a recurrent need to injure people, but since there were no foes around, he had to direct the damage to himself? Or was this a true suicidal tendency, which, when he could, he diverted from himself and, instead, inflicted injury upon others, his real or imagined foes? Our knowledge of what was internal in Herod is far too scanty to permit a reliable answer. Yet it seems well within the scope of what we do know that he was a man of high emotion who in given situations repeatedly lost control of himself. At the loss of this control, in an age and a context of Roman or Greco-Roman or Parthian despotisms, Herod absorbed the ways of his fellow tyrants, and he became fully despotic himself. Life was cheap, and to kill people was to conform to the strange mores of monarchs of those days.

As to Jewish moral teaching, which might have averted both suicide and the pattern of merciless killings, we shall see that at no time does it ever seriously enter into Herod's ken, and thereby into our account. Herod was a Jew, but not Jewish; not only was he not Jewish in any genuine religious sense, but he had no great wish to be. Through the activities of his father, Antipater, he felt, as his son, that a certain prerogative was due him from the Judean state; through his engagement to Mariamne, he felt that his aspirations were legitimate. The prerogatives inherited from his father had grown in his mind well beyond his father's. While Herod felt that in a sense he owed Judea the obligation of patriotism and loyalty, even at this time of disaster and despair, in reality he felt that Judea belonged to him, not he to Judea; the Parthians and Antigonus had deprived him of what was his. In one mood Herod was ready to kill himself; in other moments he was unshakably committed to regaining what had been taken from him. He needed to be restrained from suicide; he needed no urging toward regaining his power.

The Parthians added a humiliation to their defeat of him; they proceeded to crown Antigonus king. Moreover, they handed both Phasael and Hyrcanus over to Antigonus. Jewish legislation demanded that the high priest be free of all bodily defect and blemish. Antigonus had no wish to risk any rivalry from his uncle. He therefore accomplished the disqualification of Hyrcanus as high priest by mutilating his ears; indeed, one of our two accounts tells us graphically that Antigonus lacerated the ears of Hyrcanus with his own teeth. He then sent Hyrcanus away from Judea, to Parthia. The flight of Herod prevented Antigonus from delivering the Herodian women to Pacorus. Phasael met death either through suicide, by dashing himself against a rock, or else, being wounded in an unsuccessful attempt at suicide, he died at the hands of the physicians whom Antigonus sent, ostensibly to heal him.

Herod was in desperate straits, not only for the support and safety of his fugitive entourage, but beyond the present, for the means to reclaim his privileges in Judea. His great needs led him to extravagant, illusory hopes from the Nabateans, who were under obligations to Antipater for favors rendered. Indeed, so Josephus tells us, the Nabateans owed a monetary debt to Antipater. When the fugitives reached Nabatea, Herod made known his wishes for a refuge, and for financial help. The Nabateans, however, neither acknowledged an obligation of any kind nor wished to attract the unfavorable notice of the Parthians. They peremptorily ordered Herod out of their territory. Therefore he had a score to settle with them some day.

One course alone now lay before Herod, to turn to the Romans for assistance. He sent his family to the safety of the fortress at Masada, and he set out for Egypt, a Roman possession. Perhaps Antony was still there. The Nabateans quickly learned his destination, and, recalling the avidity of the Egyptians for Nabatean territory, they tried to intercept him in order to inform him that they had changed their mind about helping him, but Herod crossed into Egypt before the Nabateans could overtake him.

At Pelusium some minor and unexplained obstacles impeded him, though only briefly, but Herod's eminence was already such that he won a favorable response to his expressed wish to be taken to Alexandria. Antony was now back in Rome; from Cleopatra, Herod received, in addition to the promise of a ship, a notably warm welcome. Indeed, it may well have been more personally warm than Herod wished. Josephus informs us that Cleopatra detained him in Alexandria; he implies, though not clearly, that she wished some liaison with him; he relates that she solicited him to command an unspecified expedition, possibly to lead troops which would be part of Antony's projected campaign against the Parthians. If Cleopatra indeed wished, or even proposed, some affair with Herod, it is easy to understand that Herod, intending to proceed to see Antony at Rome, had no wish first to make Antony's mistress his own, and then come to Antony as a petitioner. Cleopatra was later to have another opportunity.

Since it was winter, the sea journey to Rome was a dangerous one. Storms diverted Herod's ship from its course, and forced him to the island of Rhodes for a short sojourn. There he managed to procure a new ship, despite his lack of funds, and he moved on to Brundisium (Brindisi), and then to Rome.

When he made his appeal to Antony, the Roman had a number of reasons for being responsive. Not only did Antony remember the favors of Antipater, but he was moved by a hatred of Antigonus and by the desire that someone move against this pawn of the Parthians. Again, he felt some compassion for Herod in view of the vicissitudes through which he had passed. Antony, moreover, admired Herod's abilities. In addition, according to one of the two accounts in Josephus, Herod promised Antony a considerable bribe, payable at a later time. As for Augustus Caesar, the co-ruler with Antony, it was only necessary that Herod provide a reminder of the services which Antipater had rendered Julius Caesar, and Augustus was persuaded to acquiesce in Antony's wishes.

So Antony and Augustus convened the Roman Senate. They arranged for two orators to present Herod to that noble body, and there to expatiate on his affirmative qualities and on the rascality of Antigonus, the Parthian tool. Then Antony proposed that the Senate, in view of the impending campaign against the Parthians, in which Herod could and would assist, name Herod king of Judea. The Senate voted unanimously in favor of the proposal, and Herod was given the honor of being escorted from the Senate by Antony and Augustus, graciously walking one on each side of him.

So, from then on, it was King Herod. Except that Herod still lacked the throne.

It took at most a week for Herod to receive the kingship and the grants of money. If the question is raised that Mariamne's brother Aristobulus, as a Maccabean, had a more legitimate claim to the throne than Herod, then one understands a sentence in Josephus that avers that Herod never requested the kingship for himself, but supposed, rather, that the Romans would reserve it for Aristobulus. The effect of this sentence is to suggest that the kingship was an unsought gift, possibly even a surprise to Herod. Many modern scholars have regarded this sentence as a prevarication stemming from the court biographer of Herod. If it is correct that Herod went to Rome to obtain the throne, then one needs nevertheless to understand why the Romans bypassed Aristobulus. The answer would appear to be that the Romans were much more interested in an experienced warrior such as Herod than in an unknown youth, Aristobulus, the merit of whose claim was only its legitimacy. If we charge that Herod stole the throne from Aristobulus, he did so with warm Roman consent and approval.

Herod's company of fugitives, at Masada under the command of his brother Joseph, were undergoing a siege by Antigonus, and were on the verge of capitulating. A timely rain brought the besieged some badly needed water; also, there marched southward from Syria the Roman general Ventidius, presumably to bring aid to Joseph; Ventidius had defeated an army of the Parthians in 39. Ventidius encamped near Jerusalem, as if to invest the capital. Ventidius had little desire, however, to move on to the relief of Masada; moreover, he conceived the idea of soliciting a bribe from Antigonus in return for not attacking Jerusalem. Antigonus paid the bribe to Ventidius, and the Roman general returned to Syria, but appointed an underling general, Silo, to remain in the vicinity of Jerusalem to receive continuing bribes to share with and transmit to his superior.

Herod sailed from Italy, in late 40 or early 39, and landed at Ptolemais, some ten miles north of Mount Carmel. There he managed to collect an army of both Judeans and foreigners, and he set out to march through Galilee and reclaim it. The Galilean Jews apparently flocked to him, presumably because they had suffered under Antigonus. The Romans, meanwhile, commanded Ventidius and Silo to assist Herod, but the former was apparently busy on some campaign against the Parthians, while the latter persisted in remaining near Jerusalem, so as to be available to receive Antigonus' bribes.

Herod's first military objective was not Jerusalem, but the relief of Masada. For his southward drive he needed to neutralize the coastal town of Joppa in order to protect his flank. He asked Silo for help in the siege of Joppa. Silo left the vicinity of Jerusalem to join up with Herod at the coast, but the residents of Jerusalem pursued and attacked him; Herod, thereupon, had to come to the rescue of Silo. Herod managed to take Joppa and he moved on to Masada, where he lifted the siege and freed his fugitive family. And now the populace of parts of Judea seemed eager to join with him, not only because he seemed to be again in the ascendancy, but because it was felt that with him as king, the country would enjoy some long period of stability in place of the disorders involved in the Roman challenge of the fading Parthian control.

Herod, with the assistance of Silo, moved to besiege Jerusalem, and encamped on the western side of the city. He ordered his troops to proclaim to the inhabitants within the walls that he had come for the good of the citizens and the welfare of the city, that he bore no grudge even against those who were openly his foes, and that he was prepared to forget the offenses committed against him by even the most determined of his enemies. Antigonus, inside the city, had a ready reply. It was against Roman practice, he said, to bestow kingship on a commoner, especially when there were people of royal blood in addition to Antigonus who might be offered the throne; this was probably an allusion to his nephew, Mariamne's brother Aristobulus. Moreover, Herod was not only a commoner but also an "Idumean, a half-Jew." A new civil war was inevitable.

We need not trace the ensuing warfare in its details. The moment did not seem propitious for an onslaught on Jerusalem, for Silo turned out to be a reluctant and disappointing ally; it remains uncertain whether this was because of Antigonus' bribes or because of sheer disinterest. His activity included items such as the looting of Jericho, where the inhabitants had withdrawn within its walls in fear of an assault by Herod. Indeed, throughout the winter of 39–38 Silo's army remained in comfortable quarters, demanding supplies from Herod, and receiving them clandestinely also from Antigonus. In sum, Silo left completely to Herod the task of reconquering the country. First Herod took hold of Idumea to the south. Next he moved northward to Galilee, where the garrisons of Antigonus fled before him, though some guerrillas, again described by Josephus as brigands, resisted him. Among these were people in great numbers who had taken refuge with their families in caves. These latter presented a formidable military problem, for the caves were inaccessible, and the attackers needed to be lowered in cribs from the tops of sheer cliffs to gain entrance into the caves. The depth of the bitterness of feelings in this intra-Judean war is revealed in a brief story. The father of a family of seven children disdained Herod's offer of amnesty, and, instead, standing at the entrance of the cave, he summoned his children to emerge, one by one, and he slew them in turn, then his wife, and then himself. Herod finally conquered the resisters. The Jewish opposition to Herod, where it existed, was relentless, and Herod was relentless in destroying it.

There was still another Roman general in the area, also assigned to assist Herod, a certain Machaeras.[5] Like Silo, Machaeras found some profit in dealing with Antigonus. He showed little reluctance in slaughtering Jews, even those partisan to Herod, and the latter was on the verge of complaining to Antony. The assistance of the Romans up to this point was one of Herod's major impediments. Machaeras somehow managed to dissuade Herod from informing Antony.

Indeed, Herod desisted from completing the reconquest of his own country in order to march his troops eastward to Samosata, a city on the Euphrates River, which Antony was besieging. He left behind him some forces under his brother Joseph, but these were cut to pieces by soldiers of Antigonus, and Joseph himself fell. When the news of the defeat and death of Joseph reached Galilee, the partisans of Antigonus there were able to stir the district into renewed upheavals, and these partisans acted without restraint toward the collaborators of Herod. Uprisings against Herod moved southward to Idumea.

But when Samosata was captured, Herod set out for Judea, not having learned about the death of his brother. Josephus relates that Herod had had a dream which foreshadowed this death, a dream so dreadful that it had caused him to spring from his bed in horror; immediately messengers reached him with the tidings about Joseph that confirmed the dream.

A Roman army accompanied the returning Herod, and a second one joined him in Galilee, possibly as a reward for his services at Samosata. He began now to destroy his foes with great efficiency. Slowly he reconquered much of the land; by defeating an army of Antigonus in Samaria, he was ready for the only remaining task, the retaking of Jerusalem. As his victories had accumulated, so his forces had grown in number.

Two stories of miraculous escapes from death may well have had an effect, especially on superstitious portions of the populace, in enlarging his forces, for these escapes implied that divine guidance was with Herod. One story tells simply that, prior to the battle in Samaria, Herod was in Jericho, entertaining a large company at dinner, and just after the guests departed, the building collapsed, but miraculously no one was hurt. The other story is that Herod went to a bathhouse, accompanied only by an unarmed servant. While Herod was naked in the bath, several of his enemies took refuge in the bathhouse and, sword in hand, passed through the very chamber where Herod was, but were so concerned with seeking their own safety that they paid no attention to the unarmed king.

In moving against Jerusalem, Herod prepared an assault from the north, where Pompey had earlier made his attack. The troops began the task of erecting earthworks and towers.

Herod, meanwhile, left the vicinity of Jerusalem and went to Samaria, and there he was married to his betrothed, Mariamne. This step, in the midst of the siege, reflected his confidence in the outcome of his impending attack on Jerusalem; moreover, his marriage to the royal Maccabean was a timely gesture, calculated to turn the minds of Judeans from opposition to partisanship.

The battle for Jerusalem, according to Josephus, was one of the bloodiest in all Judean history. The partisans of Antigonus fought with extreme bravery and desperation, but Herod had too many troops, especially in view of the Roman forces with him. The city finally fell on a day which Josephus describes as "the Fast," presumably but not certainly the Day of Atonement; there were other fast days in the sacred calendar besides this pre-eminent one.

Antigonus was, of course, captured, and he was sent in chains to Antony, who was then at Antioch in Syria. A Roman source (Dio Cassius XLIX, 22) narrates that Antony had Antigonus scourged on a cross, a punishment never before meted out by the Romans to a king, and then had him executed. Josephus relates that Herod was fearful that Antony might take Antigonus alive back to Rome, and that there Antigonus might be able to present his cause before the Senate, with the plea to the Romans that he, Antigonus, was of royal blood, but Herod a commoner. Herod sent a large bribe to Antony, and Antony obliged him by executing Antigonus.

The Maccabean dynasty ended in the year 37 B.C. The rivalry of the brothers Hyrcanus and Aristobulus in 67 had opened the country to Roman occupation; now, thirty years later, the dynasty itself came to its end, and a new dynasty, that of Herod, came to the throne.

Notes

1. His name is elsewhere spelled Sameas. Rabbinic literature mentions two great sages, Shemaiah and Shammai, and efforts are on record to identify the one or the other with Samaias. Rabbinic literature lacks all allusion to this incident; it also fails to provide us with secure dates regarding these two worthy men. The rabbinic tradition regards Shemaiah as earlier than Shammai, but by how much we are not informed. Many scholars take Samaias to be Shemaiah, and only a few take him to be Shammai. Possibly he was neither.

2. The two accounts by Josephus confront us with a discrepancy. In one, when Herod finally came to Jerusalem. Hyrcanus himself acquitted him without the trial being held, and then Herod went to Damascus to join Sextus Caesar. In the other account, paraphrased here, the trial actually commenced, and Hyrcanus adjourned the proceedings so that Herod could flee to Damascus.

3. An error in the Loeb Classical Library, *Josephus* VII, p. 606, note a, reads E, east, in place of W, west.

4. It is conjectured, with justice, that the marriage of Aristobulus' son to Hyrcanus' daughter Alexandra had been a gesture, which turned out to be futile, designed to create or cement good relations between the warring brothers. Also, it will be recalled that Aristobulus had been poisoned at Rome and Alexander executed by Pompey at Antioch (see above, p. 47).

5. Not to be confused with the fortress Machaerus.

Part III

ⓇⓇⓇⓇⓇⓇⓇⓇⓇⓇ

The Monarch and his Palace

37-27 B. C.

3

No mention is made in the sources of any formal ceremony of coronation. It is quite conceivable that such a ceremony could have taken place only if sufficient troops were present to deter Herod's foes from using the occasion for assassination.

Herod had no illusions that his throne was secure; indeed, he may well have reckoned, even then, that to retain the throne would be more difficult than it had been to gain it. The quality of anxiety which we have glimpsed was so much a part of Herod's personality that inevitably it was subject to increase as a result of his progression from aspirant to the throne to its occupant. Whatever in his nature was suspicious was destined to grow and to deepen, for in acquiring the throne Herod had come to possess what others wanted and what they also deemed themselves more legitimately appropriate for. And somehow, in the frame of his anxiety and suspicion, there needs to be fitted the circumstance that he, a commoner of Idumean background, had married a genuine Maccabean princess, and he was proud that he had risen to that height, and also resentful that there had been a height to which he had felt the need of rising.

Yet the immediate task before him was to pacify the country, and thereby to stabilize and ensure his throne. There were, of course, scattered cities still to retake, to deprive of their independence, and to weld into his Judea. There was still the touchy international situation to handle, for he needed to steer a middle course between his necessary dependency on Rome and that self-interest which suggested that he ought to do some manipulating on his own.

But first and foremost was the task of unifying his country after its two and a half decades of internal strife. The country still contained both pro- and anti-Herod partisans, but these amorphous groupings by no means exhausted the number and variety of the parties of Judea. We saw aspects of the divisions in the populace (above, pp. 26ff.) when we spoke in a preliminary way of Pharisees and Sadducees. But before we look more closely at the various parties, we need to face a problem, namely, that we do not possess any single source from the precise age of Herod that brings together all the information we would like to have. If we utilize only Josephus, we are preeminently in the realm of royal history, of politics, international relations, and machinations for royal power. Using other sources, for example the writings which failed of inclusion in the Jewish Bible, or the later rabbinic literature, we gain additional information about religious developments. We are able to see from the rabbinic literature the unfolding results, in the age after Herod, of impulses which began surely as early as the time of Herod or even earlier. But we do not possess the sources to enable us to see unmistakably, in exact relationship and in unassailable chronology, the trends and tendencies which existed in Herod's time. As examples of such uncertainty, let us look at two areas where we need to tread warily, the Sadducees and the synagogue: Respecting the Sadducees, our information is always indirect, coming to us from Josephus, rabbinic literature, and from the New Testament, but not from a single Sadducean document, for not one has survived, assuming that some were written. Granted that we can trust the limited characterization of the religious tendencies of the Sadducees from non-Sadducean sources, the data that we possess scarcely characterize them fully. It is not enough to know about them that they rejected both the doctrine of resurrection and also the opinion that Scripture was validly susceptible of nonliteral interpretation; we ought to know much more. We might reason, probably correctly, that the Sadducees represented royalty and the upper social classes, including the priests in Jerusalem. But were the Sadducees, throughout the period when they constituted a group, always the same, or did they conceivably represent in one decade something which was quite different in a later decade?

As to the synagogue, we need to orient ourselves first to a definition. "Synagogue" is a Greek word and in the word itself there is nothing that suggests something Jewish, for it means only "the act of assembly," and does not in itself describe who is assembling. At some point after the age of Herod, the word "synagogue," already used for the *act* of assembly, became the name also of the *place* in which the assembly took place. Archeological evidence demonstrates that the synagogue was certainly an edifice in the second Christian century, but we do not know for sure before then whether the word "synagogue" implies an act of meeting or a place. If, then, we grant that for some indefinite period antecedent to Herod, the synagogue was only the act of assembly, certainly it existed in that form in Herod's time. But whether the synagogue was or was not a building, it is of utmost importance to distinguish between the Temple at Jerusalem and the synagogue. The Temple was a place of animal sacrifice, buttressed by prayer, and presided over by hereditary priests, the chief of whom, the high priest, was, at least in principle, a direct lineal descent of Aaron, the brother of Moses. Scriptural prescription provided that there could be one and only one Temple, and it needed to be in Jerusalem,[1] and while we know, as we mentioned above (p. 48), that in 154 B.C. a certain Onias had founded a temple in Leontopolis in Egypt, this exception serves to underscore the fidelity of Jews to the limitation that there could be only one legitimate Temple, that at Jerusalem. A synagogue was not a temple, for it lacked both a sacrificial system and direction by priests; rather, the synagogue was the center where Jews assembled, especially in regions remote from Jerusalem. In place of sacrifice and priest, the synagogue assemblies centered around the study of sacred Scripture, and around the instructors skilled in the contents and significance of Scripture. Study, rather than mere reading, was a necessity, for, on the first level, Scripture was in the Hebrew language, but Jews in Palestine had almost universally adopted Aramaic, a near relative of Hebrew, as their spoken tongue, though they had of course preserved the knowledge of Hebrew at least as a literary language; study was required, then, for simple comprehension. Outside Palestine, as in Alexandria, Scripture had been translated into Greek. On a more profound level, however, genuine comprehension required a certain mastery of the contents, and true mastery implied such rudimentary consideration as the correlation of materials on the same subject, which are scattered in Scripture; for example, the laws that begin in Exodus 20 and continue throughout the remainder of the Pentateuch are in some ways directly repetitious and in some ways the repetitions are marked by differences; one who brings together and correlates such passages faces the need to explain to himself the significance both of the mere repetition (for why must a law be stated more than once?) and also of the repetition with a difference, or, furthermore, the presence of surface contradictions. Or, to go a step further, the impulse toward correlation could yield the observation that in the case of certain laws, Scripture provides merely a general principle, without particulars, but elsewhere a series of particulars without the statement of the general principle. The student with a logical mind could, on the one hand, seek to learn by deduction from a series of particulars what the general principle might seem to be, and by what precise process of inference it could be deduced; on the other hand, he might feel the impulse to move from a stated general principle into his own deduction of the particulars that followed logically.

Furthermore, Scripture was to be meditated on, as implied in Deuteronomy 6:6–7: "These words, which I command you this day shall be on your heart, and you shall teach them to your children, and discuss them, when you sit in your house, when you are out walking, and when you lie down and when you rise." Such meditation was an act of piety, which necessarily stimulated the imagination. Thus, the imposing figure of Abraham, who at maturity, as Scripture has it, heard the divine call to depart from his father's home in Ur, must have had a boyhood, even though Scripture is silent about it; and the same Abraham, departing with his son Isaac whom, in the trial of his obedience to God, he intended to offer as a sacrifice, clearly faced the universal problem of husbands about to leave home as to what to say to one's wife. Meditation on Scripture, then, resulted in the clarification of ambiguities inherent in the legal materials, and in the imaginative embroidery of the narrative materials, and especially in the enhancement of the character of Abraham, Isaac, and Jacob, Moses and David. Accordingly, the study of Scripture in the synagogue went far beyond the mere comprehension of the literal; it became a broader, more extensive, and deeper discipline, comprising in its own way such concerns as ethics and morality. As to the skilled instructor, he is known to us by two titles, the earlier of which is "scribe," and the later one, arising perhaps a half century after the death of Herod, "rabbi." We face the issue that the title of rabbi is later than the time of Herod, but proto-rabbinism is earlier; however, if we ask at what stage it was, and at what state the synagogue stood in its development, in Herod's time, the honest answer is that we do not know.

Similarly, we encounter obstacles, on the one hand, to full clarity about Pharisees and Essenes, and, on the other hand, we are not certain exactly how much of Scripture was already fully and universally accepted as Scripture in Herod's time. To give an overprecise statement of Judaism in the age of Herod is to expose oneself to implying that there is more secure information than exactness would permit; to abstain from a broad delineation of the religious and cultural movements is to ignore the probabilities and to make a rather rich religious and cultural texture more barren than it needs to be. It is therefore better to attempt to describe the probable situation at the time, with the proviso that our reconstruction is sometimes less certain than we would like.

Josephus informs us that when Herod conquered Jerusalem, he found the populace divisible into his adherents and his opponents, and the latter he proceeded to exterminate. If we associate with the vague terms, pro- and anti-Herod, other terms such as pro-Maccabean and anti-Maccabean, we are still in the realm of probability; and if we align the Sadducees with the pro-Maccabeans and the Pharisees with the anti-Maccabeans, all this is inherently probable. In such alignments, the first group would include the upper classes, the royal families, the priestly groups, and the people closely identified with the Temple in Jerusalem. The second group would include the middle and lower classes; hence the religious parties were also social groupings. The synagogue, at least in Palestine, needs to be regarded as closely related to the middle-class Pharisees, and possibly its subsequent rise to eminence was their achievement. So useful and natural was the synagogue that it came to find a home even in Jerusalem in proximity to the Temple. As we saw above, the Pharisees and Sadducees opposed each other on the question of the validity of the results of meditation and study, since the Sadducees were scriptural literalists, but the Pharisees in the synagogue necessarily broadened their study of Scripture with a growing body of inferences which were not stated specifically in Scripture. In this light, the well-known difference of opinion on resurrection, which Pharisees affirmed and Sadducees denied, was more than just the bare question of a single item, but involved a basic approach. Even respecting resurrection there were two levels of distinction between the groups. The Pharisees made the double affirmation, first, that resurrection was a tenable belief, and second, that it was susceptible of inference from the Pentateuch.[2] The double denial of the Sadducees included not only the rejection of the belief as untenable, but also the rejection of its possible inference from Scripture, for the Sadducees rejected inference and accepted only the explicit statements of Scripture. Seen in this light, then, there emerges the decisive difference between the Pharisees and the Sadducees respecting Scripture and inferences from it; within their common Judaism their difference on Scripture represented a direct antithesis. The Pharisees justified their validation of inferences from Scripture, such as this one concerning resurrection and also of many others, by developing the theory that when God had revealed the laws to Moses to record in writing, he had simultaneously revealed orally to him a body of clarifying and edifying material. The "oral revelation" to Moses was quite as authoritative as the written Scripture, and, accordingly, a doctrine such as resurrection was contained in this second facet of the two-faceted totality of revelation. The inferences, then, were not human but divine, and to the Pharisee the "oral Torah" was as authoritative as the Pentateuch itself; to the Sadducee, the oral revelation had no standing or validity whatsoever.

Yet, as we have said, the Sadducees and Pharisees each constituted some kind of entity, some kind of collective group, and they presented the all too frequent social phenomenon of groups in opposition to each other in matters beyond the basic divisive factor. It is likely that the strength of the Sadducees was centered in Jerusalem, where the court and the Temple were, and quite as likely that away from Jerusalem it was the Pharisees who exerted the largest claim to popular support.

It is a matter of historical record that the Sadducees ultimately became weakened and then totally disappeared, and that the Pharisees emerged as the dominant, indeed the only remaining party—but all this required another century to accomplish. In Herod's time the Pharisees were already quite strong; the conjecture of some scholars is probably correct that they were strengthened by Herod when he first came to the throne, and with some reason. The Sadducees, representing the royalty and the upper classes, were presumably partisans of Herod's Maccabean foes, and therefore Herod was partial to the Pharisees, and, wishing their support, contributed to their strength. The only concession necessary on the part of Herod was to relinquish to the Pharisees the domination of purely religious matters, and therefore to restrain them from interfering with his authority in political affairs. Two sages, Samaias and Pollion, appear momentarily in the account of Josephus as the men whom Herod honored above all; this Samaias, p. 64, had earlier spoken against Herod when the latter had been summoned to face charges before the Sanhedrin.[3] But Herod lacked friends and these two men did not, so Herod discreetly courted them. Assuming that these two men were Pharisees, or at least pro-Pharisees, we see that Herod chose to court them, and to regard the Sadducees as enemies.

But it was not only Pharisees who were to be found in

some numbers away from Jerusalem; in addition there were other segments of the population. Before one undertakes to speak of these groups, one must begin with the caution that such groupings were not rigid nor mutually exclusive, and just as today a man can be simultaneously a Rotarian, a Mason, a Republican, and a Harvard alumnus, so the ancient groupings require our understanding that they did not necessarily all exist on the same level. Indeed, it might be more appropriate to speak, rather, of tendencies than of groupings. Such is the case especially respecting the Essenes, about whom information is at once limited and contradictory, for what Josephus relates about them cannot square in some important details with what Philo of Alexandria (*c*. 20 B.C.–*c*. A.D. 40) had related a half century before Josephus began to write. It would appear, however, that the Essenes represented a tendency already ancient in Jewish life, the rejection of urban civilization and the espousal of a unique simplicity, even to the point of creating a communal life in an aggregate center on the west bank of the Dead Sea; they are loosely to be connected with the Qumran community of the Dead Sea scrolls. The Essenes numbered affiliates throughout Judea who did not enter the monasterylike center in the south, but remained in their home communities throughout the land. Some scholars take a cue from Josephus and see an influence of Greek monasticism on the Essenes, a view that is properly to be contested as unnecessary, since native Judaism would have furnished the impulse.

We must understand that Pharisees, Sadducees, and Essenes were all Jewish groupings, and the distinctions among them represented a narrowly limited range of emphasized matters, and not total distinction. In this light, the Essenes may well have been an extremist group with some Pharisaic coloration; perhaps they were the Pharisees who abandoned civilization; perhaps they ceased to hope to control religious affairs in Jerusalem, or even to respect them, and hence came to regard the Temple and its priests with disdain, preferring to have nothing to do with them, rather than conform to the Pharisaic tendency to try to influence or even regulate the Temple affairs. Certainly one does not set Essenes and Pharisees against each other in the same way that one would set the Essenes and the Sadducees against each other.

We need to recall, moreover, that although Scripture, the Old Testament, was already well along the way in its formation, and that already the populace had attributed a special sanctity to the Pentateuch, to the prophets, and to some if not all of the Hagiographia, literary activity had by no means ceased. Some of the literature still being produced failed to elicit a sense of genuine sanctity in Judea, but certain books, on being translated into Greek, came to be regarded as sacrosanct in Alexandria, as for example, the accounts of the Maccabean rebellion known as First and Second Maccabees.[4] This new literature was heterogeneous in its form and in its content, for it included narratives and poems, histories and didactic counsel. It also included a recurrent form of writing to which scholars have given the name "apocalyptic." This kind of literature needs explanation, and the people who produced it need some description.

Within Scripture, scholars ordinarily reserve the word "prophetic" for writings which were early (such as Amos, Isaiah, Jeremiah, and the like) and they use the word "apocalyptic" for the prophecies of the later period. In external form, prophecy was simple, plain, and straightforward in what it had to say, but the apocalyptic was marked by abundant symbol and even by cryptic utterance. Again, prophecy dealt either with the present or with the immediate future; a prevailing concern in apocalyptic writings was the remote future, the events to unfold at the end of time. Prophecy dealt with the trespasses of Israel and Judah, and God's impending punishment; apocalyptic dealt with trespasses of alien nations against Judea and against Jews, and it described, however cryptically, the advent of divine succor to rescue Jews from their foes and to effect the downfall of the enemy. To put this in another way, an apocalyptic writing such as Daniel could serve to rally Jews to patriotic enterprise, promising God's help in the Jewish wish to defeat the Syrian Greeks; or it might be directed against the Romans, as in other apocalyptic works, of which the best known example is the New Testament Revelation of John. A veritable flood of apocalyptic writings was produced in the era with which we deal. A good many have survived to our day, even though not admitted into the Bible, but more were lost; we know about them through allusion to, or quotation from, them in the writings of the church fathers and in the lists preserved by Byzantine chroniclers.

Behind the apocalyptic literature there lay a human conviction and desire for independence or freedom and it is quite reasonable to suppose that some of this literature was either produced, or else adopted and venerated, by those groups neatly denounced by Josephus as brigands, but whom we should regard as patriotic guerrillas. These random bands of activist patriots occasionally seem to us to be guilty of what from our standpoint is an apparent contradiction, for they were simultaneously certain that God would do the fighting on their behalf, and at the same time insistent on doing their own fighting. However much we may see a political aspect in the men who took up arms in rebellion against Rome, or against Herod, we err if we lose sight of the essential religious character of such rebellions. In this light, the leadership in the rebellious movement was of great consequence, for a leader needed not only to have sterling human qualities such as bravery and

determination, but also he needed to appear to his followers to have God's sanction and support.

We can at this point introduce the confusing word
"messiah." The word means "the anointed one," alluding
to the Jewish ceremony of proclaiming a monarch through
his public anointment with oil. Yet long before the age of
Herod, the term had taken on a new connotation, for when
kingship had ended in the sixth century with the Babylonian conquest of Palestine, "messiah" came to be the
term not so much for the reigning monarch as for the man
who was awaited to emerge to re-establish the terminated
monarchy and to become the king. The Messiah, then,
was the future king, whose advent depended on God's plan
and timetable. The first chore of the Messiah was to break
the hold of the conqueror, and the second to restore the
proper royal dynasty to the throne, either by the Messiah's
becoming the king, or, as a related pattern of thought had
it, through his designating the king. In either case, the
question arose among the Jews as to the valid credentials
of the intended king, and a chief requirement put on him
was the possession of royal blood through descent from
David. Neither the Maccabean kings nor Herod possessed
this important credential, and the critics of the Maccabeans
and the foes of Herod chanced to agree in asserting that
descent from David was an inescapable necessity for the
proper king.

When in some region of Judea or Galilee, especially in
the hill country, a local guerrilla distinguished himself
through his bravery and accomplishment, the hope or ex-
pectation could arise that he would move from regional
distinction to wider, more significant notice; the query
could then arise as to whether or not this might be the
long-awaited Messiah. And since it was God who was to
set the timetable for the occasion when the Messiah would
appear, certain supernatural concomitants came to be ex-

pected, some before his appearance, some at the given moment, and some immediately after. A biblical passage, the last two verses of Malachi, stated specifically that the prophet Elijah would return to earth in advance of the day of God's great judgment, and this passage either bred, or else served as the scriptural basis for, the spreading double-belief that Elijah would reappear to herald the coming of the Messiah and that the advent of the Messiah was designed to encompass more than the mere ascent of a king to the throne, and would include also the ushering in of God's great judgment day. As to the latter, normal human experience had led to the observation that righteous people often suffered and that the wicked prospered: the great judgment day was expected to come in the future and to adjust all such inequities, both those of the present and even those of the past. In this light, those people who had unjustly prospered or suffered, and who had died, could seem to be quite beyond reward or punishment, unless they could be restored to life and then made to stand trial before God. Among those, especially the Pharisees, in whom the conviction was strong that God's justice could not be forever restrained however tardy it might seem, there arose the association of resurrection with the inevitable day of God's judgment. In a sense, to abstain from believing in resurrection was equivalent to believing that God was perpetually barred from executing the merited justice. Yet since minds may agree on principle, but disagree on details, there were those men who supposed that God's final judgment would precede the time when resurrection would be general, and only the just would be resurrected for the judgment, while others held that a general resurrection of all the dead would take place, to be followed immediately by God's judgment on all men. In either line of thinking, the advent of the Messiah was bound up with resurrection and God's judgment; and since the latter was often deemed to take the form of a climax in the flow of time, it was often thought of as destined not for the immediate future but the remote; it was a far-off event which would separate time as the present age knew it, and give way to a timelessness, after being ushered in by the climactic events.

Yet the additional step could be taken, and was, of modifying the idea of a climax in the remote future by associating it with the needs, the yearnings, and the convictions of the present. The conclusion could be, and was, that now, at long last, the long flow of time had been sufficient to bring the remote future near at hand, and now one stood at the moment when the future and the present were on the threshold of coalescence. The reign of wickedness, under which the righteous suffered, was in its last moments; righteousness, through God's intervention, was about to transform the disordered world, for no longer would an unjust man be king, and no longer would Satan rule through his human puppets, but God's kingdom on earth would shortly, very shortly, be established.

That is to say, the abstractness of messianic thought necessarily became specific and concrete at the moment when a particular man arose to some regional eminence, and the queries arose whether or not this man was the long-awaited Messiah. A characteristic query was: Did Elijah precede him? Manifestly, if Elijah must precede the Messiah, then the particular man could not be the Messiah unless demonstrably Elijah had appeared to prepare the way. But how could men recognize Elijah? No one was still alive who could recall him over the centuries; and even if tradition had conveyed what the appearance of Elijah was, the possibility existed that Elijah would appear in some guise or even disguise, and fail of recognition by those who judged only by surface things. If a man were to be acclaimed as the Messiah, it followed that the immediate past had witnessed both the coming of Elijah and also the beginnings of the great climactic events; and what better beginning to climactic events was there than a signal defeat of the Romans? Yet to acclaim a given man as the likely Messiah could be at best tentative, for the auspicious beginnings needed to be followed by the full array of all that was expected. The man proclaimed or acclaimed the Messiah who did not proceed to destroy the power of Rome and to re-establish the Davidic monarchy, and to precipitate the miraculous ingathering to Palestine of Jews scattered throughout the world, would ultimately stand revealed as a deluded person, and one who deluded others, for unless the messianic age promptly arrived, then the man was not the Messiah.

The first necessity in the question of a Messiah was the recognition of him. Accordingly, ancient prophecies were searched for those cryptic signs by which the enlightened could move to the momentous matter of recognition and acclamation. Where the ancient prophecies seemed incomplete or insufficient, new apocalyptic ones were created. Yet how could one believe in these new writings? The answer arose that these were not really new, but were quite ancient, and their authors were not men of the time but the great worthies of the past, such as Abraham, Moses, Isaiah, and even Enoch, who "walked with God, and he was not, for God took him" (Genesis 5:24). To these apocalyptic writings which have survived, and which did not make their way into Scripture, whether in the Hebrew or the Greek collection, modern scholars have given the name of Pseudepigrapha, "false titles," in recognition of the practice of attributing such books to the ancient biblical characters. Since messianic movements were essentially religious, and only incidentally political, the messianic hopes and expectations spurred the writing of "apocalyptic books." In turn, the apocalyptic books spurred messianic acclamations and hopes and expectations.

There was no such grouping in Judea as the "apocalyptists," and to speak of "apocalyptic Judaism" as if it were a discernible category of people is to speak nonsense, and to deny apocalyptic writings to Pharisees or Essenes quite preposterous, for a particular apocalyptist might have been one or the other, or else influenced by one or both and not himself securely within a particular category. We should conceive of Pharisees and Essenes as both constituting what we might exaggeratedly call "enrolled members," but also as constituting a general influence that extended beyond the enrolled group.

It is likely that the usual source of apocalyptic writings was the guerrillas. These were desperate men, pushed into activity by the disorders and oppressions; because they were impelled by desperation, their fortitude was powerful and their dedication extreme. Motivated by their zeal, they are known collectively as Zealots. Ordinarily this term is reserved for the period a century later, the time of the rebellion against Rome from A.D. 66 to 70, and its use by Josephus in that connection is contemptuous name-calling. Perhaps at that later date the Zealots had become a well-marked group, and in all likelihood they were much less than that in the time when Herod was intent on gaining the throne, but the tendency existed as early as the age of Herod. These guerrillas are known also as the *sicarii*, "dagger men," and also as "the Fourth Philosophy." The *sicarii* were more or less assassins who carried their daggers hidden under their togas. The name Fourth Philosophy is absurd; it derives from Josephus and from a defect in his character, for so eager was he to laud Jews to Roman readers that he described them glowingly as all philosophers; after exhausting three categories for Pharisees, Sadducees, and Essenes, equating these with philosophical schools recognizable to the Greco-Roman world, he went on to describe a "fourth philosophy," originating from a certain Judas the Galilean, as being Pharisaic in outlook, but as having a special attachment to liberty and a scorn of death (*Antiquities* XVIII, I). This Judas was the son of the Hezekiah whom Herod had executed; the Fourth Philosophy was Josephus' quaint nomenclature for those whom he elsewhere denominated as brigands, whom we would persist in calling guerrillas.

One other trend of the times claims our attention, even though we see things most hazily. It is the founding of what were later to be known as *yeshibot*, "academies." The rabbinic tradition tells us almost nothing about the founding of the schools which were to be the vital, productive institutions out of which religious leadership and a sense of direction were to emerge after the destruction of the Temple at Jerusalem a century later. The rabbinic tradition describes its past in terms of a succession of *zugot*, "pairs" of luminary scholars, each of which received the transmitted religious-academic tradition from the preceding pair. We possess the names of the early sages, and also an aphorism or two from each of them, but we have inherited no information of a chronological kind, nor any data relating to the academies themselves. A very few sages are mentioned by Josephus, and thereby we are enabled to see the chronological pattern, though dimly. This is so in the case of Samaias and Pollion, whom we cannot, however, identify in any certainty with the sages of rabbinic literature. Two men, Hillel and Shammai, can be definitely placed in the age of Herod, though precisely where, we do not know. The two represent the development not merely of academies but of rival ones; within their common Pharisaic suppositions the two quasi-academies represent an almost unique set of clashing and contradictory opinions. Much later the rabbinic tradition related that these two academies presented no less than 365 differences of opinion; a convenient heavenly voice, though attributing a full divine inspiration to the tradition of Shammai, declared in favor of the opinions of the tradition of Hillel.

The obscure academies, and the dimly discerned synagogues, and the barely visible sages turn out to be the factors which abided with effective force beyond the age of Herod and which provided Judaism with its bases for the continuity that stretches into our own time and that gave birth to Christianity.

The above-described categories of the populace, and the trends, need to be regarded as typical and not as strict divisions of society. But if we understand the trends as marked tendencies in the populace and hence as real factors, then we can perhaps begin to summarize what faced Herod: First, a divided Jewish population, ranging from the direct hostility of the Maccabeans and the Sadducees, through the perhaps suspended neutrality of the Pharisees and the disinterest of the Essenes, and at another extreme the explosive guerrillas, often spurred on by messianism. As before Herod's time, there were still cities that were either all Gentile or partly Gentile, and they were an eyesore to him. Moreover, although the land had been impoverished by the bitter wars, tribute was still due to the Romans.

What must strike us most forcefully is the observation that Herod himself is scarcely related to the internal religious movements, and that he was certainly no part of them. Indeed, one might suppose that the taunt made to him by Antigonus that he was only a half-Jew worked in him not to elicit a retort of his full Jewishness and its subsequent demonstration but, rather, influenced him to show that even "half-Jew" exaggerated the case. Herod erected a wall, as it were, between himself and the inner life of the Judaism of the time, and he maintained his connection with Judaism only at the point where there was a direct impingement on him. Thus the guerrillas were a threat, for Herod could lose his throne or his life to them, or else displease his Roman masters by failing to quell messianic disorders. The Temple in Jerusalem was a source of revenue, both for his own needs and for the funds he had to transmit to the Romans, and therefore the office of high priest was one which needed his attention; himself ineligible for it, as the Maccabeans had not been, for they were of the right priestly lineage, he needed to be able to control both the office and the person who held it. It was more convenient to conform with the Temple ritual and appear related to it than to risk offending sensibilities by abstaining from the cult. To a limited extent, therefore, Herod was reconciled to an external practice of Judaism, but never with mind or heart or soul.

Rather, Herod was a harried, suspicious man, constantly in fear of assassination, and constantly confined within the limited authority which the Romans extended to their "client kings," which status Herod wanted to transcend. Like many a man whose authority is limited, he felt the need to exercise that limited authority to its fullest extent.

Herod had gained the throne. But could he keep it? Only if the popular uprisings were kept to the minimum and quickly destroyed when they appeared. Only if he could successfully handle the surviving Maccabeans—for so long as male Maccabeans were alive, Herod's legitimacy as king would be challenged in the eyes of the Jews, and possibly even by the Romans. With the death of Antigonus there remained alive only a few Maccabeans: the aging Hyrcanus II, Herod's brother-in-law Aristobulus, and some young children known to us as the "sons of Baba." Herod was destined to face the issue of whether or not he could manage to manipulate these Maccabeans to his own purposes, for if he could not, then the alternative was an unpleasant one, from which an insecure, impulsive man must not shrink, however ruthless his chosen action might appear to be.

To handle the affairs of state, both his own experience and whatever wisdom or shrewdness he had learned from his father were destined to be called on, and to the fullest extent. But, paradoxically, Herod had to conduct the public affairs in the context of a private family life. His immediate family was his queen Mariamne, her mother Alexandra, and his siblings: his sister Salome who resided in his palace with her husband, Herod's uncle Joseph; and his surviving brothers to whom he had given assignments away from Jerusalem. The palace, then, was largely feminine, and two of the three women, his mother-in-law Alexandra and his sister Salome, were neither especially silent nor inactive. Moreover, Antony, through whose grace Herod ruled, was the lover of Cleopatra, and the Egyptian queen was both an acquiescent mistress to the Roman and also a monarch in her own right. She had clear ambitions for power and for territory, and Herod's territory, immediately adjacent to Cleopatra's, had sporadically belonged to Egypt.

When Herod, on becoming the king, executed some of the leading citizens of Jerusalem, he accomplished the double objective of ridding himself of foes and also of showing potential enemies what fate could lie in store for them. The Sanhedrin he either tolerated, provided it confined itself to purely religious affairs, or, if one follows those scholars who infer from the silence in Josephus about the Sanhedrin, he may even have abolished it, and taken for himself both its judicial and legislative functions.

For perhaps a year or two, from 37 to 35, except for tribute money, Antony left him alone to effect whatever

internal consolidation Herod could achieve. But now Cleopatra became avid for territory. In particular, she wanted
some portions of Syria, of Judea, and even of Nabatea.
One did not, of course, say to Antony, "I want this," for
to do so was both too direct and also too fraught with
recognizable and distasteful ambition. One said, instead,
that such and such a governor of Syria, or such and such
a ruler of Judea, was insufficiently competent, or insufficiently loyal, and hence it was in the interest of Antony
to shift this territory to a person as demonstrably competent and loyal as Cleopatra. So Antony presented Cleopatra
with territory aong the coast of Judea, and also the rich
region around Jericho. Herod had no choice but to comply
with the directives from Antony. He also had the shrewdness to see that Cleopatra, however friendly or even amor-
ous she had once been, nevertheless coveted his domain.

Hyrcanus, it will be recalled, had been captured by the
Parthians, along with Herod's brother Phasael, who had
died by suicide. Hyrcanus was then residing in a Parthian
city—Josephus calls it Babylon, but it was hardly the
ancient city of that name—and was there the recipient of
the respect and honor which even captive royalty enjoyed. The Parthian Jews treated him with great respect
and solicitude. Yet Hyrcanus seems to have wanted to
return to Jerusalem. From his standpoint, Herod was the
son of his loyal friend Antipater; Herod was the defender
of his claims against the deceased usurping brother and
nephews; moreover, Herod owed him a debt of gratitude
for having saved him from whatever punishment the Sanhedrin might have been bent on, some ten years earlier,
after the execution of the Galilean Hezekiah. Therefore
Hyrcanus could expect a welcome, and safety, in Judea.
The Jews in Parthia did not hesitate to counsel Hyrcanus
against returning; they enjoyed the privilege of having
him in their midst, and they lavished many honors on him.

They reminded him, now that his ears had been cut off, that he could not regain his old office of high priest, and hence he would not receive more homage in Jerusalem than they were providing in Parthia. As to the debt owed him by Herod, they commented that it had been incurred when Herod was still a commoner, and that kings, once they attain high office, are prone to forget the favors of a bygone day. But Hyrcanus longed to be reunited with his daughter Alexandra, and with his granddaughter Mariamne and her brother Aristobulus, and to see his great-grandchildren, whom Mariamne had begun to bear to Herod. So Hyrcanus, who at no time appears to have been guilty of craftiness, preferred to return to Jerusalem, and he either saw no danger there or else brushed it aside.

As for Herod, there is the remote possibility that he saw in the prospective return of Hyrcanus not only a complete absence of danger to his throne but, indeed, a means of strengthening his position, through a public display of a warm relationship between himself and the legitimate Maccabean. Or, perhaps Alexandra and Mariamne expressed to him their desire to have Hyrcanus back in Jerusalem. Yet still another consideration prompted Herod to want Hyrcanus back in Jerusalem; if some plot against Herod might center around Hyrcanus, it would be easier to nip it in the bud in Jerusalem than to let it grow large in Parthia, for in Jerusalem he could keep Hyrcanus under constant surveillance. So he wrote warmly and affectionately to Hyrcanus, and he sent an ambassador to the king of the Parthians, bearing gifts, with the request that the Parthians allow Hyrcanus to return to Jerusalem.

So Hyrcanus came back, and Herod received him with extravagant and unlimited courtesies, allowing him an empty pre-eminence at the public feasts and in general handling Hyrcanus with that regard and those honors that would commend Herod to the populace and to the two

Maccabean women in his household. The office of high priest was open and it needed to be filled. Stray items in the various accounts in Josephus prompt the unverifiable suspicion that Herod wanted the lucrative office for himself, and it was to that end that he is alleged to have arranged for the concoction of a family genealogy that made him a scion of a priestly family that had gone into exile in Babylon. If this allegation is true, then Herod nevertheless abstained from following out his desire, not alone because the artificial genealogy would be scorned, but because he was aware that to seize the high priesthood for himself would excessively affront the Jews.

A candidate for the high priesthood was near at hand, his brother-in-law, Aristobulus, then a young man of perhaps seventeen or eighteen. Since Aristobulus was the descendant of recent high priests, the populace would not reject his credentials. Indeed, so apt a choice was Aristobulus, that at first Herod chose deliberately not to appoint him, for it was scarcely wise to project into prominence a legitimate Maccabean around whom a movement to unseat Herod might arise. So Herod passed Aristobulus by. Instead, he selected for the office a Babylonian Jew, Ananel, who came from a priestly family, which had the virtue in Herod's eyes of obscurity. Moreover, Herod was sure that he could control a high priest as unlikely as Ananel.

It was a shrewd move. Or, rather, it might have been a shrewd move, except for Herod's feminine household. That Herod should have contemplated an appointment without having discussed it seems unreasonable and unlikely, and, if he discussed it, then his bypassing of Aristobulus was an act of commission, not of omission. The response Mariamne made to Herod's choice is not disclosed to us, but we are told in clearest terms that Alexandra considered the bypassing of Aristobulus an indignity beyond bearing; she was persuaded that Aristobulus, and Aristobulus alone, should have received the appointment; for him to be brushed aside meant that a Maccabean had been scorned by an Idumean commoner, and a nobody from Babylon had been designated for the high honor due to her son.

That Alexandra made vocal protest to Herod is extremely likely; there is no reason to doubt that she spoke her mind, both forcefully and witheringly and belligerently. That Herod would have preferred her silence is understandable, and he could command it, but he could scarcely enforce it without drastic measures out of proportion to the matter. He chose simply to ignore her complaints and her pointed words, and he assumed that she could do nothing but become resigned to his royal prerogative. But Herod misjudged matters, for Alexandra determined secretly to ask Cleopatra to intercede with Antony on behalf of Aristobulus. Whether there already existed some relationship between Alexandra and Cleopatra we do not know; quite possibly there did. But if there was no such antecedent contact between the queen's mother and the Egyptian queen, Alexandra sensed correctly that Cleopatra, with her eye on Herod's territory, was the apt person to whom to convey complaints about Herod. Alexandra needed to be sure that her letter to Cleopatra would not be intercepted, and she managed to send the letter to the Egyptian queen through the help of a musician.

Antony did not immediately grant the request conveyed by Cleopatra to intercede on behalf of Aristobulus, but an agent of Antony's, Dellius, a devious and unscrupulous man, was involved in affairs that brought him to Jerusalem, and Alexandra came in touch with him. The two devised a plan, which if Alexandra knew it in all its details, marks her as a woman of extravagant wickedness; it is likely, however, that she was being duped by Dellius. His proposal to her was that in view of the great beauty possessed by both Mariamne and Aristobulus, portraits of the two should be painted, and these sent to Antony, who, on observing the beauty of the brother and sister, would be unable to say No to the mother's request.

But Dellius had a different, or at least an additional, motive, which, to speak plainly, made him nothing other than a procurer. It was to be expected that Antony would desire a beautiful woman such as Mariamne; whether he would risk the outraged wrath of a Herod from one side, and the jealousy of Cleopatra from another is quite a different matter. But it was not alone Mariamne whom Dellius proposed that Antony invite, but also Aristobulus. Guided by Dellius, Antony wrote an innocent letter to Herod, proposing that Aristobulus should visit him. But Herod was by no means ignorant of Antony's bisexual proclivities, and of Antony's extreme sensuality. He therefore wrote to Antony in the only way possible, telling him that disorders could arise in Judea if Aristobulus were to go out of the country.

Herod was quite satisfied that he had acted in a noble way in protecting Aristobulus from Antony. Yet Mariamne began to press him, and with some vehemence, to designate Aristobulus the high priest. Herod began to view the invitation of Antony to Aristobulus in a somewhat new light, indeed, in what to Herod was the only valid light: it was part of a plot to unseat him, and Aristobulus had manipulated the invitation so as to persuade Antony to appoint him king in place of Herod. There lay before Herod alternate courses, either of which was bad. To maintain Aristobulus in obscurity without office and honor meant that Mariamne and Alexandra would continue to press him, and that Alexandra—Herod had excellent spies! —would continue her maneuvers through Cleopatra. It was less bad, accordingly, to consider the second alternative, namely to placate Alexandra and Mariamne by naming Aristobulus the high priest, and thereby to neutralize Aristobulus, at least to the extent that as high priest Aristobulus could not legally leave Judea, and embark on unobserved plots. So Herod alerted his followers and advisers to what he was about, explaining to them his decision to appoint Aristobulus. Respecting Ananel, there was the problem that normally a high priest served until his death. The pretext that Herod found for removing Ananel fitted neatly into the situation; he explained to Ananel that he had appointed him only on a temporary, caretaker basis because of Aristobulus' youth, and now it was time for Ananel to step aside and let Aristobulus come into the high office.

Alexandra, on the one hand, was pleased at the elevation of her son and, on the other hand, the word came to her, as Herod wanted it to come, that he had grave suspicions about her. A humble apology to Herod could simultaneously express her gratitude and at the same time assure the able and generous Herod that now that her son had received his elevation, she would henceforth be completely obedient to her son-in-law. So she made her judicious apology, commenting that it was the nobility of her family which, she supposed, had given her the right and the freedom to act as she had done, and undoubtedly she had acted imprudently and hastily. So Alexandra and Herod became reconciled to each other, at least openly.

But Herod remained suspicious of Alexandra, even after he had deposed Ananel and Aristobulus had come into the office. He gave orders that Alexandra was to confine herself within the palace and to abstain from meddling in public affairs. He set guards about her, and obligated them to report to him the most trivial of her activities. Alexandra lived in a state of virtual slavery, and of terror, and the need and wish to escape was born in her. She con-

trived to smuggle a letter, again to Cleopatra, and the
Egyptian queen sent back a reply urging that Alexandra
and Aristobulus come to Egypt. The invitation was heartening to Alexandra, but to get out of Judea was a formidable task, possible only by some deception through which
they could slip by the notice of Herod's guards. The plan
which Alexandra devised has its comic overtones. She had
two coffins made, one for her to hide in, and the other for
Aristobulus; faithful servants were to carry the coffins out
of the palace at night, and then mother and son were to
make their way to the coast and board a ship for Alexandria.

But one of her loyal servants disclosed the plan to another, thinking that the second knew the plan and was
prepared to help carry it out. This second servant, however, was already under suspicion by Herod, for there was
some notion that he had been in on the plot when Malichus
had poisoned Antipater. Accordingly, this servant reckoned that by informing Herod of Alexandra's plan he
could assure Herod of both his former innocence and his
present fidelity.

Herod allowed Alexandra's plan to proceed, but only to
the point that mother and son were caught in the very act
of trying to escape. Herod now had a basis on which to
punish Alexandra, and without limit. The impulse to do so
collided, however, with his anxiety about Cleopatra's subsequent move, when the Egyptian would hear about the
punishment. Generosity to Alexandra would commend
him favorably to Cleopatra, and it could give him time to
think matters through, and to devise a prudent, safe way
to deal with mother and son. Especially with the son. For
Aristobulus was potentially a good candidate to overthrow
Herod.

Nothing is as welcome to an undecisive and fearful person as a delay which takes the guise of ingenious strategy.

As in other situations, Herod found himself gripped in indecision and anxiety, and unable to act; then when he did act, it was impulsively. He might have left the situation with respect to Aristobulus unresolved for a long, long time. But the fall pilgrimage festival, Sukkot (Tabernacles), brought the customary throngs to Jerusalem, and at the Temple the young high priest, dressed in the rich vestments, officiated in the sight of the multitudes. Any high priest would have been impressive in this situation; a Maccabean, young, comely, tall, and above all, a symbol to the populace, was extraordinarily impressive. The adoration of him by the people was manifested most plainly, and their joy in having him as high priest spoke so vividly that everyone could understand it, and by implication the dissatisfaction in the occupant of the throne was equally plain.

Shortly after the eight-day festival, Alexandra entertained both Herod and Aristobulus at Jericho. In September or October Jericho can be hot; it chanced that Jericho was hotter than usual. A swimming party in the Jordan or perhaps in some inlets from it, in some fishponds, was a natural proposal, eagerly responded to by a number of young men who were in the company. It was good sport, and it was cooling, and the exuberant young men turned to the usual water pranks. Herod and Aristobulus first remained aloof, possibly because it was unseemly for the king and the high priest to disport naked with commoners. But toward dusk Herod prevailed on young Aristobulus to go into the water. The pranks continued, and very shortly some of the young men held Aristobulus under water, as if it were all a game, and Aristobulus was drowned. An accident, of course, a regrettable accident. Ananel was restored as high priest.

The death of Aristobulus brought a deep mourning to all of Judea. For Alexandra, it was one more bitter calamity in a life replete with them. She felt inclined to suicide, but she was deterred by a single motive, to get revenge for what she was sure was an act of murder. She carefully abstained from expressing this latter conviction, for to do so could only result in countersteps which would destroy any opportunity for whatever vengeance she might some day decided upon. As for Herod, he was beset by a mixture of remorse and the well-founded fear that the death of Aristobulus would not be accepted as an accident. He provided a most elaborate funeral, and he publicly shed copious tears in order to persuade the persuadable that he was in deepest grief. His anxious remorse brought to his grief enough authenticity to be convincing to many. Possibly it convinced Mariamne.

But not Alexandra. To Cleopatra she wrote an account of the death, indeed of the murder, of Aristobulus. In turn Cleopatra promptly passed the allegation on to Antony, in a form as hostile to Herod as she could muster, and Antony was slowly brought to the point of feeling that he must inquire into matters. In 34 Antony, then in Laodicea on the coast of Syria, sent the command to Herod to appear in order to answer questions about the strange death of Aristobulus. This was precisely the outcome that Herod had feared, and his knowledge, or guess, that it was Cleopatra who had prompted the command from Antony filled him with additional terror, for however warm Cleopatra had been to him when he had been in Egypt, he knew that she wanted even more, indeed all, of his territory.

Herod could not disobey a command from the Roman Antony, so there was no choice but to go. And going meant danger, for it lay in the power of Antony not only to remove him as king but even to pass the death sentence on him. Herod was required, then, to go on a trip, from which there was good likelihood that he would not return. He could go only after making the preparations, as it were, for what could ensue in case Antony were to decree his execution; that is to say, he had to write his will.

At this point in the account of Josephus we encounter a passage for which his readers are scarcely prepared. One can understand that Herod needed to leave instructions about his preference for the succession to the throne, since by this time Mariamne had been his wife for three years and had borne him some children—perhaps two of the four she bore him—and Herod might well have indicated his wishes about the throne and these children. Yet Josephus confines himself to only one matter, Herod's wishes with respect to Mariamne in case of his death. That this should be the solitary item reflected from Herod's testament is surprising, but even more surprising is the character of this item, contained in instructions which Herod entrusted to Joseph, his uncle and brother-in-law, the husband of his sister Salome. It consisted in this, that should Herod die, Joseph was to slay Mariamne immediately. The instruction, on first encounter, reveals the mixture of deep love and jealousy Herod felt for Mariamne, in his shrinking from the thought of his queen's belonging to any other man. There is very little in Josephus' previous narration to suggest any depth of passion on Herod's part for Mariamne; the relative abruptness with which this passage appears forces one to modify the inference natural up to this point that in marrying Mariamne Herod was preoccupied exclusively with the inherent advantages, and had little or no interest in Mariamne. However unseemly jeolousy may be regarded in the table of regrettable human frailties, it serves nevertheless as an indication, or even as some measurement, of love; and granted the truism that human motives are involved, nevertheless one can usually conclude: no jealousy, no love; much jealousy, much love; unrestrained jealousy, unrestrained love. The manner in which the relation between jealousy and love can often lead to unpredictable sequals is quite another matter from the bare issue of the interrelation of love and hatred in a stable and ongoing situation, as was destined to develop later. Here we deal with our need, without adequate previous preparation, to assimilate the contention of Josephus that Herod so loved Mariamne that, faced with the prospect of his death, he took steps that she should never belong to another man.

Josephus then proceeds to add another fact. Josephus says that at the bottom of Herod's instruction to slay Mariamne in the event of his own death was his knowledge that Antony had fallen in love with her on having heard of her beauty. Perhaps through oversight, Josephus makes no mention here of the portraits sent to Antony, and he has previously given us no hint of Herod's direct knowledge of the specific maneuvers of Alexandra through Cleopatra. It is a most natural inference, however, that he suspected Antony of harboring a lust not only for the now dead Aristobulus but for Herod's own wife. The question arises, then, of whether the command of Herod that Mariamne was to die if he himself died was as much Herod's desire that she belong to no other man, as his desire to deny her to Antony.

That Herod's attitude was influenced or shaped by his knowledge of Antony's character is a possibility. At the same time, however, it could well have been his attitude toward any person who was the Roman commander. It has been suggested that it was not Herod's love for Mariamne, not the mixture of love and jealousy that prompted Herod's instruction but, rather, his fear that a liaison between Antony and Mariamne would result in Mariamne's possession of a kingdom far greater than Herod's —and hence it was a completely different form of jealousy that prompted his thought. But this is speculative and uncertain. Herod was Antony's friend but also his vassal, and he knew his Roman.

Herod made the inevitable journey to Antony. Before him, and with Cleopatra always on the scene, Herod set forth a defense of his actions, a defense which was in reality no defense. He pursued the line of reasoning that if a king were required to render an account of his government to some superior, it amounted to the denial that the man was the king; it was proper, so he argued, that those who give authority to a king should permit that king to use the authority given to him. He took care to accompany this line of logical argument with handsome gifts to Antony. As for Cleopatra, Herod found it possible to imply that, in addition to her being motivated by a desire for Judean territory, it was improper for her to meddle in Roman affairs outside her own domain.

Antony was too much the Roman conqueror to let a mistress, even Cleopatra, trespass into his imperial prerogatives. He, and he alone, would make the decision. First, in order to silence Cleopatra, Antony gave her some territory in Coele-Syria. Then he turned to reassure Herod of his continuation in high favor. Whether in direct exchange for this urgently needed assurance, or perhaps in pure gratitude for it, Herod accompanied Antony for part of the way east, where Antony was to campaign against the Parthians. Then Herod set out for home, satisfied to have passed through the crisis so safely.

In Jerusalem, meanwhile, Joseph carried out Herod's mandate to watch over Mariamne, with the result that he was in her company a great deal of the time, to the acute displeasure of his wife-niece, Salome. To this sister of Herod, the attentions her husband was paying Mariamne were an indignity, especially since between Salome and Mariamne there had passed more than once words of dispute and even of recrimination, for Mariamne had not hesitated to allude to her own high birth, and to the low birth of her royal husband and of her in-laws. To Salome's resentment that her husband was paying undue regard to Mariamne was added Salome's growing weariness with Joseph, and her wish to get rid of him. It was but one step, therefore, for Salome to move from the opinion that Joseph was paying too much attention to Mariamne to the belief that he was paying her improper attention. Moreover, there was no better retort (to save for future use) to a queen who boasted that she was high-born than the intimation that she had carried on an illicit affair with a mere lieutenant of her royal husband, with a man of birth quite as low as the king's, or even lower.

As these currents of feminine hatred began to swell in the palace in Jerusalem, the rumor arrived, prompted by enemies of Herod, that Antony had tortured Herod and had then executed him. At this point, Alexandra had to make a choice, whether to reply on her hope and supposition that the populace would quickly rush to acclaim Mariamne as the ruler, or whether some other person would arise to seek the throne for himself. In her estimation, the populace presented a threat, a danger, and not a source of support to her. On the other hand, it would not be too long, so she reasoned, before Antony would seek out Mariamne, and then become enamored of her, with the sequel that Mariamne would come into full royal power in Judea. She thereupon suggested that Joseph approach the guards stationed in Jerusalem with the request that the Romans maintain the full security of the palace. Mariamne joined her mother in advocating an appeal to the Roman garrison. But Joseph had Salome and her mother, Cypros, also available for unsolicited counsel, and both Salome and Cypros knew of Alexandra's suggestion. The proposed appeal to the Roman garrison implied to Salome and Cypros not only the future ascendancy of Mariamne, but thereby also the loss of their own position and wealth. They contended to Joseph that Alexandra's proposal lent itself to interpretation as an act of deliberate disloyalty to Herod, a disloyalty that could have serious consequences if the rumor about Herod's death proved unfounded. So Joseph was faced by contradictory outspoken advice.

In the midst of these machinations by women against each other, letters arrived from the still living Herod describing his vindication before Antony. Once the rumor of Herod's death proved baseless, Alexandra and Mariamne desisted from their proposal to call in the Roman garrison, but neither Cypros nor Salome intended to let this proposal be forgotten, since it bordered on the traitorous. As for Joseph, his precise role in these machinations is quite unclear, but inasmuch as Salome's distaste for him was increasing, it is reasonable to suppose that he did not flatly reject Alexandra's proposal, but instead gave it at least some passing consideration, and out of this circumstance, Salome would be able to add to her allegation of a liaison by him with Mariamne the further allegation of her husband's disloyalty to her brother.

It was to a palace filled with multifarious rivalries and animosities that the triumphant Herod returned. Instead of receiving a warm and applauding welcome, he found himself plunged into turmoil. From Salome and Cypros he learned of Alexandra's proposal that Joseph summon the Roman garrison; and while there was no intimation that Joseph had complied with the suggestion, there was also no indication at all that Joseph had begun to plan to carry out Herod's injunction to slay Mariamne, on hearing of Herod's supposed death. Clearly, then, Joseph was guilty of disobedience, or at least of noncompliance; while Joseph would have been in an untenable position had he proceeded to slay Mariamne, he was in almost as poor a position through having desisted. Now Salome breathed to Herod the allegation of the adultery, with the intimation that it involved frequent and repeated occurrence; the alleged adultery took place in a context of a deeper and more traitorous trespass by Joseph.

Herod did not confront Joseph with the compound allegations; indeed, he did not allow Joseph into his presence at all. Rather, he gave orders to execute Joseph, and the orders were promptly obeyed. As to Alexandra, he increased the severity of the restrictions which he had already decreed for her, and she now became a prisoner in the palace. It was she on whom his anger settled, for, so he could see, it was she who was the true cause of all the mischief, especially in the light of her proposal to call in the Roman garrison.

But even with Joseph executed, there abided with Herod the allegations of Mariamne's adultery. In the depth of his love for her, and his intense jealousy, he found himself in profound inner unrest. He could not believe the allegation, simply because he did not want to; he could not discredit it, for it came from his mother and his sister. He summoned Mariamne, and he laid the charges before her openly. Mariamne made her denials, first asserting her innocence, and then accompanying her assertions with explanations. Finally, however, she resorted to the device of an oath, solemnly swearing that she was innocent. Slowly Herod began to believe her, and, having offended her by confronting her with the allegations, he sought to remove the affront by abject apologies, and by renewed protestations of his love and of his admiration for her character, especially for her sense of modesty and propriety. At length the two both found the bitter tears they were shedding a suitable gateway to reconciliation, and they joined in a most tender embrace, as if all was explained or forgiven, or forgotten.

Only Herod could not cleanse his mind entirely of suspicion. He believed Mariamne, and at the same time there abided in him a residual disbelief. He was reassured about her fidelity, but not quite completely. He could momentarily quell his jealousy, but he could never exorcize it.

It does not appear that he contemplated at all that step of prudence by which to eliminate the frictions in his household, namely, the expulsion of his mother and sister from the palace. Perhaps family loyalty was too strong to admit of such drastic action. Or perhaps it was well, since Mariamne could not forget she was a Maccabean, that she always be reminded by the presence of bitter foes in the palace that he, not she, was supreme in Judea.[5]

After the execution of Joseph and the reconciliation with Mariamne, Herod came into a period of a little tranquillity. It was broken, however, by an incident which Josephus abstains from relating in order, but much later harks back to. He tells that at the time when Mariamne was still alive, an allegation was made against Herod's brother Pheroras, by whom we do not know, that Pheroras was bent on poisoning Herod. Herod launched an investigation, and although he used an adequate amount of torture, he could find no proof of the plot.

That an accusation of this kind could be credibly made, even though it failed to be sustained, against his own brother and beneficiary, should illumine for us the often tenuous nature of Herod's hold on the throne. If one could not trust one's own brother, but needed to abide in omnipresent suspicion even of one's family, then whom could one trust? To be the king meant to wear a perpetual mantle of distrust and suspicion, and such a mantle became Herod's customary garb.

But, furthermore, one can conjecture that the accusation was true, and failed to be sustained simply because Herod, perpetually a victim of family solidarity, declined to believe those allegations against his own kin and rushed to believe in the case of those who were not of his blood.

We do not know precisely how much Herod was shaken by this incident, for Josephus does not tell us. Yet we shall see that it was a harbinger of similar, more involved, events which were to unfold with some repetition.

At about this time, Herod faced the impending visit to Judea of Cleopatra. Antony at the time was making further preparations for his wars in the east, now against Armenia. Cleopatra's gift from Antony of territory in Syria was not as much as she asked for, but only so much as Antony felt would appease her and still provide him with the appearance of some independence of mind. She had accompanied him part of the way east, but now she determined to return to Egypt, and in order to do so by land, she needed to traverse Judea. The message arrived that she was coming, so Herod was faced with the prospect of a royal visitor, avid for some of his territory, and still the mistress of Antony, his own master. However much Herod needed to welcome her, she could scarcely have been welcome.

Cleopatra at that time was thirty-five years old, Herod some four years older. By our standards she was still a young woman, and certainly by any standard she was young enough to retain still the attractions of femininity. Of her early life and youth we own few details, but thereafter, for a period of seventeen or eighteen years, we have many more, for in these years she went through experiences that in more ordinary mortals could consume a half century. She was the daughter of Ptolemy XI, one of a dynasty of tyrants whose dissolute life and misrule had led to constant rebellion. When Cleopatra was eleven, a revolt in Alexandria unseated her father; it was through the intervention of Gabinius in 58 B.C. (narrated above, p. 44) that her father regained his throne, and then Gabinius pro-

ceeded to drain Egypt of its wealth. Ptolemy XI reigned
for about six years after recovering the throne, dying in
51. He was succeeded by Ptolemy XII, Cleopatra's younger
brother, who, in 52 or 51, also became Cleopatra's husband.
But after Ptolemy XII had ascended the throne, disputes
arose between him and his sister-queen, especially on
matters of royal policy, on which Cleopatra had strong
opinions. Also, she came to the conviction that she could
rule with greater skill than her husband-brother. She fled
to Syria, assembled troops there, and returned to Egypt in
49, in order to unseat her brother. With the help of Julius
Caesar, she succeeded, and she became the ruler of Egypt
and also the mistress of the Roman. Ptolemy XII died
through accidental drowning in the Nile, and Cleopatra
then married a still younger brother, Ptolemy XIII, at the
instigation of Julius Caesar. At that juncture Caesar departed for his eastern campaign against Pontus (of which
he reported, "I came, I saw, I conquered"). When Caesar
returned to Rome, Cleopatra went there to join him, and
there she gave birth to the boy, Caesarion, widely believed
to be Caesar's son. After the murder of Caesar in 44, Cleopatra returned to Egypt. It was in 42 that her liaison with
Antony began, a liaison punctuated by many forced separa-
tions, mostly occasioned by Antony's military expeditions
in the east, but also by his need, in 40, to interrupt the
military expeditions in order to marry Octavia, the sister
of Augustus Caesar. After 40, Antony was again in the east
and he resumed his affair with Cleopatra. Accordingly,
Cleopatra was with Antony when the Roman summoned
Herod to him in 36.

The liaisons of Cleopatra with the Romans Julius Caesar
and Mark Antony were by no means clandestine affairs;
they were not matters of the delighted whispers on the
part of the knowing, but were quite open matters, publicly
and universally known. It was known, too, even then, that

Cleopatra possessed a certain magnetic force which had bound first Caesar and now Antony to her, and she had already achieved her place in the assessment of men as the epitome of a woman's capacity to enthrall a man.

We speculated above as to whether or not there might have been a brief liaison when Herod had been in Egypt in 40, for Josephus seems to be on the border of suggesting that there was, but this is no more than a mere intimation, and by no means a clear one. The anxiety of Herod about the prospect of Cleopatra's visit in Judea in 36 seemed to hinge on something quite beyond the political implications; indeed one might infer that Cleopatra's hostility to him in the preceding years rested on something more than her wish for his territory.

Josephus sets the stage in *Antiquities* for the visit of Cleopatra by providing a short résumé of some of her deeds, though attributing to her some murders which occurred only later. He tells that so mad was Cleopatra for money that she would despoil a temple or a sepulcher to gain it. No place was too holy for her to ravage for its wealth, nor too profane to escape her cruel treatment if thereby material gain could be achieved. She was, he assures us, a slave of her lusts, and she wanted everything that she could think of. For the most part she gained from Antony whatever she wanted, and one can explain this, Josephus assures us, only by recognizing that he was in some way or other bewitched by her. Yet, he adds, at times the gross injustice of her demands confronted Antony with the choice of appearing to be a sick man through acquiescing to her, or, of appearing well through denying her some of her requests. He had given her Jericho and its environs, one of the richest areas in Judea.

Jericho lay somewhat west of the Jordan River, seventeen miles from Jerusalem and perhaps five miles from the north end of the Dead Sea into which the Jordan flows.

It was some eight hundred feet below the sea level, at the foot of the descent from the Judean hills on which Jerusalem nestles. The tropical climate of Jericho made it "the city of the palm trees," as Scripture describes it. Even in ancient times it was known as the source both for dyes and for the drug of the balsam shrub. A winter palace located there could have provided Maccabean kings and Herod himself with a convenient place to retire to, and we can conjecture that there was such an edifice at Jericho; modern archeology has uncovered what appears to be a sumptuous gymnasium, or some comparable building, coming from that age.

It is to Jericho that Josephus allocates the events of Cleopatra's visit, moving one to speculate whether or not Herod had received the Egyptian queen in the palace at Jerusalem; but we do not know. Germane to this question is the further speculation, was Mariamne at all on the scene, either at Jerusalem, in an unrecorded portion of Cleopatra's visit, or at Jericho, when Herod entertained Cleopatra there.

Josephus does not clarify these uncertainties, but he narrates plainly that at Jericho Cleopatra attempted to entice Herod into an affair. She did so quite openly; in another woman one would say brazenly. Perhaps an open affair was her preferred device to get Herod completely into her power. We are not told whether she was prompted by a general lust, for the satisfaction of which Herod chanced to be conveniently available, or through having conceived some passion for him in particular, but Josephus records the opinion that Cleopatra seemed overcome by love for Herod.

If such was indeed the case, then one must comment that Cleopatra normally had little difficulty in finding herself so overcome. Long behind her lay her affairs, according to Plutarch, with Pompey as well as with Caesar. Plutarch, in his biographical essay on Antony, in his *Lives*, tells us that her affair with Antony had begun even prior to their meeting, for the emissary sent by Antony to summon Cleopatra to appear before Antony to explain her alleged partisanship for Cassius in the intra-Roman war, observed her beauty and manner, and advised her that she not only had nothing to fear from Antony, but would have great influence over him. The emissary suggested that she appear in her best attire, that is, as anything but a suppliant. Then Plutarch comments that when Julius Caesar and Pompey had had her favors—most scholars assume that the supposition of an affair with Pompey is groundless—she was young and inexperienced, being at the time of her first liaison with Caesar about twenty. In the lapse of the half dozen or so years, that is, from Caesar's death to Antony's summons of her, she had now come to the time of life when feminine beauty reaches its full maturity. Plutarch reports, moreover, that Cleopatra's beauty was neither "astonishing nor without equal," but ascribes her ability to capture men to the attraction of her person and the wit of her conversation, and that the manner in which she did things was entrancing. Her voice, we are told, was a pleasure merely to hear, and her gifts as a linguist—surely Plutarch exaggerates how many languages she knew!—added to her attractions.

It was, then, no ordinary woman whom Herod was entertaining, but a shrewd, grasping, ruthless queen, an invitation to whose couch promised unequaled and unparalleled pleasures, but also the prospect of the most dire consequences. Anyone in a situation such as Herod found himself in would forever alienate Antony by acquiescing in Cleopatra's proposal, and at the same time he could hardly expect Cleopatra to abstain thereafter from dominating him as she dominated Antony.

Josephus informs us (*The Jewish War* I, 477) that, in

the succession of women Herod married, he normally chose a wife for her beauty rather than her family; in the case of one of his marriages, as we shall see, he apparently first considered but rejected taking the particular damsel by force and later preferred nuptials instead, and here Josephus comments that no consideration ever prevented Herod from following his pleasure. But Herod was apparently not an adulterous profligate, as was his master Antony; only his abundant marriages would incline us to view him as a man of marked sexual sensuality.

How much Herod was attracted to Cleopatra and privately desired to consummate the proposed liaison, we have no way of knowing. To the extent that he was attracted, to that extent he was afraid; and his fear triumphed over whatever desire he had. Indeed, still another fact inclines one to suppose that his wish to acquiesce was a strong one, for though he determined to decline the favors, he conceived the intention of seizing Cleopatra and of putting her to death, a clear indication that he needed to resist her attraction. If we can trust Josephus, Herod not only projected doing so, but even discussed it with his associates. These immediately pointed out to him that should he slay Cleopatra he would earn the relentless hatred of his master Antony. To this Herod replied that in the long run Antony would be grateful, since it was manifest that Cleopatra would scarcely remain faithful to Antony. His advisers then proceeded to enumerate for him the terrible harvest he would reap from insolently slaying the most desirable woman in the world, the paramour of the great Roman Antony; and, moreover, they could see no advantage accruing to Herod from such an action. His best course of action was quietly to resist Cleopatra's wicked proposals; to act uprightly in the face of her offer by rejecting it was to combine honor with prudent foresight.

Herod was, then, too fearful to accept Cleopatra's favors. He denied himself the pleasure which Julius Caesar and Mark Antony had had, for they were great Roman generals and rulers, but he was only a petty Near Eastern prince who reigned through the grace of Rome. He gave her gifts, and he escorted her to the border of Egypt. Certain imposts which Antony levied on him to pay to Cleopatra, Herod paid with some honesty.

For the period from 36 to 31 Josephus is silent about events in Judea, save for this visit by Cleopatra. The relative quiet of the country had brought some recovery of its prosperity, and Herod collected a great amount of taxes, and created a large and well-equipped army.

The Roman world, we will recall, was then governed by its "Second Triumvirate," with Antony dominant in the east, Augustus Caesar controlling the west, and Lepidus holding North Africa. In the west before 40 there had arisen difficulties and even insurrections, and the suspicion existed in Rome that Antony's first wife, Fulvia, who had remained in the Eternal City when Antony went to the east, was carrying out conspiratorial maneuvers on behalf of her absent husband. But in 40 Octavius and Antony had met at a conference at Brundisium, and had there arrived at a reconciliation of certain of their disputes. Moreover, Fulvia having died in that same year, Antony had then married Octavia, the sister of Augustus, as we have related, but had gone back to the east and taken up again with Cleopatra. In the west, the island of Sicily had been seized by Sextus Pompey, a son of the great Pompey, and Sextus and his great marauding fleet were a thorn to Augustus; it was not until 36, a matter of almost four years, that Sextus Pompey was defeated. In the same year, Antony had begun his eastern campaigns against the Parthians, campaigns which ended in disaster. Mutual recriminations set Augustus and Antony, both of them "consuls," against each other, for Antony had sneered at the slowness of Augustus' conquest of Sextus Pompey, while Augustus had sneered at Antony's failures in the east. Some scholars suppose that Antony was bent on supplementing Rome with Alexandria as the leading city of the empire. Yet beyond these political events, there was personal animosity between Augustus and Antony. The latter divorced Octavia about the year 32, and, having already lived with Cleopatra in Alexandria for a period of two years, he then married her and acknowledged the paternity of two sons born to her; moreover, he greatly displeased Augustus by recognizing Cleopatra's son Caesarion, then a boy of fifteen, as the son of Caesar, and as the heir presumptive to Cleopatra. That is to say, the rivalry between Rome in the east and Rome in the west around the year 32 took the form of personal rivalry and animosity, and jealousy of power and wealth. With these personal motives added (and with Lepidus deprived of his power by Augustus), warfare between Rome in the east and Rome in the west was inevitable.

The war between Antony and Augustus was precipitated by an act of the Roman Senate. At Augustus' instigation, the Senate passed a declaration of war against Cleopatra. Antony, of course, had been giving her territory, and, further, he had even written a will assigning some of the eastern lands to the children she had borne him.

Augustus mustered a fleet of 250 vessels, and an army of something more than eight legions, a legion usually numbering six thousand men. Antony and Cleopatra raised a mercenary army of about thirty legions.

Whether or not Herod thought through the question of which side he would espouse, Augustus' or Antony's, is not told to us. How aware he was that he might be backing the side destined to lose is also unknown. Since he had been raised to his throne by Antony, and since Antony was the ruler in the east, Herod had little choice of sides. He raised and equipped a sizable army and offered it to Antony. Antony, however, declined his offer, and enjoined on him an expedition against the Nabateans, this in all probability at the instigation of Cleopatra, for it was to her interest that the Judeans and the Nabateans, both of whose territories she coveted, should weaken themselves by warfare.

The Nabatean kingdom at this time had extended its sway northward, to the area east of the Jordan and within Coele-Syria, and there the Judean and Nabatean armies confronted each other, at a village which Josephus calls Canatha in *The Jewish War* and Cana in *Antiquities*.[6] The rival armies were drawn up in battle array. Nearby, however, were the forces of Cleopatra, to whom portions of Coele-Syria had been given by Antony. These Egyptian forces were commanded by a general named Athenion. A furious onslaught by the troops of Herod routed the Nabateans, but the troops who gained this signal victory were young and inexperienced; the first obligation on them was to follow Herod's orders to consolidate their position. Instead, they rushed into hot pursuit of the retreating and defeated Nabateans. Athenion and his troops then executed a surprise attack on the forces of Herod, and promptly the Nabateans, and also natives of the area, joined in the battle. What was at first a Judean victory turned into a staggering defeat, and the army of Herod was virtually annihilated. Herod had failed in the mandate given him by Antony to subdue the Nabateans; it was no small come-down that he could thereafter do little more to carry out Antony's mandate than to make sporadic, minor raids against the Nabateans.

This bitter, vexing defeat was a major disaster, and we can understand that Herod was utterly shaken by it. Moreover, he faced the need to negotiate with the Nabateans (exactly to what end we do not know, but presumably to work out a long-range truce), and he sent ambassadors to them; this was in the spring of 31. Now a new disaster struck Judea, an earthquake of tremendous destructiveness, causing the death of thousands of people; *The Jewish War* numbers them at thirty thousand, the *Antiquities* at ten.[7] When the Nabateans learned the extent of the damage caused by the earthquake, they concluded that Judea was enough weakened to become the ready prey to their own ambitions. They thereupon slew the ambassadors with whom they were discussing peace, and proceeded to invade Judea. What they did not know was that Herod's residual army, being encamped in a field, escaped the devastation of the cities; it remained intact, though frightened, both by the earthquake and by the impending Nabatean invasions. Since morale was understandably low, it fell to Herod to restore courage to his troops and to his subjects. Josephus tells us that Herod met this need through a speech that he delivered to his people; the speech, which he purports to quote, is somewhat different in *The Jewish War* from that in *Antiquities*. The speech in *Antiquities* (XIV, 127–146) sets forth Herod's candid admission of the need to encourage his people in view of the untoward incidents of the immediate past. It then asserts that the impending war with the Nabateans is a just one. It was he, so Herod says, who protected the Nabateans against Cleopatra's design to absorb their territory, this by his personal gifts to Antony, and, having preserved the Nabateans, it was unfitting now to become subject to them and to pay them tribute. The wickedness of the Nabateans in beheading the ambassadors was such as to shock the world, for ambassadors were universally sacred and inviolable, even in the case of nations hostile to each other. Hence, the Nabateans, guilty of gross injustice, could scarcely hope to triumph in a war. If, he continued, there were people who said that though God was on the side of the Judeans, the Nabateans had both more courage and more troops, then the reply had to be that at Canatha, it was the Judeans who had demonstrated the greater courage, until the betrayal by Athenion. And if some supposed that the recent earthquake might have frightened the Judeans, then perhaps the way to look at the earthquake was to regard it as a snare through which to entrap the Nabateans. The earthquake was not so destructive as to lead to the conclusion, to which some had come, that it was brought by God to punish the Judeans, for if one followed that reasoning, one needed to see the termination of God's wrath in the termination of the earthquake. It was God's will, said Herod, that the Judeans proceed with this war, and that was why the troops in the field were spared the deaths which occurred in the cities.

The speech in *The Jewish War* (I, 373–379) is similar in substance, though its language is quite different. It was unreasonable, so Herod is portrayed as saying, to be as disheartened by the Nabatean invasion, a human visitation, as by the visitation from heaven, the earthquake. This earthquake was a snare, for the Nabateans were relying more on the disaster to the Judeans than on their own strength. Moreover, the overconfidence of the Nabateans, coupled with the presumed Judean diffidence, provided a setting in which the Judeans could arouse themselves and defeat the Nabateans. Furthermore, the slaughter of the ambassadors was sure to bring God's wrath down upon the Nabateans. Finally, "Let every man move forward, not for wife and children or our endangered country, but to avenge our envoys." Having delivered this heartening speech, Herod offered at the Temple the appropriate sacrifices ordained in Holy Writ.

William Whiston (1667–1752), who translated Josephus into English, has a footnote to the speech in *Antiquities:*

"This piece of religion . . . is worth remarking, for it is the only example of this nature, so far as I remember, that Josephus ever mentions in all his large and particular accounts of this Herod." It is, of course, not to be ruled out that the pious incident is historical; yet one can have his doubts.

Nevertheless, one need not doubt that the recent double disaster constituted one of the gravest sets of stresses and strains through which the insecure Judean monarch passed. Not only had he failed to carry out the mandate of Antony, a circumstance which scarcely strengthened his hold on the throne, but he could not help but be anxious about the events shaping up between Antony and Augustus. The failure to defeat the Nabateans could well earn him the displeasure of a victorious Antony; his strong backing of Antony would scarcely endear him to a victorious Augustus. So if, in the mounting insecurity, Herod encouraged his people by a contrived speech, and himself by a hypocritical act of religious devotion, we can well understand it.

The military engagement with the Nabateans took place at a site which in ancient times was known as Rabbath-Ammon, but in Herod's day as Philadelphia. Today it is Amman, capital of Jordan. It lay northeast of the Dead Sea, about twenty-three miles east of the Jordan River. A fort, decisive for the impending full-scale battle, was the center of some preliminary skirmishes. When the battle was joined, the Nabateans, apparently having little stomach for warfare despite superior numbers, followed a primarily defensive strategy, and with some success. But when the troops of Herod mounted a ferocious assault, the Nabateans began to give way, and then panic overtook them, and they trampled their own troops to death. To add to their discomfiture, the Nabateans began to suffer acutely from the lack of water, with the result that the bulk of them surrendered; a few days later the remainder capitulated. Herod's victory was complete; it was crowned, indeed, by the action of the Nabateans in naming him as their Protector—whether this title was merely honorific or implied some ruling authority we do not know.

Herod returned to Judea in great triumph. In his palace, however, the same feminine machinations were going on as before, but now perhaps at even greater extremes. Especially was this the case respecting Alexandra. And unsettling as was this continuing domestic strife, even more unsettling was the news from afar. In September, the two forces, those of Augustus and the combined militia of Antony and Cleopatra, encountered each other off the west coast of Greece, at a place called Actium, a promontory at the entrance of the Gulf of Ambracia, just north of the island called, today, Leukas. It was the hope of Antony to entice Augustus Caesar into a land battle, for there lay Antony's possible advantage, but in a sea battle Antony would face a fleet superior in both armament and naval skill.

Augustus had set up a naval blockade to hem in the forces of Antony and Cleopatra. The ships directly under Antony tried to run the blockade, and to return to Egypt, but they were overwhelmingly defeated. The ships under Cleopatra managed to make their way through the blockade, and returned to Alexandria. Earlier, we saw that Herod, contemplating the slaying of Cleopatra, intended to justify it on the allegation that she would not remain faithful to Antony; out of this passage in Josephus the conclusion has been drawn by some historians that Cleopatra treacherously abandoned Antony at Actium; most modern historians discount this allegation, and conclude, instead, that it was at Antony's direct behest that Cleopatra took her fleet away. Antony was able to join Cleopatra in Alexandria. The two were forced, however, to recognize the hopelessness of their military situation, and, moreover,

Cleopatra faced some imminent internal uprisings. To avert these she ordered the execution of her sister Arsinoë, and arranged for the murder of her boy-husband, Ptolemy XIII. But Augustus' ships approached Alexandria. Then, as we can also read in Shakespeare's imaginative retelling in his *Antony and Cleopatra*, Antony stabbed himself to death, and Cleopatra died after being bitten by a deadly asp. In the year 30 Augustus became the full master of Rome and all its possessions.

It was within the realm of possibility now that Augustus would wish someone on the throne of Judea more directly of his own selection, someone without the record of having offered assistance to Antony. As Herod surveyed matters, not only did his tenure as king depend on the favor of the Romans, but also the Romans would raise the question of who might be available to succeed him. Obviously his throne might revert to the dynasty from which he had taken it, the Maccabeans. Of these almost none had survived the various struggles, except, of course, the aged and innocuous and blemished Hyrcanus. To an insecure Herod, the mild and retiring Hyrcanus began to loom as a direct threat. Moreover, Alexandra began to persuade Hyrcanus that he should take some steps to protect himself, her, and their line, the children born to Mariamne and Herod. She proposed to Hyrcanus that "they"—exactly who, we do not know, but presumably Hyrcanus, Alexandra, and Mariamne—should seek refuge with the Nabateans, until such time as the issue of the throne would be settled by the Romans in the new situation of Antony's defeat. Hyrcanus gradually yielded to the importunings of his daughter. He composed a letter addressed to the ruler of the Nabateans, and he entrusted it to a man named Dositheus, a devoted servant to him and Alexandra, and whose near kin had been maltreated by or through Herod. That is to say, Dositheus seemed a reliable vessel. But after Dositheus was given the letter, he promptly took it to Herod. The king, on reading it, determined on his strategy. He sent Dositheus on to the Nabateans, with instructions to bring back to Herod the reply which they would make. The Nabateans readily acceded to the request of Hyrcanus in their written reply, and they even promised to send troops to meet him on his southward journey and to escort him in safety to their domain. Dutifully, Dositheus handed the reply of the Nabateans to Herod.

At this point in the narrative of *Antiquities*, we encounter a second story. In addition to the account summarized in the above paragraph—which, if reliable, implies that Hyrcanus, through acceding to the importunings of Alexandra, sealed his own doom, for in a sense he was guilty of plotting against Herod—Josephus provides another version. This divergent story contains no word about the two suspicious letters. Rather, from time to time, Hyrcanus had received the gifts normally exchanged among royalty, and one such gift consisted of four horses sent by the Nabateans, a gift innocently given and innocently received. To Herod the receipt of the gift was the equivalent of bribery and therefore of treason. Whether on true but flimsy charges or on entirely false ones, Herod ordered the execution of the Maccabean.

What is even more germane than whether or not Hyrcanus was plotting against Herod is the observation that even if Hyrcanus were plotting, the slaying of the aged man was a punishment that Herod could have omitted, and the plotting ignored. Surely Hyrcanus could not have posed a threat of any dimension; and to slay the very old man was needlessly to anticipate the inevitable working of nature. And to slay Hyrcanus without touching his daughter Alexandra is difficult to understand, unless at that moment Herod was unwilling to affront his wife by harming her mother.

But what we must above all remark is the curious juxtaposition in the account of Josephus: Herod delivers an eloquent speech to encourage his people, he offers sacrifices at the Temple, he bests the Nabateans, and then he slays Hyrcanus! Granted that this sequence of events reflects an age of disorder, the response of Herod reflects an even greater disorder, indeed, a disarrayed mind, one on the verge of losing its ability to sort out experiences and analyze and classify them, one that instead resorts to the most primitive of instinctive responses. The throne which he occupied seemed to many not legitimately his, and nothing in the world was more precious to him than that throne, and nothing would deflect him from a frenzied defense of his throne, even against those, like Hyrcanus, who had no intention of taking it from him or of weakening his grasp on it.

Having slain Hyrcanus so that Augustus could not readily find a royal candidate with whom to replace him, Herod prepared to visit the Roman whose opponent he had backed, and to humble himself before him. In a literal sense, Herod needed first to put his household in order, for he could not absent himself from the capital and leave the warring women under the roof of the palace, on the one side Mariamne and her mother Alexandra, and on the other side his sister Salome and his mother Cypros. Moreover, there were enough vestiges of internal dissidence within Judea to give him pause, or even anxiety. He determined to put the kingdom in charge of his brother Pheroras while he was away. Cypros and Salome he deposited in the fortress at Masada, on the bluff overlooking the Dead Sea. Mariamne and Alexandra he put at the fortress of Alexandreion, some fifty miles north-northeast of Jerusalem. Perhaps his children by Mariamne—two sons (a third had died as a baby) and two daughters—were sent to Alexandreion also.

This separation from each other of people precious to Herod and unremittingly hostile to each other, was unquestionably a necessity, a product of the strife of the household of Herod. But even beyond this large measure of feminine animosity, the relationship between Herod and Mariamne had come into its own distortion. From her standpoint, however much she might originally have loved her husband, he stood revealed as the murderer both of her brother Aristobulus and now of her grandfather Hyrcanus; and if originally there had been any love on her part, it had changed into hatred. Her aspersions on the lowly Idumean origin of her husband and of his sister were no longer mere bickering which can ebb and flow and constitute a nuisance rather than a menace; now her scorning words were fraught with the utmost of implacable enmity. Yet much as Mariamne had hated her sister-in-law, and scorned her, even more she had come to loathe and despise Herod. On the other hand, he had not ceased to love Mariamne; Josephus tells us that so great was his love for her that he was quite unaware that she was the cause of the turmoil in his household; indeed, he was as unremittingly enamored of her as before. Josephus puts it that he loved her to the same extent that she hated him.

The fortress of Alexandreion he put in the charge of an official, Joseph,[8] the royal treasurer, and a certain military man, Sohemus. These were routine assignments. He left the additional mandate that should Augustus decree his own death, Joseph and Sohemus should proceed to make an end of Mariamne and Alexandra, and then should try, as best they could, to preserve the throne either for Pheroras or for Herod's sons.

So Herod set out for the island of Rhodes to call on Augustus. He found it prudent not to wear the royal diadem in the presence of Augustus, for by not wearing it he implied that he was, at least in comparison with Augustus, merely a commoner. Josephus preserves for us what purports to be Herod's statement of his case before the Roman, and, if we regard the speech as authentic, then we must regard it as a signally judicious utilization of honesty, or at least of a large measure of it. Not only did Herod not deny that he had assisted Antony, though, of course, he said, in limited measure, through supplying food. The fact was that Antony had made him king, and therefore he admitted having had an unswerving loyalty to Antony. Only the instructions from Antony to attack the Nabateans had prevented Herod from being present at Actium, in opposition to Augustus. Indeed, so Herod went on, he had not deserted Antony even after Actium—as presumably Cleopatra had done—but he had remained a friend and even a counselor. Respecting the latter—and here either Josephus or Herod prevaricates—he had advised Antony to slay Cleopatra, by which action Antony would find the remedy for his disasters. Had Antony complied, then he, Herod, would have supplied Antony with money, with fortress walls for his self-protection, and with an army to oppose Augustus, an army which Herod himself would lead as a brother in arms. So we read in the version in *The Jewish War*.

The other version, that in *Antiquities*, depicts Herod as suggesting that, if Cleopatra were out of the way, Antony and Augustus might have composed their difficulties. But Antony would not listen to Herod. Meanwhile—now Herod became theological and pious—God had granted victory to Augustus. There was only one reasonable conclusion to Herod's speech: "I shared in Antony's defeat. Since his downfall, I have put aside my diadem. I have come to you with my hope for safety dependent on my straightforwardness. I trust that an inquiry will ensue, not as to whose friend I have been, but how loyal a friend I was." This second version appends another sentence: "I will be the same loyal friend to you."

Whether the speech alone, or the speech and other considerations,[9] such as the generosity of heart attributed to Augustus, won over the Roman, we do not know. The result of the encounter, however, is quite certain. Augustus restored the diadem to Herod's head. More than that, Herod won Augustus' approval, and even some warmth of friendship. And a few months later he entertained Augustus in proper measure when Augustus passed through Judea. Augustus had a decree issued which confirmed Herod as king.

Herod's triumph, then, was complete, and a refutation of his terrible fears. He returned home from Rhodes, in 30, in high exultation, filled with the desire to convey the glorious news of his full vindication to his beloved Mariamne.

But at Alexandreion, Mariamne had come to the climax of her hatred for her husband. The military man, Sohemus, succumbed gradually to a certain flattery from Mariamne and Alexandra, and he turned from being a guard over them into their compliant servant. Moreover, Sohemus was aware that Herod might never return alive from the visit to Augustus at Rhodes, and, should the throne pass either to Alexandra or to Mariamne, he stood to gain power by the gratitude that they would feel toward him. Or, if Herod should survive, Sohemus was confident that Mariamne so controlled him that Herod would never go against her expressed wishes, and she would protect his interests. Therefore, Sohemus entered into the most friendly of relations with the women. In that context, he disclosed to Mariamne the instructions which Herod had given that, in the event of Herod's death, Mariamne must die.

In the confusion in Josephus, two contradictory motives are given for the instruction by Herod. On the one

hand, this is depicted as jealousy, in that he did not wish
Mariamne, in surviving him, to belong to another man; on
the other hand, this is depicted as a hostile desire, motivated by Herod's wish to bequeath the throne to his children, and not to Mariamne or her mother. While Sohemus
had been sworn to secrecy by Herod, he did not hesitate
to disclose the secret instruction to Mariamne. Her immediate inference was that she was in a situation similar to
that of her grandfather and her brother, who had died as
victims of Herod's hatred of Maccabeans. She began to
express openly her hope that Herod would be rejected by
Augustus at Rhodes, and she did not hesitate to proclaim
that it was intolerable for her to continue to live with him.

Herod was unaware of these developments, and, continually infatuated with Mariamne, he supposed that she
was still infatuated with him. Hence it was to her at his
triumphant homecoming that he planned to give the good
news of his success, and he wished to report to her first
and in private. Their reunion took place, so it would seem,
in Jerusalem, at the palace; an exultant Herod began to tell
Mariamne the story of his great achievement. But Mariamne, far from sharing his joy, seemed sorry to hear what
he was telling, and she was quite unable to conceal the
resentments which she felt. So Mariamne turned the sweet-
ness of his triumph into raw bitterness.

In his frustration Herod found himself, in the ensuing
days, in moments when he hated her unreservedly. Yet
such moods passed and his infatuation reasserted itself; he
found himself going from one extreme to the other. It was
in his power to punish her for her insolence; he was quite
incapable of bringing himself to the point of forgetting or
ignoring his infatuation. Moreover, the throne was precious to him, and there was always the danger that if he
harmed his Maccabean wife, he would thereby spur rebellious upheavals in Judea.

It was not that Herod bided his time. Rather, he remained a prisoner of his indecision, for he knew that he must in some way resolve the situation in which his queen openly scorned him (and his family), and at the same time he could not move to the point of action. Both Salome and Cypros witnessed the occasions of Mariamne's open scorn, and Herod, in listening to them, needed all the inner restraint he could muster to abstain from an impetuous assault on his wife.

So it went for almost a full year, the placid nature of the country at that juncture in startling contrast with the turmoil in the palace. Then a set of connected incidents brought matters to a head. On a certain day, at the noon hour, Herod lay down on his bed to rest. He sent for Mariamne to join him. She came into the room, but she refused to lie down with him, apparently as she had been consistently refusing, despite his manifest desire for her. Moreover, she proceeded to revile him for the murder of her grandfather and her brother. The incident pushed him nearer to a reluctant decision.

Salome, the sister, learned of the matter, and she observed the extraordinary extent to which Herod was disturbed. She sought out Herod's cupbearer to act out a role long before arranged between her and him, to come to Herod, at a high moment of Herod's frustration, with the report, a completely false one, that Mariamne had sought the cupbearer's assistance in preparing some love potion, some aphrodisiac to give to Herod. Salome knew that Herod would see the immediate connection between a love potion designed to stimulate his desire, and Mariamne's deliberate, continued refusal to give him his conjugal rights. The cupbearer delivered the tidings, with the predictable result that Herod was moved from disturbance into violent indignation. He summoned the eunuch who was Mariamne's personal servant, to question him about the whys and wherefores of Mariamne's hatred of him. The eunuch professed ignorance about the love potion. Under severe torture he ventured the explanation for Mariamne's hatred: it was occasioned by something that Sohemus had told her. It could only mean that Sohemus had revealed the secret instruction to kill her. To Herod there could be only one explanation for the betrayal by Sohemus of his confidence, an explanation undoubtedly hinted to him by Salome, that Sohemus and Mariamne had been intimate. Immediately Herod ordered the execution of Sohemus, and immediately it was carried out.

With Mariamne, however, he determined on the indignity of a public trial at which the queen would face the accusations of adultery and treason, and the disgrace of the matter of the love potion—and it could be implied, moreover, that this potion was nothing less than a poison.

We are not informed about the trial, neither as to where it took place and whether or not before the Sanhedrin, nor who the judge was. Some modern accounts suppose that Herod himself was the judge—an unnecessary and improbable extravagance, contradicted by Josephus' speaking of the members of the court in the plural, for Herod thoroughly controlled the judges. Mariamne was, of course, found guilty. The members of the court, and Herod himself for a while, favored as punishment her incarceration in the prison of one of the fortresses in the land. But Salome and others argued to Herod that he must put Mariamne to death, clinching their point by the contention that as long as she lived, the populace could rally around her in revolt. So Herod acquiesced in the execution of Mariamne.

In the Greek literary tradition, known either to Josephus or to his literary assistants, it was quite permissible for an author to increase the pathos of an already pathetic situation. Surely what Josephus proceeds to relate is legendary.

Alexandra, the mother, immediately prior to the execution, was naturally greatly fearful for her own safety. Now she pretended to a change of her loyalties, and she joined in the calumniation of her own daughter. While Mariamne was being led to her execution, Alexandra publicly cried out in reproach that Mariamne deserved her punishment, that she had been an evil woman, insolent to her husband, and ungrateful. This item we must dismiss as legend, for it in no way comports with the character of Alexandra. Mariamne, the account continues, remained silent, neither responding nor reacting to her mother's outburst. In quiet dignity, without change of color of her face, she went impassively to her death, and by this means exhibited to the spectators the nobility of her birth.

However admirable Mariamne was, in terms of her beauty and her chastity, certainly she was lacking in understanding and in humility, and in a sense she used Herod ill, for he had uniformly treated her with kindliness and indulgence. Dependent on him, either she disdained to understand that she was not a free agent or else the impulse to belittle his relatives, and to score him off in retaliation for his slaying of her relatives, was more than she could resist. Her manner provoked him; and she might have had the insight to know that the animosity to her of his plotting relatives was such that it was the height of imprudence to provoke him in any way. Since she had already ceased to be his wife in every way, Herod lost very little that was real by her death. Though she was apparently guiltless of the charge of adultery, she managed to behave in such a way that the accusation, despite Herod's reluctance to believe it, seemed credible and persuasive.

Yet if Herod lost little that was real in her death, in his fantasies he became all the more infatuated with her, now that she was dead. Indeed, he passed beyond the borders of sensibleness, and into the domain of insanity, for not only did he continue to love her with all the ardor of the bygone days when their marriage had been a happy one, but he often fancied that she was still alive, and he would call for her to come to him. He gave himself, at times, to open laments at her death, laments coupled with unrelieved remorse, laments which Josephus describes as indecent.

No more vivid portrait of a disconsolate Herod exists than that which Byron gives in *Herod's Lament for Mariamne*:

I

Oh, Mariamne! now for thee
The heart for which thou bled'st is bleeding;
Revenge is lost in agony,
And wild remorse to rage succeeding.
Oh, Mariamne! Where art thou?
Thou canst not hear my bitter pleading;
Ah, couldst thou—thou wouldst pardon now,
Though Heaven were to my prayer unheeding.

II

And is she dead?—and did they dare
Obey my frenzy's jealous raving?
My wrath but doomed my own despair:
The sword that smote her 's o'er me waving.—
But thou art cold, my murdered love!
And this dark heart is vainly craving
For her who soars alone above,
And leaves my soul unworthy saving.

III

She's gone, who shared my diadem;
She's sunk, with her my joys entombing;
I swept that flower from Judah's stem,
Whose leaves for me alone were blooming;

And mine's the guilt, and mine the hell,
This bosom's desolation dooming;
And I have earned these tortures well,
Which unconsumed are still consuming!

The relevant question can be raised of whether it was his execution of Mariamne which pushed Herod beyond the bounds of sanity or whether this act, bringing to the surface the antecedent instability in him, assailed and destroyed his balance, and pushed him into the recurrent periods of separation from reality. One senses a certain incompleteness in the account of Josephus, especially respecting the full year that elapsed between the time of Herod's return from his visit to Augustus and the formulation of his allegation against his queen. In a year of temporizing and indecision, we can understand that Salome steadily fed his suspicion and jealousy, and nurtured his resentment, and the months of indecision helped to increase these. Mariamne added to his bitter frustration by withholding her conjugal obligations, thereby increasing for him the willingness, or indeed the obligation, to believe the allegation of her infidelity. But at all events, the execution of Mariamne was not simply the limited matter of the supposed adultery of a queen; to Herod this putative adultery was inextricably bound up with his hold on his kingship, for to the extent that his kingship possessed legitimacy it was through his marriage to the Maccabean, and to that extent the supposed adultery was equivalent to jeopardizing the legitimacy. That Alexandra had tried to manipulate him out of the throne was already clear and antecedently established, and the combination of adultery and sexual rejection appeared to him as if Mariamne were plotting along exactly the same lines as her mother. And since Mariamne had borne him children who through her possessed for the throne credentials which he himself lacked, it was entirely credible to an insecure man that Mariamne was engaged in some subtle effort to take the throne from him and hand it over to her children.

Accordingly, Herod was confronted with the dilemma that he loved Mariamne but that he loved the throne even more, and his love for her could tolerate almost anything but the threat that he might lose his kingship. To be the king of Judea meant to Herod to possess both status and power, and to lose the throne was to revert to being merely a descendant of Idumean proselytes, to return to being a commoner. So, he could not brook manipulation and plot, even on the part of her whom he loved, and he felt compelled to choose to have a firm grasp on the throne over possessing a disloyal and hostile queen. But since the charge of Mariamne's infidelity and disloyalty was never totally established in his mind, his remorse, once she was executed, necessarily grew and necessarily bedeviled him. Indeed, once she was dead and no longer a threat to his throne, he could blot out from his mind that it was on behalf of the possession of the throne that he had had her killed, and he could now remember only how deeply he had loved her. His brother-in-law Aristobulus had had to die, and the aged Hyrcanus had had to die, and Mariamne had had to die; and Herod had to begin to pay the price for these killings through the eruption in him of a guilt which completely shattered his stability.

But, we must ask again, was Herod unstable first, so that he slew Mariamne, or did his slaying her make him unstable and temporarily insane? On the one hand, we have glimpsed his strange tendency to delay and then to act impetuously; we have seen in him the gamut of emotional tensions, and we recounted his effort at suicide. We have seen him harassed to the point of paralysis in his home life, and at the same time caught in debilitating fear that Rome would depose him. Need we conjecture whether antecedently he was potentially insane? Is it not sufficient to assume that scarcely any man could have lived through these occasions of emotional upheaval which Herod did, and not arrive inevitably at the point where prudence and moral restraint and marriage ties disappear? What we must say of Mariamne is that she earned his hatred, and of Herod that where other men would have *dreamed* of a slaying, he proceeded to the act. His remorse and temporary insanity were in direct proportion to the months of his reluctance, and that reluctance was, in turn, a blend of his love for her and his unwillingness to accept as true that which he had come to believe was credible. The conclusion must be that antecedently he was highly emotional but not insane; it was his family, both his queen and her mother, and also his sister and his brother, who drove him into an act of madness and thereby made him recurrently mad.

As for his sons by Mariamne, boys in the early teens, it is uncertain how closely they were informed about the trial and execution of their mother while these were going on. We know, however, that later on they necessarily knew about it in all its details, and that they became partisans of their Maccabean mother. The precise whereabouts at this time of Herod's oldest son, Antipater, whom the commoner Doris had borne to him, is unclear; apparently he was in Judea, but not in Jerusalem, and privileged to visit his royal father only on the occasion of the three religious pilgrimages, Tabernacles, Passover, and Pentecost.

At this time when Herod was unsettled mentally by his remorse, an epidemic of some kind made its appearance in Judea, and leading citizens, including trusted adherents of Herod, were carried off by it. It was quite natural that there were those who saw in the pestilence a divine punishment on Herod for his slaying of Mariamne, and apparently Herod himself thought that he was undergoing the wrath of God. After a period of trying to forget Mariamne, through futilely devising elaborate entertainments and contrived feasts, he felt the need to withdraw from direct public notice, to take himself into the wilderness where, unseen, he could afflict himself; it was announced, for public consumption, that he had gone into the wilderness for the sport of hunting. Unable himself to administer the affairs of state, he turned them over to his subordinates. To his mental state of deep guilt and remorse was added some form of physical illness, a high fever accompanied by a severe ache at the back of his head; modern doctors have suggested a diagnosis of severe boils. Herod's physicians prescribed medications and diet, but the medications proved to be ineffective, and he did not possess the inner controls necessary to abide by the prescribed diet.

It is very tempting to advert to Herod's retreat to the wilderness—Josephus gives us only the bare fact and no more—and to speculate on its meaning. Perhaps on one level it was no more than a retirement from public notice, a temporary abandonment of Jerusalem designed to reduce the abundance of reports and rumors of his insane conduct in the palace. It is worth speculating on another level, however, that his recourse to the wilderness was more than this mere useful device, and was no less than a desperate quest for spiritual surcease, no less than an act of religious searching. While nothing in the account of Josephus suggests such a thing, the tradition among the Jews was that their origin was in the wilderness: in the Wilderness of Sin they had received the Torah at the sacred mountain of Sinai-Horeb; to the wilderness the prophet Elijah had repaired after his soul-searing experiences with Ahab and Jezebel (I Kings 18–19). It was in the wilderness epoch of the ancient past that the literary prophets, especially those of the pre-exilic period, had placed the golden age of the Hebrews; it was from the wilderness that there stemmed the seventh-century Rechabites, mentioned in

Jeremiah 35, holy men who urged the adoption of a simple
regimen in the wilderness as a replacement for the wickedness of the sedentary urban life of that age. The community that created the so-called Dead Sea scrolls lived a
somewhat monastic life in the wilderness of Judea in
Herod's time. Shortly after the time of Herod, the Greek
Jew, Philo of Alexandria, repeatedly advocated retirement
to the wilderness as the means not only of escaping from
"the vices of the city," but as the necessary prelude to
communion with God. It is thus consistent with all that
we know of Jewish tradition to associate the wilderness
not only with a sanctity transcending the evils of civilization, but as the place where one could most readily com-
mune with God. Nothing in our knowledge of Herod
supports the supposition of any such religious bent on his
part, and we have no echo at all of religious disposition in
any depth in him. Yet desperation then, even as now, can
well have prompted a person, when all else appeared to
have failed, to try religion, and perhaps Herod too supposed that in the wilderness some miraculous cure for his
physical ailment would come to him, and some form of
theophany would redeem him from his spiritual disquiet.
If that was Herod's hope, he was grievously disappointed.
Unhelped by his wilderness experience, he went back to
civilization. Only, he went now to Samaria, where he had
built a palace, instead of to Jerusalem where bitter memo-
ries were vivid. He was so sick physically that his doctors
gave him up.

Notes

1. The insistence on, or supposition of, one Temple at Jerusalem
is found in the Five Books of Moses. There are clear mentions,
however, of other temples in such pre-exilic prophets as Amos, and
in the Books of Judges, Samuel, and Kings. Herein, then, lies an

age-old problem. Traditional interpreters regard the existence of these plural temples as an improper deviation from the antecedent Mosaic prescriptions. Modernist scholars regard the prescriptions for a single Temple as not Mosaic but as reflecting the age after the Babylonian exile, an age in which there existed only the Jerusalem Temple, with the prescription dating from the late age but attributed to Moses. In this latter view, the one Temple was a development out of an earlier situation in which plural temples existed.

2. Resurrection is explicit in Daniel 12:2—"Many who sleep in the dust of the earth shall awaken, some to eternal life and some to shame and eternal contempt." Possibly Daniel was not then universally accepted as scriptural; yet even if it were, it would not have vied in authority with the Pentateuch.

3. Josephus, a sometimes forgetful author, attributes at this point to Pollion the speech which earlier he had ascribed to Samaias.

4. The Greek canon, through the Latin, became the Christian canon; in the sixteenth century, Protestants decided on the Hebrew collection as their proper canon, but Roman Catholics have retained the longer Greek-Latin list. The ordinary Protestant or Jewish term for the books in the Greek-Latin Old Testament, but absent from the Hebrew, is "Apocrypha."

5. The matter of the allegation that Mariamne had had an affair with Herod's trusted lieutenant is so narrated by Josephus as to present the student with problems of details, and also of substance. In *The Jewish War* I, 441–444, which was written before *Antiquities*, we are given one account, that when Herod was summoned by Antony, he ordered his brother-in-law (and uncle?) Joseph to keep watch over Mariamne, as a result of which Herod executed both Joseph and Mariamne.

In *Antiquities*, on the other hand, we have accounts of two such summonses, that by Antony (XV, 65–70, 85–87) and a later one by Augustus (XV, 183–231). In the first of the two summonses, the lieutenant designated to watch over Mariamne was Joseph, who disclosed to Mariamne Herod's orders to slay her if he perished; Herod concluded, on learning that Joseph had disclosed this intention to Mariamne, that there had been a liaison. In the second summons, the designated lieutenant was not Joseph, but a certain Sohemus, and again the matter of Herod's instructions to slay Mariamne in the event of his own death serves in precisely the same way as in the earlier case. In *Antiquities* it is after the sup-

posed liaison with Sohemus that Herod brings the matter of
Mariamne's adultery to a climax.

Is *The Jewish War* right, and was there only one incident? Is
Antiquities right, that there were two? If there were two, is it
possible that details from the one made their way, through Josephus' carelessness or through confusion in his sources, into his
other account? Scholars have struggled with these matters. There
is no sure solution, but only a certain probability. I believe that
there were two incidents, not one; I believe, however, that the
matter of the disclosure to Mariamne of Herod's instruction to
slay her in the event of his death belongs properly only to the
second incident. I have so narrated this first incident as to assume
that Salome's jealousy led to accusations of a liaison and hence the
execution of Joseph; I have not followed Josephus in relating twice
the supposition that the disclosure of Herod's order to slay Mariamne persuaded Herod of her guilt.

6. This Cana is not to be confused with the Galilean city of
John 2, which relates that there Jesus turned water into wine.

7. Some scholars hold the view that the destruction of the buildings of the Dead Sea scrolls community was caused by this earthquake rather than by the devastating war of A.D. 66–70.

8. As mentioned above, in note 5, confusion exists in the ac-
counts. There the Joseph, presently executed, was presumably
Herod's uncle and Salome's husband. The confusion about the two
Josephs—unless the two were really one—is beyond clarification.

9. Apparently Herod had prevented certain gladiators intending
to join Cleopatra and Antony in Egypt from passing through
Judea.

Part IV

⌐⌐⌐⌐⌐⌐⌐⌐⌐⌐⌐⌐

The Uses of Prosperity

27-18 B.C.

4

After the retreat to the wilderness failed to work a cure on Herod, his spiritual recovery came about in a way distinct from the piety about which we speculated. In Jerusalem, Alexandra, well informed of the condition of the king, began to plot again. The strong fortress in Jerusalem, which dominated the city, together with the possession of the Temple, conferred on whoever held them a means of controlling the kingdom. On the pretext that Herod might die and the throne not pass to her grandsons, Alexandra approached the military guardians of both the fortress and the Temple with the proposal that they vest the dual control in her. These guardians included men beholden to Herod and also men fearful of entering into any plot against him; and regardless of their political intrigues, they probably considered it impious of Alexandra to seek to control Jerusalem, despite the gravity of the king's illness. At any rate, Alexandra completely misjudged the men whom she selected to approach, for they immediately sent messengers to Herod with the news of her proposal. Alexandra's plan appeared to Herod not so much designed to safeguard the rights of his children, as she suggested, as to seize the power for herself. Sick as he was, he was not so ill as to fail to recognize still another effort to take his throne away from him. Indeed, he began to recover. Without delay he ordered the execution of Alexandra.

At that time, he was prone quickly to order executions, even of his friends, and of his relatives by marriage. After Herod had executed Salome's husband Joseph, she had mar-

ried a man of Idumean ancestry named Costobar. Herod
had designated him governor of the region of Idumea and
of the city of Gaza. On his elevation to that post, Costobar,
prompted by some ambitions of his own, had privately determined to become the ruler of the Idumeans. He had
then sought the help of Cleopatra so as to become independent of Herod; indeed, Josephus records the wish on
the part of Costobar to restore the Idumeans to the worship of their god Coze, as it had existed prior to the forced
conversion of the Idumeans to Judaism. Reports of Costobar's machinations had come to Herod, and only the entreaties of Salome and Cypros had deterred Herod from
slaying this brother-in-law too. One reads in Josephus
about the effectiveness of these entreaties with some in-
credulity, for one doubts that Herod would have tolerated
a quasi-rebellion, especially when the rebel was aligning
himself with Cleopatra, and one suspects that the account
has been influenced by the wish to supply Herod with a
justifiable motive in what was now to ensue.

At any rate, Salome and Costobar had recently become
separated from each other; indeed, Josephus informs us
that Salome "sent him a bill of divorce." Since in Jewish
practice, divorce was the prerogative only of the husband
and never of the wife, Salome was following her own bent
rather than Jewish law. Her objective now, however, was
not only to be rid of Costobar, but to destroy him. She
therefore made an accusation which was certain to arouse
Herod. It involved the Maccabean family, already mentioned, the "sons of Baba," a family that had been partisans
of Antigonus at the time that Herod had besieged Jerusalem; to Costobar, as the lieutenant of Herod, had fallen the
obligation at that time to destroy these captured opponents. Instead, Costobar had provided these Maccabeans
with a place of refuge and concealment on his farm in
Idumea. When Herod at that earlier time had inquired

into the fate of the sons of Baba, Costobar had lied, asserting on oath that he knew nothing at all about them. For
a dozen years, then, Costobar had protected the sons of
Baba by keeping them concealed. Salome, having separated
from Costobar, disclosed to Herod where Costobar had
hidden the sons of Baba. To Herod this matter, since it
involved Maccabeans, was another plot against his throne;
not only did he slay Costobar, and some other men in high
places whom he associated with hiding of the sons of Baba,
but he also slew the remnants of this Maccabean family,
the last survivors of the Maccabean lineage. Now there
were no Maccabeans[1] left to whom Herod's throne might
go. Except his sons by Mariamne.

The incident of the plot of Alexandra and the discovery
of the concealment of the sons of Baba, together with their
execution, were sufficient to enable Herod to recuperate
from his illness. He turned now from being king to becoming a dictator, reckless of the lives of people and indifferent to the laws of the Jews. Indeed, by the year 25 B.C.,
Herod's control of Judea was so absolute that he began to
cherish a new ambition, to rise above the limitations implicit in his being merely the designated Jewish king of
Judea and to reach the higher rank in the empire. He felt
that he could now become a veritable Greco-Roman, and
turned to follow that disposition rather than to cultivate the
inner life of the Judaism of his country.

We have already noted the paradox that whereas Antipater, his father, had sought ceaselessly to be accepted and
recognized as a Jew, Herod had taken his surface Jewishness for granted, and sought for a different kind of acceptance and recognition. How shall we explain the absence in him of some sense of the identification which his
father had sought? Was it missing because he was born
into what his father needed to struggle for? Or was it that
he unconsciously acquiesced in the charges made against

him by his Jewish foes that he was an outsider, an alien? Perhaps his vendetta against all the Maccabeans, including his beloved Mariamne, was a reflection of his identifying the hated Maccabeans as the symbol of authentic Jewishness, and he needed to destroy the symbol as he had destroyed the people. There was, to be sure, a Jewish populace which would need his continual appeasement so that it would not rise in rebellion and threaten his throne; there were, hence, some sensible limits which one should observe, if not out of conviction then out of expediency. But, on the other hand, Rome had designated him king, and had confirmed him as king; thereby he was an authentic Roman, no different from any other Roman, and he must act like a Roman. Roman kings were builders of cities and amphitheaters and roads and aqueducts—and pagan temples; and there was no better way for Herod to show that he was truly a Roman than to behave like a Roman king.

He recognized his need to abstain from interfering unduly in the public religious customs of the Jews. While he did nothing directly to impede these, he limited severely his own participation in them, and, according to Josephus, did nothing to promote any public expression of Judaism. He felt no restraint, on the other hand, at introducing even into Jerusalem those expressions of paganism which a century and a half earlier had divided the population into Hellenizers and opponents of Hellenism. He built a Greek theater within Jerusalem, and an amphitheater and a hippodrome just outside it. He inaugurated an imitation of the Olympian games, to be held every five years, and to them he invited the best athletes from the neighboring kingdoms, indeed, from all over the known world. The athletes naturally performed naked, against all Jewish sensibility. Costly chariot races were held; animals, especially lions, were captured for use in the arena, where men condemned to death were forced to fight with beasts, to the delight of the foreigners who attended the spectacles near Jerusalem.

He saw, as we have said, that sensible limits were necessary. Herod was aware of the grumbling on the part of Jews against the games and the theater, but this grumbling was relatively minor and on matters relatively peripheral. One item, however, threatened to become too strong an issue even for Herod. Throughout the amphitheater were hung artistic trophies, central in which stood either a figure of Augustus or else figures of warriors holding their military weapons. To the Jews these trophies represented images, forbidden in the Ten Commandments. Herod became aware of the Jewish resentment of the trophies. It did not suit him to remove them; instead, he decided to try to persuade some leading Jews that trophies of this kind were such nonsense as to merit no opposition; that is to say, the trophies were too silly to oppose. Pursuing this task, he brought some eminent Jews to the amphitheater, assembled them before the golden and silver trophies, and had some workmen pry off the silver and the gold of a few trophies to disclose the bare wood that the precious metals covered. The Jews discerned the bare pieces of wood, and they joined with Herod in laughing at the idea that such pieces of wood could ever be associated with sanctity. In short, Herod represented himself to these Jews as sharing in their derision of the trophies, and he implied that since they could all laugh at the trophies, there was therefore no need to remove them.

But if he felt constrained hypocritically to placate some eminent Jews because of the trophies, and he succeeded in doing so, there were those in the populace who, beyond placation, regarded the innovations, the arena, the theater, and the other buildings as hostile to Judaism and subversive of it. Among some men there arose the conviction that the only way to deal with Herod and his desecration of Judaism was to assassinate him. They chose the theater as the best place for their purpose, for they supposed that Herod would be unable to escape them there. They laid their plans carefully, and they lay in wait for Herod to arrive and to enter. But Herod's espionage system was an efficient one, and the plot was discovered, just as Herod was about to enter the theater. Herod prudently did not enter, but retired instead to his palace. His police rounded up the conspirators, who numbered ten. These had no wish to deny their intention or to repudiate it, for they regarded themselves as embarked on a holy and pious purpose, not on behalf of their own gain but on behalf of the sacred customs of their people, and they were prepared to die to preserve them. Promptly they were sentenced, first to torture and then to execution.

The particular spy who had disclosed the plot to Herod was known to the populace. Shortly thereafter a group of people set upon him in the sight of many; they slew him, pulled him apart limb from limb, and threw the pieces to the dogs. Herod's police set out to punish the slayers of the spy, and arrested many of the people who had witnessed the slaying, but they could not elicit the names of those who had done the deed. They resorted finally to the torture of some women who were among the witnesses, and these gave them the names of the slayers. Herod responded quickly, executing not only those who had done the deed, but also their families.

He saw that he needed the tightest of controls in order to hold the populace in check and to discourage further efforts to assassinate him. He therefore increased the fortification of his palace, with twin strongholds which he named Caesarium and Agrippeion,[2] and of the Temple, rebuilding there the fortress known as Antonia. He rebuilt the city of Samaria into a fortress, changing its name to

Sebaste,[3] "the sacred," in honor of Augustus—and he erected a temple there sacred to Augustus. The coastal city previously known as Straton's Tower he rebuilt into Caesarea.[4] Indeed, he dotted his lands with fortresses, erected always with what Josephus describes as the fineness of Herod's taste. He also expanded his system of espionage so that it was no longer restricted to Jerusalem, but now extended throughout his domains. In short, Herod created a police state.

He was the king both of the Jews and also against the Jews.

A period of surcease from foreign wars enabled Herod to accumulate wealth, from the yield of his own domains and also from the international commerce. A police state Judea was, but for the moment it was a prosperous one. Herod had an annual income which a modern scholar has estimated as the equivalent in purchasing power of some five million dollars, an immense sum. He had no reluctance to spend money, whether for buildings within his domains or, as we shall see, for buildings he wished to give to his neighbors.

All then seemed to be going well, at least as far as externals were concerned. But in 25 disaster struck Judea in the form of an unprecedented drought. Josephus speculates as to whether the disaster was punishment from God or whether it was merely the recurrence of the natural phenomena which periodically fall upon different parts of civilization. Because of the drought there was a failure of agricultural produce, and, in the resultant hunger, pestilence and disease spread throughout the land. Indeed, the seed from which a yield was hoped for the subsequent year became spoiled, so that the famine spread over a period of two years. Economically, too, the famine took its toll, especially in the inability of the cities to produce the revenues which Herod required. Since Herod had been spending liberally in his program of building, he had no reserves to cushion him against the loss of income. Already the object of the hatred of the populace, he found himself in a worse situation now, for the natural disaster was laid at his door.

What Herod still possessed was the wealth which he had built into his expensive palaces. Food was available in Egypt, governed at that time by a certain Petronius, a friend of Herod. Petronious had the disposition to sell food, and Herod, having some residual means of purchasing it, did so. He embarked then on what we would describe today as a welfare program, and on a considerable scale. To the very poor and the aged he distributed food at government cost; to those with some money he made it available on what appears to have been an equitable system of rationing. He provided also winter clothing for those unable to provide it for themselves. And he distributed seed to the farmers.

The disaster of the famine provided Herod with a challenge of huge proportions, a challenge which he met so successfully that one senses in Herod a tremendous ability in both conception and execution. Had he failed to rise to the occasion, he might well have found rebellion spreading throughout his domains, a rebellion fed by the hunger and want of the two dismal years. Not only did he rise to the occasion, but he took especial care to have the populace understand that it was from him that their help was coming. Animosity turned to gratitude, and gratitude dissolved a large measure of the built-up hatred; indeed, Herod was able to create the image of himself as that of a king unbrokenly solicitous for his people, so as to imply that the acts of violence and cruelty of the past were not only exceptions to his usual manner, but were the results of the provocations to which he had been exposed. Outside Judea his fame as an able monarch spread, probably through some propaganda machine.

The famine, then, which might have toppled him, became instead the means of stabilizing his hold on the populace. And since, except for his sons, there were no longer any Maccabeans left by whose slaughter he could alienate the population, Herod stood on the threshold of a period of tranquillity and approval. The restoration of prosperity enabled him to send a body of five hundred picked soldiers to assist a Roman attack on Arabia Felix; he also reverted to his program of building. Moreover, he became enamored at this time of a beautiful woman, of a priestly family, the daughter of a certain Simon the son of Boethus; she too bore the name of Mariamne. Josephus reports that Herod had some thought of making this woman his mistress, or even taking her by force. Such a course, however, would reopen the allegations of violence and despotism, especially since the family were not mere nonentities, so that it was more prudent to marry her. Unhappily, her family, though of some account, were not as eminent as his own royalty had now become, and, once having married above him, he felt that he could not now marry beneath him. The solution lay in raising the status of the family. This Herod accomplished by a simple device: for a second time he deposed the high priest Ananel, and appointed in his stead Simon, the father of the woman. This done, he proceeded to the wedding with Mariamne II.

His building program continued. Not only did he continue with fortresses, but he beautified the pagan cities in his domains, even to the point of building pagan temples, though he was careful not to build such temples in the Jewish cities. These accomplishments, which were considerable, were carefully reported to Augustus, and they strengthened Herod's position with the emperor. Mindful of the sensibilities of the Jews, as previous to the attempted assassination he had not been, he carefully informed them that his motive in building the pagan cities was his wish to comply with the demands put on him by the Romans, to whom he and his country were necessarily subservient; whatever trespass of Jewish customs was involved in all this Romanization was not the result of inclination or conviction on his part, but of prudence and necessity.

His chief accomplishment as a builder was the completion of the building of Caesarea, which was to take some dozen[5] years. Not only did Herod erect there sumptuous palaces and public housing, but he built an artificial harbor in which ships could lie in safety even in violent storms. Josephus mentions two statues at Caesarea, one of Rome— what is meant is uncertain—and one of Augustus. The inevitable theater and amphitheater were there, of course. But Josephus is careful to mention also a system of sewers and underground tunnels by which both the rain and the sewage could be carried off. Herod transformed a tiny coastal fortress into a carefully planned, carefully executed, elegant seaport.

If Herod's motive in all this building was to impress Augustus, he unquestionably succeeded. In 24 or 23, Caesar bestowed on him three areas east of the Sea of Galilee, Trachonitis, Batanaea (southern Bashan), and Auranitis. Able rulers were rare, and Rome was prepared to recognize ability. Moreover, Herod now determined to send his two sons by the first Mariamne, Alexander and Aristobulus, to Rome. The motive was for them to absorb the culture and education of the great capital—and also to come into the ken of Augustus. These children of Herod were his presumptive heirs, and, Roman as he now conceived himself, it was essential that through a stay in Rome they become authentically Romanized. The ages of the children at this time are uncertain, for the years of their birth are not recorded; some fourteen years had passed since he had married the first Mariamne, so that these boys were still in their early teens.

A client-king needed constantly to be in good standing with the Romans. When Augustus turned over the governorship of the east to Marcus Vipsanius Agrippa, Herod went to the island of Lesbos to call on this new governor. Disaffection, fed by the ousted ruler of Trachonitis, had brought accusations against Herod to the attention of Agrippa; moreover, this deposed ruler had sold Auranitis to the Nabateans, so that the ownership of that land became a subject of dispute between the Nabateans and Herod. The residents of Gadara,[6] a town about six miles southeast of the Lake of Galilee, proceeded to make accusations of mistreatment against Herod. Had these accusations been accompanied by upheavals within Judea, the Romans might well have taken them seriously, but a ruler was a ruler by virtue of the requirement that people be ruled, and the Romans were prepared to expect some measure of disaffection, and to tolerate it, provided the ruler handled it effectively. Agrippa was well satisfied with Herod.

About the year 20, Augustus Caesar came to Syria, and complainants appeared before him in the presence of Herod, but not only did Caesar ignore these complaints—some of the complainants committed suicide—he quickly made a show of grasping the hand of Herod in friendship. He confirmed the earlier transfer to Herod of the northeastern territories; he also made him governor over part of Syria. Josephus gives the summary that, respecting the two men, Caesar and Agrippa, who governed the vast Roman empire, Caesar preferred only Agrippa to Herod, and Agrippa only Caesar to the Judean monarch. Herod had achieved his goal, the maximum acceptance by the Romans.

Herod requested of Caesar a tetrarchy for his brother Pheroras, and Pheroras was granted the Perea, the region east of the Jordan River, and he was given a gift of a large amount of money, one hundred talents. Unimportant in itself beyond a demonstration of Herod's influence with Caesar, the designation of Pheroras as tetrarch was to figure in a minor way in the unfolding domestic horrors which Herod was still destined to endure. If there was perhaps some selfish motive on Herod's part, it was to be assured by Pheroras' presence there that the Perea would not become a center of rebellion against him. At a place called Panium, near the source of the Jordan, Herod built a temple to Augustus Caesar.

The confirmation of his authority by Caesar might well have brought Herod the reassurance of the stability of his throne. Yet his open pursuit and espousal of paganism appeared to the populace as a threatened dissolution of their religion, and Herod's agents reported to him the constant grumblings and the articulate hostility. The police character of the state was intensified; arrest and execution, whether secret or open, was frequent. Josephus relates that Herod did not permit the people to meet together, walk together, or eat together, but carefully watched everything. Herod would from time to time dress as a private citizen and wander about at night to listen in on the conversations of the people so as to guage the extent of the resentment and hostility. He resorted to the gesture of waiving a third of the taxes, hopeful thereby to lessen the animosity of the populace, but it was a futile gesture.

Fearful of those whom he governed, Herod introduced a loyalty oath; dire punishment awaited the ordinary citizen who refused to take it. The two Pharisaic scholars, Samaias and Pollion, whom we met earlier, were requested to take the oath. Pollion declined to do so, but his stature was such that Herod found it prudent to abstain from making an issue over the matter.

Also exempt from the oath of allegiance were the Essenes. Perhaps they were so marginal a group as to justify Herod's ignoring them, on the supposition that they would not influence the populace. Josephus, however, suggests still another motive, which he traces to Herod's youth. When Herod was a little boy, an eminent Essene named Menahem, a man so pious that he had the gift of foretelling the future, encountered the lad on his way to school. Menahem greeted Herod as the future king, but the boy promptly replied that he was a commoner. Menahem smiled, patted the boy on his behind, and said, "You will nevertheless become the king, and you will reign happily, because God has found you worthy. Always remember the pats of Menahem, as a symbol of the change which will come in your fortunes." As the account in Josephus proceeds, one senses that Menahem had, in the first sentence, made a prophecy of dubious validity, for Josephus goes on to tell that Menahem spoke further, in an afterthought which probably belongs to Josephus rather than to the Essene: "Your most reasonable course of action, which will bring you a good reputation, will be to practice justice, and piety towards God.[7] But I know that you will not be such a person." Menahem went on to inform Herod that a dismal end awaited him. When Herod later gained the throne, he sent for Menahem, to inquire of him how long he would reign. Menahem, however, was silent. Herod asked, "Will it be ten years, or not?" Menahem replied, "Yes, twenty, even thirty," but he did not specify the number of years. Herod, pleased at the prospect of a long reign, dismissed Menahem. Herod, so says Josephus, held the Essenes in high honor; indeed, many of the Essenes were men of such virtue that they were honored by becoming recipients of divine revelation.[8] It is quite possible, of course, that the same Herod who ignored the Temple cult, and arbitrarily appointed and deposed the high priest on at least three occasions, was nevertheless susceptible to some regard for the religious sanctity of the Essenes. But a more probable explanation is not that he had any regard for them, but that he exempted them from the oath of allegiance simply because it was wiser to ignore them than to raise an issue with them, for he knew that the Essenes would resist taking the oath.

But Herod would not have been the able king that he was if he had limited his actions to the coercion of the populace. Having tried unsuccessfully to win them over by the remission of a part of the taxes, he now conceived a bolder and more dramatic plan. It rested on his recognition that however much Jews hated the throne, and especially the incumbent, they loved the Temple. It was through the Temple that Herod proposed to gain the voluntary allegiance of the Jews.

Jewish tradition speaks, in fact, of two Temples, the first built by Solomon and destroyed by the Babylonians in 586, and the second built about seventy years later, after the return of the Jewish exiles from Babylon. There is ample reason to suppose that between 516 and Herod's decision to rebuild the Temple in the year 18, there were a number of destructions and rebuildings. The upheavals in Jerusalem from the time when Hyrcanus and Aristobulus began to vie for the throne, and the battles waged there, may well have brought damage to the surviving Temple, and one may guess that it had undergone repairs rather than a full refurbishing.

Herod's wish to rebuild the second Temple may well have brought to his mind, or elicited the pointed comment of one of his advisers, that impious hands were scarcely suitable for such an act of piety. Someone may have had the audacity to quote to Herod the words which I Chronicles 22:7–10 puts into the mouth of David, speaking to Solomon: "My son, I had it in my heart to build a house to the name of the Lord my God, but the word of the

Lord came to me, saying, 'You have spilled too much blood and engaged in too great battles. You shall not build my house for you have spilled too much blood to the ground before me. Behold, a son will be born to you, a man of tranquility, whom I will grant respite from all his foes round about, for *Solomon* ["peace"] will be his name, and peace and quiet will I provide for Israel in his days. He will build a house to my name.'" That David, according to the Chronicler, recognized himself as disqualified did not constitute a vivid precedent for Herod; quite possibly it was his belief that the need to gain the voluntary allegiance of the populace should overcome his squeamishness, supposing that he had any. This much is certain, however, that Herod saw clearly that the populace would not readily and immediately support a man with his record in an undertaking which they regarded as the ultimate in sanctity.

First of all, then, Herod needed to win the populace to the idea of rebuilding the Temple, and then to the propriety of his doing so. He assembled the people and spoke to them. Josephus quotes for us (*Antiquities* XV, 382–387) the speech which Herod is purported to have made to the people; it can be paraphrased in the following way:

"I have no need to rehearse for you the many things I have done since becoming king. These have been directed more to your security than to my own glory. I have never neglected your needs, nor did I build buildings for my own safety as much as for your own. With God's help I have brought the Jewish nation to a prosperity without precedent. You know about the many edifices I have erected both in Judea and in the lands we have acquired. Let me now speak about the greatest of all such undertakings, which will be a work of the greatest piety and excellence. When our fathers returned from Babylon, they built the present Temple. It lacks sixty cubits, however, of being the height of the first Temple, which Solomon built. This is the case, not because of any fault in our ancestors, but because that was the limit enjoined on them by Cyrus and Darius. In the subsequent time, the Greek overlords did not permit our fathers to raise the Temple to its pristine height, and they could not make the second Temple conform in its structure to the first. Now, however, since by God's will I am your ruler, and we have had a long period of peace, and have amassed riches and abundant revenues, and, most of all, since I am on such good terms with the Romans, the rulers of the world, I intend to correct all that is amiss in the present Temple. I shall make a grateful return to God for the blessings given me in the form of my kingship, in the most pious way, by making His Temple as perfect as I am able."

The blend of piety and hypocrisy is chargeable, at least in its present form, to Josephus or to his literary assistant rather than to Herod. Josephus records that the speech failed in its objective, for in place of stirring the populace to enthusiasm, they suspected that the speech camouflaged Herod's intention to tear down the Temple. Indeed, the task of rebuilding along the lines hinted at in Herod's speech appears to have struck people as grandiose beyond accomplishment. This unexpected response spurred Herod to a further public commitment, calculated to remove the suspicion; he promised not to begin to tear down the old building until he would have assembled before them all the materials necessary for the new.

To this promise Herod was faithful. Soon the wagons brought the requisite stones; ten thousand artisans—this is Josephus' number—were selected, and a thousand priests were taught the craft of the stonecutter and the carpenter. Only then did the rebuilding commence.

Josephus gives a detailed description of the Temple, one which antiquarians properly have studied minutely; the

Temple has been portrayed graphically by a number of modern designers, both with restraint and without it. The Temple itself was surrounded by courts in which Gentiles were permitted,[9] and the courts were contained within columns and porticoes. The sanctuary itself was situated within a more elaborate building, set on the highest ground of the site, and consisted primarily of two halls, often called, respectively, the "holy place" and the "holy of holies." The latter was empty (though in the first Temple, the Ark of the Covenant was kept within it), and was entered only once a year, on the Day of Atonement, and by the high priest alone. It was separated from the "holy place" by a drapery or curtain, also known as a veil; it was in the "holy place" that the altar of incense stood and the golden table for the showbread and the candelabrum.[10] Since the sanctuary was only the pair of inner chambers, we need to envisage the total structure as a very elaborate building, replete with halls and meeting rooms and storage chambers. Indeed one must conceive of the "Temple" as a whole complex of buildings, including its surrounding fortresses. It was, then, no mere minor structure that Herod erected, but something quite the reverse. The inner sanctuary took a year and a half to build; the total building, eight years.

When the inner sanctuary was completed, an elaborate dedication was held. By coincidence the dedication coincided with the anniversary of Herod's accession to the throne—or, more probably, was set for that one of four New Year days, which Jews observed, called the "New Year for Kings." Josephus, despite his penchant for impressive and exaggerated numbers, for once fails us; he says that it is impossible to tabulate the total sacrifices offered at the dedication. He relates a tradition found also in rabbinic literature (Ta'anit 23a) which tells that during the period of the construction of the Temple, rain fell only at night, and never in the daytime when it might have impeded the construction; Josephus believes that this is so, for it conforms to other manifestations of God. Josephus concludes, accordingly, that God approved highly of this Temple. As for the populace, as hostile as the ancient rabbinic literature is to Herod, it says of Herod's Temple, "He who never saw Herod's edifice has never in his life seen a beautiful building" (Baba Batra 4a). Another passage in this literature declares that this edifice was Herod's atonement for the sages of Israel whom he had slain (Midrash Rabbah Numbers XIV, 8). The populace, then, also approved highly of this Temple.

One would suppose, therefore, that Herod, having made some expiation for his trespasses, was now to be vouchsafed years of tranquillity. But his love of the throne was an obsession, and he had children with Maccabean blood, and a brother Pheroras, and a sister, Salome[11]—and these all shared in Herod's obsessive love of power.

Notes

1. The lapse of the dozen years may account for a discrepancy in Josephus as to whether these "sons" were children or men. As to the extinction of the Maccabeans, strongly stressed by Josephus, at least one exception needs to be noted, namely, that the Antigonus who had reigned from 40–37 left a daughter whom Herod's son Antipater married.

2. Marcus Vipsanius Agrippa (63–12 B.C.), the devoted friend and presumptive successor to Augustus, figures in our account below.

3. *Sebastos* is the Greek adjective which translates the Latin *Augustus*.

4. The ruins are visible today, and attest to the onetime magnificence of the Herodian city. The rebuilding seems to have taken Herod ten years.

5. Elsewhere Josephus assigns the span of rebuilding to ten years.

6. Mark 5: 1–13 and its parallels relate the healing there of a demoniac, out of whom came unclean spirits named Legion.

7. The balance of piety toward God and virtue, for example justice, to men is stock material in Hellenistic Jewish writers, for example Philo and IV Maccabees.

8. An Essene, Judas, is reported to have predicted the death of Antigonus the son of Aristobulus (*Antiquities* XIII, xi, 2); and an Essene, Simon, was able to interpret the meaning of a dream of Archelaus, the son of Herod (*Antiquities* XVII, xiii, 3).

9. An inscription in Greek, warning Gentiles not to enter within the barrier and the fence around the sanctuary itself on the penalty of death, has been found.

10. The candelabrum and the table for the showbread and a pair of silver trumpets are depicted on the Arch of Titus in Rome, spoils taken from the Temple after its destruction in A.D. 70.

11. His mother, Cypros, disappears from the accounts in Josephus.

of the fact of her execution. To them Herod
much their father as the slayer of their mother.
he young men were Maccabeans through their
they were therefore legitimately eligible for
which Herod must some day vacate. In Jeru-
still survived those who had joined in malign-
other, and such people could expect to pay the
heir calumniation, once the princes came to
e chief among those with reason to fear some
geance was Herod's sister, Salome, but there
s too in Jerusalem who had a great deal to fear.
erod had gone personally to Rome to fetch his
dicated the deep affection he had for them. The
ive of those who feared some future vengeance
ons was the destruction of this affection. Calum-
d destroyed Mariamne I, and calumniation was a
ol. The young men became the objects of a
g campaign. It was alleged of them that they were
to certain people that they were finding it im-
be in Herod's company without remembering
s he who had put their mother to death; it was
hat they disclosed to willing ears that they re-
erod's unbounded affection for them with acute
ound detestation. These sentiments, which the
en were presumed to have confided to worthy
s of confidences, were deliberately brought to the
Herod, and magnified. Whatever the high hopes
e in his sons which prompted Herod to journey
to bring them back to Jerusalem, these were now
nto an incipient hatred. Indeed, Herod found him-
by a deep love for the young men, and a growing
y toward them.
while, however, the external amenities needed to
, and since the young men were now of an age to
led, Herod married them off. The wife of Aris-

Part V

本本本本本本本本本本

Family Life

18-6 B.C.

5

In the year
twenty years
having reached the ma
could ever allow. He h
wealth and income; he
control of having buil
and having them well
domains, including area
dotted with his fortress
five, he was no longer
an old man, and we may
prepared now to enjoy tl

He journeyed to Rome
I were in school. When
twenty-two years earlier,
petitioner; now he was
high in the favor of Augu
ander and Aristobulus, n
pleted certain of the stud
Rome. Augustus Caesar re
and with appropriate court
journey was a satisfying
princes to return to Judea,
their native land.

Perhaps Herod suppose
earlier had been forgotten,
in Jerusalem, they inevitabl
the accusations against thei

recollection
was not so
Moreover,
mother and
the throne
salem there
ing their m
price for
power. Th
future ver
were other
That He
two sons i
first objec
from the s
niation ha
proven t
whisperin
confiding
possible t
that it wa
alleged tl
turned H
and prof
young m
recipient
ears of
and prid
to Rome
turning i
self torn
animosit
Mean
continu
be wed

Part V

‫צּרּצּרּצּרּצּרּצּרּצּרּ‬

Family Life

18-6 B.C.

5

In the year 18 or 17, having reigned for about twenty years, Herod could regard himself as having reached the maximum in stability that his situation could ever allow. He had the confidence of Rome; he had wealth and income; he had the populace under the double control of having built a magnificent Temple for them, and having them well in hand in his police state; his domains, including areas which were Gentile, were well dotted with his fortresses and his troops. A man of fifty-five, he was no longer young and inexperienced, nor yet an old man, and we may well conceive of him as someone prepared now to enjoy the fruits of his labors.

He journeyed to Rome, where his two sons by Mariamne I were in school. When he had first gone to Rome, some twenty-two years earlier, he had been a refugee, an abject petitioner; now he was an honored and able client king, high in the favor of Augustus Caesar. The two sons, Alexander and Aristobulus, now in their late teens, had completed certain of the studies which had brought them to Rome. Augustus Caesar received Herod in all friendliness, and with appropriate courtesy, and we can imagine that the journey was a satisfying one. It was time now for the princes to return to Judea, to accompany Herod back to their native land.

Perhaps Herod supposed that the events of a decade earlier had been forgotten, but once the princes were back in Jerusalem, they inevitably encountered the reminder of the accusations against their mother, Mariamne, and the recollection of the fact of her execution. To them Herod was not so much their father as the slayer of their mother. Moreover, the young men were Maccabeans through their mother and they were therefore legitimately eligible for the throne which Herod must some day vacate. In Jerusalem there still survived those who had joined in maligning their mother, and such people could expect to pay the price for their calumniation, once the princes came to power. The chief among those with reason to fear some future vengeance was Herod's sister, Salome, but there were others too in Jerusalem who had a great deal to fear.

That Herod had gone personally to Rome to fetch his two sons indicated the deep affection he had for them. The first objective of those who feared some future vengeance from the sons was the destruction of this affection. Calumniation had destroyed Mariamne I, and calumniation was a proven tool. The young men became the objects of a whispering campaign. It was alleged of them that they were confiding to certain people that they were finding it impossible to be in Herod's company without remembering that it was he who had put their mother to death; it was alleged that they disclosed to willing ears that they returned Herod's unbounded affection for them with acute and profound detestation. These sentiments, which the young men were presumed to have confided to worthy recipients of confidences, were deliberately brought to the ears of Herod, and magnified. Whatever the high hopes and pride in his sons which prompted Herod to journey to Rome to bring them back to Jerusalem, these were now turning into an incipient hatred. Indeed, Herod found himself torn by a deep love for the young men, and a growing animosity toward them.

Meanwhile, however, the external amenities needed to continue, and since the young men were now of an age to be wedded, Herod married them off. The wife of Aristobulus was Bernice, a daughter of Salome; for Alexander, Herod chose a bride not only from a distant place but with no claim at all to any Jewish ancestry, Glaphyra, the daughter of Archelaus, king of Cappadocia. The former marriage was judicious in that the strains of Maccabean and Herodian blood were to be mingled in the prospective grandchildren of Herod; the latter marriage was an expression of Herod's royalty, for he was a king in the Roman empire, and his son was married to a Gentile princess whose father was also a king in the Roman empire.

While his court festered with the renewed currents of subdued hostility, Agrippa, the Roman governor of the east, prepared to return from Italy to the east, and dutifully Herod journeyed to call on his friend. He invited Agrippa to visit Judea, and Agrippa accepted, with the result that Herod was able to show him the rebuilt cities of Sebaste and Caesarea, and three principal fortresses, Alexandreion, Herodium, and Hyrcania. Agrippa, treated royally, responded with royal generosity, a clear token of how deeply he was impressed with what he saw. A year later Herod, always mindful of the need to be subordinate to Rome, set out to pay still another call on Agrippa, this time at the island of Lesbos. Storm winds delayed Herod, so that Agrippa had left for the Bosporus before Herod could arrive at Lesbos. Herod gave a large sum of money to restore the fallen portico of Chius in Lesbos, and he sailed in pursuit of Agrippa to the Bosporus. Agrippa, however, had gone farther east, and therefore Herod followed him to the Pontus, where he overtook him. Agrippa was engaged in settling disorders in the Crimea, disorders which accompanied an uprising and usurpation of the throne there. For some period of time Herod stayed with his good friend Agrippa, assisting him in both the military and the civil needs, and as a consequence the mutual affection was all the more strengthened. When the affairs in the Crimea were straightened out, Agrippa accompanied Herod on an overland return to the coast of Asia Minor, to Ephesus; on this journey Herod bestowed liberal gifts on many of the cities through which the two passed. His influence with Agrippa was such that when he responded to outside requests for the favor of intercession, he did so with great success.

Either at Ephesus, or perhaps somewhere else nearby in Iona, just prior to the time that Agrippa sailed away to Samos, there took place an incident which we need to note. Jews were to be found in quite great numbers throughout that area. There was gathered before Agrippa an assembly of Roman officials and of local kings and rulers. To this assembly there came deputations of Jews with a significant grievance. They had been compelled by both the local rulers and the Roman officials to practices and procedures which they regarded as undesirable and also illegal, for these amounted to the abrogation of their right to live under Jewish law; instead they were compelled to live under local or Roman law. Furthermore, so went the complaint, on many an occasion the Jews had been forced to appear in the law courts on the Jewish holidays. The funds which they had accumulated to send to Jerusalem in support of the Temple had been confiscated. They had been drafted into the armies, or pressed to fill minor civic offices which entailed a great expenditure to the incumbent. This was all illegal, the Jews alleged, for the Romans had always permitted Jews to live by their own laws.

To Herod, these complaints, if correct, had validity, for it was a matter of previous practice, willingly acceded to by the Romans, that Jews in the Dispersion governed themselves. Moreover, the revenues from Dispersion Jews for the Temple in Jerusalem were of consequence to Herod. But, above all, even despite the absence from his make-up of any genuine Jewish sentiment, the complaints as expressed detracted from Herod's prerogatives as the king of the Jews, and it was his own royal authority, as it were, which was being whittled away, and his own eminence with the Romans which was flouted.

Herod determined to intervene. We might attribute to Herod the single motive of protecting his legitimate authority and eminence, yet we could be in error. While it is true that we find in the accounts of Herod scarcely a shred of affirmative loyalty to Judaism, that is, to the religion, he was capable of great loyalty to Jewish people, and of enormous solicitude in those areas where his own status as king was not threatened. It is almost as if his unconcern for the Jewish religion as such was balanced by a sensitive solicitude for the physical well-being of the Jews. Since he was their king, they were his people, the aggregate of those for whose welfare his abilities and personal gifts needed to be dedicated, provided that welfare did not clash with his own. To attribute to Herod a true generosity respecting the Jews is to go too far; to attribute to him a sense of some responsibility, even if blended with some self-interest, is quite consistent with the facts.

As to the form of Herod's intervention, there was in his company the Syrian Greek, the pagan of many gifts, named Nicholas and known as Nicholas[1] of Damascus, from his native city. A philosopher and historian, Nicholas had in some way wandered into Jerusalem, perhaps around the year 20, and became attached to the court of Herod; indeed, it is related that he tutored the monarch in the latter's amateur forays into philosophy. Progressively, Nicholas was to become more and more a trusted adviser of Herod, as we shall see, and later he wrote the history of Herod, which, we noted, has not survived to our day but which displeased Josephus at a number of places as being sycophantic. Nicholas, then, was a man of great talents, and

Herod thereupon designated him to present the case of the Ionian Jews before Agrippa and the assembled Roman officials and kings. Why did Herod not make the presentation himself? Possibly he lacked either a full skill in Greek or the oratorical ability; perhaps it was more seemly to his dignity for his representative to speak than for him to appear, king as he was, in the role of a mere petitioner.

The speech attributed to Nicholas, again, may well be the work of Josephus or one of his literary editors. Yet the general tone and contents are well worth summarizing. Though an abundance of Roman officials were in attendance, Nicholas directed his words as if to Agrippa alone: "It is necessary to those in distress, O mightiest Agrippa, to seek the help of those men able to end their difficulties." The Jews, he went on, had been the recipients in the past of favors granted from above, from men high in power. The present complaints related to misdeeds perpetrated on the Jews not from above but from men of no greater rank than the Jews, from tormentors who, like the Jews, were subjects of Agrippa. The persecutors were guilty of wronging both the Jews, the recipients of the favor of Agrippa, and also Agrippa himself who had granted the favor. If anyone were to ask the Jews whether they preferred life or the ability to be faithful to the ancestral customs by which they honored God, then assuredly the Jews preferred to suffer death rather than to violate the customs of their forefathers. The whole human race now enjoyed— "Thanks to you, Agrippa!"—the possibility to live in prosperity and in fidelity to the customs which each people cherished in its own background. The tormentors inflicted upon others a persecution which they would never have chosen to undergo, and they were acting just as impiously in violating the sacred traditions of others as they would have acted in neglecting the obligations to their own gods. Now came a series of rhetorical questions: "Is there any people or city or community for whom your authority and the Roman power are not a blessing? Would anyone want to revoke the favors you have bestowed? Those people who deprive others of privileges you have bestowed leave themselves open to lose their own privileges which you have given. All that the Jews ask is to share with others the right to preserve the ancestral religion without interference." These ancestral customs were not secret precepts, but, rather, every seventh day was publicly dedicated to the study of Jewish customs and laws, as a safeguard against sin. These customs were both excellent and ancient. The opponents had seized the money collected to send to the Temple; they had imposed special taxes; they had taken Jews to courts and to tribunals even on the sacred holy days. All this was a product of a hatred which was undeserved and indeed unauthorized. "Your rule establishes good will and abolishes ill will." In requesting the relief from persecution, and the continuation of rights, this was fully in conformity with Agrippa's earlier grants, and with the decrees of the Senate in Rome.

Nicholas was not content, though, to rest his case on matters of justice or history. An emotional appeal was in order, and this Nicholas presented in the form of recounting of the virtues of Herod: "What act of good will has the king who sits beside you left undone? What token of good faith has he omitted? What kind of honor of you has he failed to think of? What emergency of yours has he not regarded as of first importance? One must not pass by without mention the valor of Herod's father, Antipater, who came to the help of Julius Caesar in Egypt. One must not forget the decisive turn in the military crisis that that help furnished. And did not Caesar write to the Senate, and did he not bestow Roman citizenship on Antipater?" Such favors, Nicholas continued, were deserved and they ought now to be confirmed; indeed, even if they did not chance to be a happy carry-over from an earlier time, they would deserve to be given and confirmed now, for the reason that Herod had been so gracious to Agrippa. "He received you in a friendly way when you visited Judea; and on that visit you had the proper ritual sacrifices offered to God, and you feasted the populace, and you received their gifts in return."

This speech is well constructed, and in Greek has both fluency and eloquence, even though the cynicism of the content is obvious and the *quid pro quo* level of the concluding words somewhat apparent. One wonders if the last words were indeed spoken, for courteous as the words were, the implication that a powerful Roman needed to be grateful for the attention of a minor king has a slight ring of presumption. Yet the double argument, that imperial policy provided the precedent on which the Jews of Ionia based their claim, and that Rome owed a debt of gratitude to Antipater and Herod, carried the day. Agrippa confirmed that the claims of the Jews were just. He even added that he was prepared to cede them still more rights, provided only that to do so would not cause any trouble to the Roman government. When the meeting broke up, Herod went to Agrippa and, embracing him, thanked him. Agrippa responded with equal warmth, putting his arms around Herod and embracing him in turn, thereby treating him as an equal. This was in the sight of the petitioning Jews and the assembled officials.

The outcome, then, could scarcely have been more favorable to Herod, and his sense of security in the esteem and affection of Rome could not have been greater. He returned to Jerusalem in high spirits, arranged for a huge public gathering of the populace, from the city and the surrounding countryside, and in an address informed them of his achievements on behalf of the Jews of Asia Minor. He then set before them the general picture of the prosperity of Judea under his kingship, and he remitted a fourth of their taxes owed for the previous year. The address over, the populace scattered, but now with a feeling of benevolence toward Herod.

Within the palace, however, the dissension had grown even more acute. The directing of Salome's animosity to Mariamne's children had led to the creation of dark insinuations and of plain, vicious tales about the young men; we must remember that Aristobulus was married to Bernice, the daughter of Salome, and that Salome's manipulations were against the husband of her own daughter. From their side, the young men began to grow indiscreet, or even reckless, in their expressions of hostility to Herod and of their ambition for his throne. Salome began to receive some assistance from Herod's brother Pheroras, who previously was not closely connected with the calumnies. The household was riven by the intensifying hatred, yet with this difference, that the princes were open in their abuse and reproaches of Herod for what had happened to their mother, but Salome and Pheroras were subtle and calculating. Brother and sister even contrived to feed the hopeful supposition of the princes that their reckless talk could lead some of the citizenry to violent uprising against Herod, and the princes began to speak openly of the innocence of their mother, and of their intention to exact vengeance on her murderer with their own hands. The reports of these currents of hatred did not remain confined to the palace but became the subject of the interested gossip of the city. The gain to Herod by his journey to Agrippa was offset by the depth of the dissension in his household, which his absence from the city encouraged.

Now that he was home, and even flushed with the success of his address to the populace, to his dismay he was immediately accosted by Salome and Pheroras with the allegation that he stood in great danger from the desire of his sons to avenge the death of their mother. Indeed, Herod's elation at his success with Agrippa, of which he was naturally proud, was abruptly diminished by a new dimension of anxiety about his status with the Romans, in that Salome and Pheroras gave him frightening particulars of the plot against him; the princes were going to use Archelaus of Cappodocia, the father-in-law of Alexander, as the means of reaching Augustus Caesar and of bringing charges against Herod before him.

In the chagrin at the bitter situation which marked his homecoming, Herod might well have taken some immediate action. Again, however, it was his way to delay things, and to lapse into deep inner disturbance and unsettlement. The alternatives respecting his sons were these: either to confront them directly, and even to punish them; however, this not only went against the deep affection that he had for them, but involved the possibilities that the populace would resent the punishment of the princes with Maccabean blood and that Rome would look askance at the matter; or to let things alone, and to hope that he could in some way bring his sons to a different attitude. The fact seems to be this, that Herod did not know what to do, and therefore for a period of time he did nothing.

He then took a step which he supposed would ameliorate the situation. It will be recalled that his oldest son, Antipater, did not reside in the palace, but only visited the father on the occasion of public festivals. Now Herod brought Antipater to court, hoping that the presence there of his oldest son would suggest to the children of Mariamne, who were younger, that succession to his throne was neither their exclusive nor necessary right, and that they would be well advised to curb their reckless tongues, if they expected to be treated on an equal basis with Antipater by the father.

That Herod's son Antipater was born to him by a commoner may have led Herod to suppose that this oldest son would feel some sense of inferiority in the palace and so would be passive and submissive. If so, Herod misjudged his son Antipater, who was neither passive nor timid, nor devoid of ambition and shrewdness. To the manipulations by Salome and Pheroras there were now added the machinations by Herod's oldest son. Antipater quickly discerned the extent to which Herod had become alienated from Mariamne's sons, and he saw the opportunity to set himself markedly in the first place in his father's affections and in the line for succession. Antipater first considered but quickly rejected the method used by Salome and Pheroras, whose way was to bring ugly charges against Alexander and Aristobulus directly to Herod. Instead, Antipater reasoned that to do so himself might make him suspect, for Herod might regard him as promoting his own cause. Rather, Antipater saw to it that people whom Herod trusted brought the king an endless succession of reports about Mariamne's children. Antipater was prudent enough not to let his friends invent false charges, but had them confine the reports to an exaggeration of verifiable misdeeds. Consequently, Herod was faced more and more by reports of the continued grief of Mariamne's children over the injustice to their mother, and of their determination to seek vengeance.

As is natural in the court of any king, there were those courtiers who regarded Antipater as the young man to whom the future belonged, the young man whose good will was desirable. So Antipater began to gather his own following. The more Herod was fed the continuing reports about Alexander and Aristobulus, the more he exhibited his growing partiality for Antipater. When Antipater's power had increased sufficiently. Herod brought the mother, Doris, into the palace, and back to his bed, as a further humiliation of Alexander and Aristobulus. One wonders if he gave thought to the possibility that such humiliation by its very essence could only exacerbate all that was already amiss. Moreover, Herod began to mention Antipater in his letters to Caesar, a fact which was scarcely kept a secret. In the year 13 Agrippa left the east to return to Rome; Herod sailed to meet him en route, and he took Antipater with him. At Herod's request Agrippa agreed to take Antipater to Rome with him, to present him to Caesar. Herod provided Antipater with an abundance of presents to bestow in the Eternal City.

It was a golden opportunity for Antipater to be in Rome, and to be near to and in touch with the Roman power which would some day speak decisively on the succession to Herod's throne. Armed with rich presents and with his father's letters of introduction, Antipater had little difficulty in rising even above the favorable portrait of him which his father's letters had painted. He grew in esteem and influence in Rome. Yet in being away from Jerusalem, he felt that he was losing the opportunity to continue to malign his half-brothers. Also, inheriting his father's insecurity, he began to worry that while away from Jerusalem, his half-brothers might manage in some way to decrease the gap between them and Herod. Unable in person, for the time, to feed Herod's suspicion of and hostility toward Mariamne's sons, Antipater resorted to letters that were calculated to add to Herod's hatred, especially since these letters were cleverly composed as expressing Antipater's earnest concern for his father's welfare.

Herod's antipathy for Alexander and Aristobulus, nurtured at home by Salome and Pheroras and by mail by Antipater, grew to the point of being unbearable. Herod nevertheless was reluctant to take action, partly through the paralysis of his will, and partly through his fear of the unknown sequels which might attend any drastic punishment he might deal out to his sons.

Nowhere else does the pathetic insecurity of Herod appear more clearly, or more dramatically, than in what he now determined to do. He made the decision to journey to Italy, to consult Augustus Caesar about Alexander and Aristobulus. Indeed, Herod took the two sons with him, and the three appeared before Augustus, either at Rome or at the city of Aquileia. Where Antipater was at the moment, we do not know.

So Herod, the great and ferocious king, set before the greater and more ferocious Augustus the plaintive tale of his misfortunes in the two sons: not only were they full of hatred and animosity, but they even intended to take over Herod's throne—and here Herod threw in an important reminder, that Augustus had granted him the right to choose and name his heir to the throne; by implication the plotting of the brothers was thereby a defiance of the will of Caesar. Yet it was not the plotting to seize the throne that Herod felt Augustus needed to address himself; rather, it was the extent of his sons' hatred of him, which could be gauged by their willingness to forgo both the throne and their lives for the sake of killing their father. If we can trust the account in Josephus—and there is no reason here not to—Herod proceeded to pour out before Augustus all the accumulated bitterness of the preceding months of dissension, hostility, and debilitating restraint. He excused himself for the ugly words he spoke, conceding that they would pollute Caesar's ears. He asked Augustus the rhetorical question, what harsh treatment could these sons complain that he had meted out to them? And how could they blame him for those cruel acts, to their mother and to others, especially since he had acquired his realm through great pain and dangers? And how did they dare, even though they were princes, to tamper with the mastery of a realm which was his own, either to hold on to or to give to that one of his children worthy of it? Indeed, his sons seemed not to understand, so Herod said, that the throne was a prize awaiting that son of his who would distinguish himself in filial duty. All the more was it unfilial for his sons to plot for the throne, or even to contemplate their inheriting it, for the mere contemplation implied an excessive attention to the prospect of his death. He went on to lament before Augustus that his ungrateful sons had received rich presents, servants, and a life of luxury. He boasted that he had arranged brilliant marriages for them. But, he went on, the greatest token of the quality of his affection for his sons was his abstaining from punishing them, despite his having the authority to do so. Finally, he was aware that in bringing his sons before Caesar, their common benefactor, he was giving up both the rights which a father, treated undutifully, possesses, and also the privileges of a king who discovers a plot against himself; instead, he was bringing his sons before Caesar as if he and his sons were equals. He asked the favor of Caesar that should the sons succeed in a plot against him, he not be left completely unavenged; but most of all, he asked that he be spared living a life of fear, and he asked that his sons not escape punishment for having committed the worst crimes known to mankind.

The pathos of Herod's words to Caesar is too clear to need commentary, except for the reminder that they arose from the inner turmoil of affection mixed with hatred, of pride in the throne that he would bequeath and his obsessive need to hold on to that throne. Also, the months of anguished indecision may well have pushed Herod again beyond the confines of full sanity.

To the young men, the charges made by Herod were

reason enough for them to fear what might ensue. It appears that in Jerusalem they had rejected the imputation of filial impiety on the grounds that they were justified in hating their father for slaying their innocent mother; in this scene before Caesar nothing could have been less appropriate than for them to repeat the charges against Herod which they had made so recklessly at home. Unable to muster an adequate defense for their actions, the brothers wept copiously and miserably, and presented themselves as abject, youthful, confused, and diffident princes. Josephus records that although the bystanders were moved to pity the young men, they were even more moved by the deep emotion which Herod had displayed.

At length, however, Alexander found words to speak, addressing them to his father in the presence of the tearful audience. "Father, your good will to us is manifest, even in this trial. If it had been your intention to take severe action against us, you would not have brought us before the Savior of all mankind." We may assume that Caesar enjoyed hearing the title which Hellenistic kings reveled in. "In view of your authority as both our father and our king, your bringing us here signifies your wish to save us, not to execute us. Hence, we are now all the more in anguish, for we could not bear to live if we believed that we were guilty of wrongdoing against a father such as you. To die in innocence is less bad than to live under the suspicion of guilt. If we can speak in candor, perhaps we may be able to speak to you persuasively, and, at the same time, escape danger; but if we are to continue to remain under suspicion, then there is no gain in our surviving beyond even today." Alexander then addressed himself to Herod, commenting on the accusations made against them. "If a king has young sons whose mother has been put to death, nothing will keep the father from suspecting them of plotting against him. Suspicion, though, is one thing, and acts of impiety are another. Can anyone convict us of preparing a poison, or of having prompted a conspiracy, or of bribing servants, or of writing letters against you? Yet each of these things, though never done, has come to be reported against us. When a palace is not united, it is disastrous for the kingdom; and the throne itself, which you intend to bestow as a reward for filial piety, manages to imbue evil men with hopes and there is no restraint against their vicious actions. No wrongdoing on our part can be shown. About the calumnies against us, if you wish to dispose of them, you must be willing to give us a hearing. Have we been boldly outspoken? Not against you— that would have been wrong—but only against those who have had something to quote even when nothing has been said. Did we lament our mother? Not because she was put to death, but because, dead, she was slandered by worthless men.

"Do we want the throne which belongs to our father? To what end? We have royal honors; would it then not be misplaced zeal to desire them? Or, if we do not have them, we do have hope of them, have we not? Or, do you suppose that we could expect to gain the throne by putting you out of the way? The earth would not let us walk on it, or the sea sail on it. Would the piety of your subjects or the religious feelings of the entire nation permit parricides to assume the control of the state and to enter the sacred Temple you have built? And even if these things were brushed aside as insignificant, could anyone guilty of your murder escape punishment as long as Caesar lives? Your sons, begotten by you, are neither so undutiful nor so foolish. Perhaps, though, they are caught in a situation unfortunate for you.

"What is it that has the power to lead you to believe impious things of us? Our mother is dead; but that should act as a caution for us rather than stir us to plot. There is more we could say in our defense about what we have done, but in reality there is nothing to say about deeds that were never done.

"Accordingly, in the presence of Caesar, ruler of all mankind, and now a mediator between us, we suggest an agreement. If you, father, will, in all earnestness, bring yourself back to freedom from suspicion of us, we are willing, even in an unhappy way, to live on under the onus of the false accusation of grave crimes. If, though, fear abides in you, then you must continue to live on in your blamelessness, but we assert that we do not wish to live at the cost of an injustice to him who gave us life."

The effect of this mendacious eloquence was to persuade Caesar that he had been right in disbelieving Herod's charges; he saw, also, that Herod was touched, even moved, by Alexander's defense of himself and his brother. The bystanders were completely convinced by Alexander's skillful words, especially since the charges seemed incredible, and the young men were handsome, in the full bloom of their manhood, and they naturally evoked great sympathy—and Herod, antipathy. The humility of the brothers added its own measure of persuasion, for defiance was remote from their expression as they looked at the ground dejectedly and continued to weep. Indeed, the whole situation was abruptly changed, for it was Herod who now required some defense, especially in light of his inability to prove any charges against his sons.

Caesar then acted out his role as mediator. On the one hand, so he said, the youths were assuredly cleared of any charges, but, on the other hand, they should have so behaved toward Herod as to prevent such charges from arising. Turning to Herod, he urged him to set aside all suspicion and to become reconciled to his sons, for it was wrong to believe things so evil of a person's own offspring. Not only would a change of heart cure all that was wrong on both sides, but each side should affirmatively cultivate good will toward the other; first, they should apologize, and thereafter determine to show a fuller concern each for the other. Caesar then gave a sign to the youths, and in response they were about to fall at Herod's feet in supplication. Herod, however, took them in his arms, embraced them each in turn—and all present were deeply affected by this gesture of reconciliation.

So Herod and his two sons left the presence of Caesar together, and presently Antipater joined the three of them, the latter declaring himself pleased at the reconciliation.[2] It was incumbent on Herod now to give a lavish gift to Caesar; it amounted to three hundred talents, earmarked to provide bread and circuses for the people of Rome. In return Caesar gave Herod half of the revenue of Caesar's copper mines in Cyprus, and the right to manage the other half. Moreover, he gave Herod the renewed right either to designate one of his sons as his successor or—and this was new—to divide his kingdom among all of them.

Most laconically Josephus passes over a matter one could wish he had dwelt on at some length. He relates that Herod wished to distribute his kingdom to his sons immediately, but Caesar forbade him to relinquish control of either his kingdom or his sons during his lifetime. (I confess that I find myself doubting this statement of Josephus, for it smacks of coming from a source that sought to vindicate Herod for the evils which were still to arise, by recording his wish at this time, as it were, to retire.) But on the other hand, Caesar was concerned for tranquillity in the empire, and hence he did not want Herod to relinquish the throne at that time. Possibly Caesar deemed it a sufficient outcome that he had allowed Herod the unusual privilege of naming which son would succeed him at death; normally a "client king" did not possess this privilege, and any heir to the throne needed approval by the Roman

Senate. To let Herod retire could plunge Judea, and even all Syria, into disorder.

The usual date given for the reconciliation of Herod and his sons is 13 B.C. or, preferably, 12, when Herod was just over sixty. Why did Herod propose that he divide his kingdom at that time? If it seems out of keeping with his obsessive love of power, it is intelligible as a desperate effort on his part to find some way of living in peace in his palace. Suppose, for example, that each of the three sons with whom we deal in the present context—there were other sons, as we shall see—could have had his own area, such as Galilee, or the Perea, or Judea, and each could have had his own palace, Herod, by scattering his household in such a way, might have found some domestic peace. Had this happened, his remaining years would have been different, for bitter as was his experience up to this point with his household, it was fated to worsen, and to eventuate in those acts which, even more than the incidents we have already related, have bequeathed to us a portrait of Herod as a man of insane cruelty. When Caesar required Herod to remain king he doomed him to circumstances so intolerable that Herod was to be unable to withstand what was destined to arise.

In the midst of the brief spell of reconciliation, Herod and his sons sailed for Judea, stopping at an offshore island, Elaeusa, in Cilicia in Asia Minor, where Herod met King Archelaus of Cappadocia, the father-in-law of Alexander, who had apparently arranged to meet Herod so as to celebrate the happy reconciliation of his son-in-law with Herod. Archelaus appears to have kept himself closely informed about events in Judea.

On arriving in Jerusalem, Herod arranged for another public appearance and address, directed mostly to reporting the kindnesses shown him by Caesar and to reviewing his own benefactions to the populace. He closed his speech by admonishing his sons, the court, and the populace to cultivate concord and harmony. Then he announced publicly the prospective succession to his throne, naming Antipater first, and then Alexander and Aristobulus. He himself nevertheless was to continue to rule, he said, and he spoke of the circumstance that he was not so old as to be hampered by age, nor had he lost any of the capacities that a king must have. Moreover, he issued a stern warning against those who might attach themselves to his sons with the objective of bringing about his downfall; a fearful punishment would await any who gave himself to such efforts. "It is not jealousy of my children which impels me to restrict the attention paid to my sons, but my awareness that such attention promotes recklessness in young people." Turning to his sons, he said, "I give you now royal clothing and retinues. I pray that God preserve my decision, provided that you live in unity." Publicly embracing his sons, he then dismissed the throng. His address, thus, was a passionate plea for unity, but in part the ears on which it fell were deaf.

Not only was concord elusive, but, so says Josephus, divine intervention could be the explanation for the ever deepening discords—unless, he says, hedging, it was simply Tyche, "fortune." This divine intervention, if that is what it was, was a punishment, a result of a matter concerning the Tomb of David. Herod had learned that during the siege of Jerusalem by the Syrian Greeks in 135 or 134, the then king, John Hyrcanus, had opened the Tomb and taken from it three thousand talents, a tenth of which he used to bribe Antiochus to lift the siege; some of the remainder of this great wealth John Hyrcanus used to establish a mercenary army. Herod was always in need of money, for his benefactions quite probably exceeded his income; he was led to believe that John Hyrcanus had taken only a small portion of the wealth that was in the

Tomb, and he determined to make his own quiet, unobserved entry to acquire whatever wealth remained. To his
disappointment, the Tomb did not contain any more
money, though it did yield some gold ornaments and other
things of value. In the course of his careful search for
money, Herod penetrated the Tomb as far as the coffins
of David and Solomon—the text of Josephus implies but
does not state that Herod broke open these coffins—but
now a supernatural occurrence ended the foray into the
Tomb. A sheet of flame destroyed two of Herod's body-
guards, and Herod became terribly frightened, and immediately ended the search. In remorse, he built an expensive
white marble memorial at the entrance of the Tomb.[4] But,
comments Josephus, possibly because of this evil deed, the
dissension in the palace increased.

From the one side, Alexander and Aristobulus resented
the priority of primogeniture publicly accorded to Antipater and, from the other, Antipater resented the rank accorded to his half-brothers, though inferior to his own.
Antipater was apparently signally unscrupulous; at no time
is there a good word spoken of him in Josephus. Antipater
managed to keep the brothers off balance by continuing,
as in the past, to arrange for accusations against them to be
made by people other than himself. At the same time he
defended the brothers to Herod, thereby persuading Herod
that he, Antipater, was the only one who was tireless on
behalf of Herod. These defenses by Antipater usually
took the form of indirectly confirming the allegations
which he seemed to be rejecting as he reported them; and
gradually Herod was becoming convinced, especially
through Antipater's defense of the brothers, that Alexander was plotting to murder him. Antipater grew in
power, to the point that Herod commended the royal
treasurer to Antipater's friendship; not only did Herod
consult more and more with Antipater on royal affairs,

but he began to consult even with Antipater's mother, Doris. The sons of Mariamne regarded this development as the greatest possible indignity to them and their royal birth.

But the full account of the parties to the dissension requires a reminder that Antipater was able to rely upon his aunt Salome and his uncle Pheroras as his partisans against the sons of Mariamne; in addition, however, Alexander's wife, Glaphyra, the royal daughter of King Archelaus of Cappadocia, felt herself quite superior to her sister-in-law Bernice, Salome's daughter. The winds of antagonism and hatred blew in every conceivable direction, especially as Herod added to the list and number of his wives, none of whom seems to have suited the other residents of the palace.

To this elaborate dissension was now added still another dimension. Pheroras was betrothed to Salampsio, the daughter of Herod and Mariamne I, but he fell in love with a slave girl. Herod became indignant at his brother; he broke the engagement and married the girl off to his nephew Phasael, the son of his dead brother Phasael. Yet after a lapse of some time, when the ardor of Pheroras for the slave girl seemed to Herod to have cooled, Herod now offered his brother the hand of another daughter born of his marriage to Mariamne I, a girl named, like Herod's mother, Cypros. Pheroras was able to see the wisdom of acceding to his brother's royal wish, and though he had begotten a child by the slave girl, he put her aside, and arranged to be married to Cypros a month later. Promptly, however, he resumed his relations with his mistress, instead of marrying his niece-princess. Herod was hurt and indignant; the court, quick to discern that Pheroras had fallen from favor, proceeded to provide Herod with an abundance of calumnies about him.

In still another current of intrigue, Salome persuaded

her daughter Bernice to withhold from her husband Aristobulus his conjugal rights. Bernice became a spy for Salome, reporting to her the random comments of her husband and his brother, and alleging that the brothers spoke of nothing but their hatred of Herod. Moreover, she reported their boast that when once they had attained the throne, they would make village clerks out of those sons born to Herod by his increasing number of wives.

In the context in which almost every one was plotting against someone else, Herod remained the center, the one to whom the allegations and charges and countercharges were made. His suspicions increased in breadth and depth, and he found himself more and more unable to distinguish between the credible and the incredible—and he began to believe everything that he heard.

The calumnies, hitherto general, then took a peculiar specific turn. Pheroras came to Alexander with the allegation, brought to him, so he said, from Salome, that Herod was smitten with passion for Alexander's wife, Glaphyra. Since Herod was always generous and bestowed gifts lavishly on all his family, including Glaphyra, Alexander now began to interpret the gifts to Glaphyra as having only one possible meaning. Unable through jealousy to restrain his anger, Alexander went to Herod and openly made the accusation, which was supported, he said, by the word of Pheroras. Herod's anger now turned to fury. He summoned Pheroras and confronted him with Alexander's report. Pheroras did not deny that he had spoken to Alexander in the terms in which Alexander quoted him; what he said—and this was in the presence of Salome—was that he had got his information from her. From Salome there came an immediate emotional explosion and a denial. Pheroras, she charged, was plotting against her because of her effort, on behalf of Herod, to persuade Pheroras to get rid of the slave-girl and to marry Cypros. She tore her hair and she beat her breast.

Yet Herod's response to all this hideousness in his family was relatively mild. He did not punish his brother and sister, even though he had come to hate them; he only banished them from his court. Especially in the case of Pheroras was this a mild punishment, for Herod could recall from the days when Mariamne was alive that an allegation had been made against Pheroras that he was bent on poisoning him. At that time Herod had launched an investigation, abetted by some judicious torture, but had found no proof of a plot against him. It was prudent now, however, to get Pheroras and Salome out of the court.

Soon, however, they were back, and Salome became involved in an affair of the heart. Already twice widowed, each time because Herod had executed the husband, she fell in love with a Nabatean, Syllaeus, who was the virtual ruler of his country under its king, Obadas. Between Obadas and Herod there had arisen a state of advanced hatred. Syllaeus was a young man, much younger than Salome. He had come to Jerusalem on some commercial mission, possibly to negotiate a loan and, on being entertained by Herod at dinner, he met Salome. In the ensuing days they met again at a series of dinners, and their conduct was such as to indicate that some kind of relationship, or at least some understanding, existed between them. What the eyes of the court guessed at was made specific in the gossip of the women of the court, and the reports about Salome's indiscretions with the young man reached Herod. The king turned to Pheroras for information, and the latter, after observing the conduct of the lovebirds at a dinner, confirmed to Herod that Syllaeus and Salome were deeply involved in a passionate affair. The business negotiations between Herod and Syllaeus reached a point of completion or of pause, and Syllaeus left Jerusalem for

Nabatea, only to return after two or three months, with the request to Herod that he be allowed to marry Salome. He urged upon Herod the advantage of such a marriage, since his own control of Nabatea had grown to the point that reciprocal advantages could accrue to both kingdoms. So Herod inquired of Salome what her disposition was; she quickly agreed to marry Syllaeus.

But now Herod interposed an objection: Salome was Jewish, Syllaeus not. We do not know whether or not this same obstacle presented itself in the case of the marriage of Alexander to Glaphyra of Cappadocia. Perhaps it did, and perhaps Glaphyra became converted to Judaism. But perhaps it did not, for it appears probable that Herod did not insist on conversion in the case of the marriage of his son to a Greek princess of consequence, for the offspring of Alexander and Glaphyra either were not or else ceased to be Jews, as is related in *Antiquities* XVIII, 141. Herod could, inconsistently, demand conversion in the case of a marriage involving a Nabatean, whom he probably regarded as of a lower rank. One suspects that the issue of religion was merely a pretext. Syllaeus, however, was unwilling to convert, asserting that to do so would prompt the Nabateans to stone him to death. So Syllaeus departed without marrying Salome, and he felt aggrieved to the point of wishing to repay Herod for frustrating his desire. How he did so, we shall see presently. But with the marriage abandoned, and the illicit relationship not given its veneer of legality, the courtiers had a renewed occasion for gossiping about Salome and her affair with the young Nabatean. Even Pheroras joined in, for he openly accused his sister of lewd conduct with Syllaeus.

Salome did not allow her state of culpability to reduce her to quiescence or to retirement from her machinations; since Pheroras had evaded marrying Cypros, Salome now proposed that Cypros be given to her son, whom she had

borne to Costabar. Promptly Pheroras objected, proposing
instead that Cypros should marry his own son, contending
that if the princess married the son of Costabar, the latter
would use the situation to avenge the death of his father
at Herod's hands. The eventual outcome was that Cypros
was married to Pheroras' son, not Salome's. The account
in Josephus is unclear; perhaps the ultimate decision by
which Cypros was married to Pheroras' son was reached
only after that princess was first betrothed to Salome's
son;[5] or perhaps we must be content with knowing that
there were ugly intrigues, the details of which remain
confused.

So the rivalries and the animosities of the court were
by no means one single channel but, rather, a series of
brooks and creeks and rivers that flowed, as if in defiance
of all principles of geography, in a variety of directions.
Not only was Herod subjected to the pain of observing
these animosities, but he was called on to move from reluctant decision to further reluctant decision, and each
decision seemed to involve him in something kindred to
punitive action against his nearest and dearest. Without
restraints to his own morality, he was caught in the coils
of the immoralities of his precious family.

To the incidents of adultery in his family, both the real
and the merely alleged, but still safely within the confines
of heterosexuality, there presently was added a matter of
pederasty. How inconsistent this Grecian practice was
with Judaism seems not to have attracted the notice of
Josephus. The pederasty is presented as if it was to be
taken for granted, and the focus is on jealousy and on
plotting, not on the sexual deviations so abominable in
Jewish eyes. Herod was served by three eunuchs whom
he was "immoderately fond of by reason of their beauty."
One was his wine-pourer, the second his waiter at meals,
and the third a sort of *valet de chambre*. These eunuchs

Alexander managed to draw to himself, bestowed great presents upon them, and used them for pederastic purposes. Soon this act of poaching on his own preserve was reported to Herod. Outraged, he had the eunuchs put to torture. They promptly confessed to the acts, but at first they made no other allegations against Alexander. When the torture was increased, however, they appended an accusation: Alexander had broached to them the idea that they should become loyal to him, for they had no future with Herod since the latter was old—old despite the dyeing of his hair. Moreover, so they reported, Alexander had set before them the consideration that he was next in line for the throne, not only because of his lineage, but also because people of substance and power, including officers of the army, and even friends of Herod, were already joined to him in anticipation of certain significant events soon to take place.

To Herod's sense of outrage about the eunuchs, these disclosures added a huge measure of fear, indeed of terror, and he was certain that there now existed a true conspiracy, a real plot against him. Again, he slipped past the borders of sanity. Uncertain that he or anyone else could fend off every effort at assassination, he abstained from directly confronting Alexander, lest he immediately set off some disastrous events; instead he increased and broadened the espionage throughout the palace. That terror which he himself felt he now passed on to those within the palace, and each person who had enjoyed the calumniation of others was forced to wonder how dangerously he himself was being besmirched. The more influential the person, the more he underwent Herod's suspicion and animosity, even if his life might be spared; the less influential the person, the easier it was for Herod to condemn that person to immediate death.

The calumniated, provided they were sufficiently uninfluential, were put to death; but with the passing of some time Herod became aware of having executed innocent people. He might thereupon have chosen to desist from his indiscriminate executions; instead, he turned on the erstwhile informers and executed many of them. Completely unable to discriminate between the loyal and disloyal, and between the honest and dishonest, he found himself becoming more and more bereft of even his trustworthy lieutenants.

No one made as great a contribution to Herod's lack of equilibrium as his son Antipater. As before, when Antipater had disdained direct accusation, so now too he abstained from specific allegations, contenting himself with merely ascribing to this person or that some attachment to Alexander, fully aware that even innocent attachment was in Herod's eyes the most guilty form of treason. Because of Antipater, more espionage and more executions were required. Next, there came to Herod's ears the report, via Antipater, that Alexander regarded his own native gifts, such as his handsome, large frame and his expertness with the bow, as lamentable liabilities rather than commendable assets, for his superior endowments were what prompted Herod to envy and to the jealous acts of cruelty. Alexander bragged, so Herod was told, that when he went hunting with Herod, he deliberately missed the target, for it pleased Herod's vanity to excel in marksmanship.

But beyond such trivia and backbiting of mere nuisance import, there came a report to Herod that Alexander and his brother Aristobulus had arranged matters so that, on some hunting expedition, they would ambush Herod and slay him, and then Alexander would flee to Rome and there lay claim to the throne of Judea. This report terrified Herod. Moreover, Herod was brought a letter, supposedly from Alexander to Aristobulus, in which the writer accused Herod of unjust partiality for Antipater, especially in the matter of Antipater's financial allowance.

These latter allegations seemed to Herod sufficient basis for arresting Alexander, and this he did.

Yet to arrest Alexander was one thing and to punish him another, especially since the consent of Augustus was necessary. Herod was unable to bring himself to fix on an extreme punishment, so for the while he did nothing at all. Feeling the need of some further basis to justify his having imprisoned Alexander, he resorted to additional espionage and additional torture and additional executions. The instruments of torture now yielded a harvest; it was alleged by a certain young man that Alexander had sent messages to friends in Rome asking that they prevail upon Augustus Caesar to summon Alexander, so that he could there report that Herod had entered into a friendly relationship with the king of the Parthians, and would support them against Rome. The tortured young man reported, moreover, that Alexander had had a poisonous drug prepared in Ascalon.

These disclosures increased Herod's terror, but they also provided some surcease for his uneasy conscience, in the sense that the plot against him was apparently even worse than he had supposed, and his cruelties therefore necessary. The poison needed to be found, and Herod instituted a relentless search for it, though in vain.

Alexander was, of course, questioned. After protesting his innocence long and loud, he faced squarely the reality that he could not persuade his father of his innocence. Reconciled to being executed, he resolved to do something to injure Herod and the kingdom. He wrote a four-part book, in which he desisted from continuing to deny the allegations against him, and, instead, confessed to them. But, ingeniously, he went on to give the names of those who had been in on the plot with him. These included Pheroras, and also some of the king's leading councillors; also named was his aunt Salome, who, he wrote, had even forced her way into his chamber one night and had lain with him, in which enterprise he had been an unwilling participant.

That Alexander's book purported to be his confession lent credence to the accusations which he had made. So large was the number of highly placed people whom he accused, and so frightened were they, that in self-exculpation they turned to support against each other the accusations which Alexander had made. Imprisonment and execution increased, and no one in the palace had reason to feel safe. Yet, anxiously fearful of Herod as everyone around the court inevitably became, in no other person did anxiety become as powerful and as obsessive as it did in Herod. Though Alexander was in prison, Herod was readily able to imagine him advancing toward him with drawn sword, or, even worse, standing directly over him, sword in hand. The court was not content to ascribe mere hallucination to Herod; it was convinced now of his full insanity.

At this juncture, Archelaus of Cappadocia, having learned of the imprisonment of his son-in-law, came to Judea to see what he might accomplish. Shrewdly recognizing that it is impossible to appease an insane man, and that to appeal to Herod, or to try to dissuade him, would only increase Herod's obsessive hatred of Alexander, Archelaus determined on a course exactly opposite of what might have been expected. Thus, on being closeted with Herod, Archelaus spoke of his admiration for Herod's leniency to Alexander, for he had supposed that Alexander had long since been executed. Archelaus even proposed something new: together Archelaus and Herod needed to inquire into the possible guilt of Glaphyra, and the two needed to strengthen each other, should such a guilt emerge, to be assured that Glaphyra as well as Alexander would receive extreme punishment.

Herod had expected excoriation and accusation from

Archelaus. Since his conscience was uneasy, hence his long delay in punishing Alexander, he welcomed these words of Archelaus, for he felt justified now both in having imprisoned Alexander and also in having abstained so far from executing him. Archelaus proposed that Glaphyra's marriage to Alexander be dissolved, and Herod became the solicitous father, concerned for his wayward son. In tears, Herod begged Archelaus not to take that extreme step, nor to be unforgiving of Alexander's misdeeds, for Alexander was still only a young man.

Archelaus had been given a copy of Alexander's four-part book; now he began to give its supposed true interpretation to Herod. The book showed clearly, so he said, that a young man, innocent of any malice, had been corrupted by evil people who wished to manipulate him, and that chief among these wicked people was Pheroras.

Herod's hatred of his brother had by now been manifested so often that Archelaus unquestionably knew that he was pursuing a tack that would appeal to Herod. It was therefore a chore of no magnitude, once Archelaus had got Herod's ear, to divert Herod's wrath from Alexander to Pheroras. Since nothing was secret in the court, Pheroras quickly learned that he was emerging as the chief culprit. Knowing that now a mere appeal to Herod would be futile, Pheroras cast about for some way out of his difficulties. He donned black clothes, as if in mourning, and he visited Archelaus, throwing himself on the mercy of the king of Cappadocia. To the appeal from Pheroras, Archelaus gave his response: Pheroras must promptly go to Herod, confess sole responsibility for all that had transpired, and Archelaus would be present at the confession to speak in behalf of Pheroras.

So Pheroras went to Herod, as he had done often before, and in tears threw himself at Herod's feet, begging Herod's pardon. Archelaus kept his promise; he immediately began to speak, not so much directly in behalf of Pheroras, as more generally about his experience and his accrued wisdom. The events in Judea, he asserted, happened very often in kingdoms, and they had happened in Cappadocia. He himself had suffered injuries from his own brothers, even more grievous than those which Herod had suffered from Pheroras. And just as Archelaus had then tended toward a natural fraternal affection rather than to revenge, so he now counseled Herod that it was better to cure an infected limb than to amputate it. So Archelaus succeeded in reconciling Herod and Pheroras.

His larger objective, the complete reconciliation of Herod and Alexander, was now feasible. There remained for Archelaus only the extension of his shrewd procedure of denigrating Alexander to Herod, so that Herod could feel the need to defend his son. Archelaus set forth to Herod that he was still indignant with his daughter and son-in-law, and that he would separate them from each other; he would, however, allow Herod to choose for his daughter whatever husband Herod might select, so that thereby he and Herod could continue in their warm friendship for each other. To this Herod replied that he hoped that Archelaus would not terminate the marriage of Alexander and Glaphyra, for Herod was prepared to welcome the return of his son Alexander to his affections; furthermore, the couple already had children, and, moreover, Alexander was deeply attached to Glaphyra. Above all, however, Glaphyra could, in the future, act as a restraining force on Alexander, and could help him to discern the error of his ways. So Archelaus succeeded in prompting Herod to petition him for exactly that outcome which Archelaus desired. Archelaus took his departure, carrying with him rich gifts, both of money and of eunuchs, and, so Josephus adds, a concubine.

Josephus relates in *Antiquities*, in a half-sentence, that

Herod made a journey to Rome to set before Caesar an account of the matter of the imprisonment of Alexander; in *The Jewish War* there is a full sentence to the effect that Archelaus advised Herod to make this journey, personally to report to Caesar, this as an addendum to a written report which Archelaus had already sent to Augustus. Josephus, however, tells us nothing at all of this journey. We can assume that just as the reports of the difficulties in Jerusalem were known in Cappadocia, so to some extent they were known in Rome, for rumors about royalty spread rapidly in the empire. Inasmuch as Herod returned from this journey to Rome without having lost anything perceptible through having gone there, we can conclude that his mission was a success.

Perhaps, too, the intervention of Archelaus into the Alexander affair resulted in restoring Herod to some clarity of mind. Yet it seems inescapable that Herod's standing with Caesar was weakened by this need to go and explain, and unquestionably Herod's anxiety increased about retaining the throne and about retaining the right to bequeath it as he wished. The unfolding events suggest that this was the case. Even worse for Herod was the circumstance that Agrippa had died in 12 B.C., and therefore Herod no longer possessed this influential advocate and intermediary.

On Herod's return from Rome to Jerusalem, he discovered that the long peace which he had enjoyed was now threatened by disorders that needed to be put down. The Nabateans were involved in the disorders, and Syllaeus, to whom he had denied the hand of Salome, was in Rome and alert to avenge himself on Herod. In Trachonitis, the region east of the Sea of Galilee, the rumor spread that Herod had died, and, accordingly, a revolt broke out. Herod's generals put down the rebellion, but some forty of the rebels escaped to Nabatea; there they were warmly received by Syllaeus' people, and given a fortified town to dwell in. These rebels made frequent forays against Herod's territories, but, on pursuit, always managed to flee to the safety of Nabatean territory. Since Herod was unable to punish the offenders directly, he carried out a notable slaughter of the kinsmen of the rebels in Trachonitis. But the forays against his territories from Nabatea continued. Herod turned, therefore, to the Roman officials in Syria with the request that they order the Nabateans to turn the rebels over to him. Syllaeus, back again in Nabatea, was now virtually its ruler, and he turned down the request. Herod now had reason for wrath against the Nabateans; moreover, at the time that Syllaeus had been in Jerusalem, he had persuaded Herod to make a substantial loan to Nabatea, a loan as yet not repaid. Herod, accordingly, added to the demand that the rebels be turned over to him the further demand that the loan be repaid. Again the Roman officials were consulted; they proposed a kind of compromise about the rebels, namely, that the Nabateans turn over Herod's subjects to him, and that Herod turn over to the Nabateans their subjects whom he held; Josephus tells us, however, that Herod possessed no Nabatean subjects. As to the loan, Syllaeus was to repay it in thirty days.

But Syllaeus left for Rome without paying the debt. The Roman officials in Syria thereupon gave Herod permission to invade Nabatea to attack the rebels, but Rome itself was unaware of the granting of it. He attacked the walled town where the rebels were quartered, and he captured it; now, however, he found himself suddenly attacked by the Nabateans. These he quickly defeated, and he then punished them. He settled Idumeans in Trachonitis to keep the rebellious populace subdued. In the interest of prudence he wrote a report to the Roman officials in Syria about his invasion of Nabatea; they in turn made their

investigation, and the facts seemed to bear out what Herod
had reported.

But Syllaeus found a warm welcome in Rome. When
reports came to him about Herod's invasion of Nabatea,
Syllaeus presented himself to Caesar to make allegations
against Herod. He exaggerated greatly the number of
casualties suffered by the Nabateans after their attack on
Herod, and he suggested that Herod had been on the
offensive. He added that Herod had seized that particular
moment to attack Nabatea because its king, Obadas, was
feeble and disabled, and because Syllaeus was away; indeed, Syllaeus asserted, he was away and in Rome for only
one reason, to keep Caesar informed about the possible
rupture of imperial peace in that portion of his empire—
and the cause of the rupture, of course, was Herod.

Caesar abstained from a full inquiry into the background
and facts about Herod's invasion of Nabatea; he confined
himself to the single allegation that Herod had improperly
invaded that kingdom. Herod's representative in Rome had
no opportunity to explain the circumstances of the invasion, and no chance to allude to the permission granted by
the Roman officials in Syria. It is a token of the decline of
Herod's prestige with Caesar that he summarily wrote to
Herod in sharp rebuke, and his letter included a passage
to the effect that while formerly he had treated Herod as
a friend, now he would treat him as merely a subject. To
Herod the possible danger to his life from his plotting son
was a matter against which he could take some hopeful,
preventive action, and even counter the threat; and even
should he die in some intrigue, his honor would, as it were,
remain intact; to lose face with Augustus Caesar, however,
was to stand on the threshold of disgrace and dishonor.
In the case of Herod such disgrace was the worst kind of
defeat, for he had devoted himself above all else to courting the favor of Rome. To come face to face with the

awareness of the decline of his esteem in Augustus' eyes was to undergo the most crushing of experiences.

A client could not fight Caesar. All he could do was to plead his case. A forlorn and abject Herod had no choice; so plead he must.

Matters, however, worsened, for Syllaeus sent on to Nabatea the reports of Herod's reduced influence with Caesar, and the Nabateans promptly joined with the rebels of Trachonitis in new attacks on Herod's territories. Herod, dismayed and fully affrighted by Caesar's hostile letters, felt constrained to send an embassy to Rome to plead his cause, but Caesar declined to receive them. Syllaeus meanwhile enhanced his position with Caesar, especially when Obadas died.

The Nabatean throne was then occupied by Aretas IV, but in advance of receiving Caesar's consent to do so; and, moreover, Herod found in him an unconscious ally, for Aretas had reason to consider Syllaeus a dangerous rival. Aretas sent letters to Rome with allegations against Syllaeus, including the charge that Syllaeus was an adulterer on a grand scale, a disloyal servant to Obadas whose royal power he had virtually usurped and, further, that Syllaeus had in fact brought about the death of Obadas by arranging for the poisoning of him.

Syllaeus, however, was quite generous in his distribution of gifts and bribes and he managed to keep the allegations by Aretas from coming to the attention of Caesar. Disorders arose in Nabatea, but Aretas did not have a sufficiently tight hold on his throne to be able to quell them; Herod might have crushed the rebels, but he was fearful of further wrath on the part of Caesar if he proceeded without imperial consent. The whole situation in Palestine deteriorated all the more.

In the campaign against the Nabateans which had displeased Caesar, Herod seems to have led his troops himself, as is clearly implied in the language of Josephus. The date of that untimely invasion was 10 or 9 B.C., and Herod was then either sixty-three or sixty-four. To be able to lead an army suggests that he still possessed a large measure of his physical vigor; nothing in the accounts implies that he was not in full possession of his physical powers. Yet at about this same time, when he was scarcely in possession of mental balance, we know that his physical health began to decline, with manifestations of that decline emerging immediately after the invasion of Nabatea.

Herod now faced three dangers, first, the complete loss of status with Caesar, second, the disruption of his full control of his territory which he had conquered or had been awarded, and, third, the strife in his palace. It was an urgent necessity, even a desperate need for him, to get the ear of Caesar in some way, especially now that his embassy had returned without having been received. We may well ask, why did he not himself go to Rome? We do not know. Perhaps he despaired of the ability to persuade Caesar; perhaps he thought that, in going, he had more to lose than to gain, for if he went to Rome, Caesar might have used the occasion of the visit to depose him. Unable or unwilling to go, Herod chose as his emissary for a renewed effort Nicholas of Damascus, for the latter was not only a shrewd negotiator, but in addition his reputation as a writer and philosopher made him somewhat known even in Rome. So Nicholas set out for the Eternal City.

At the time of the visit of Archelaus of Cappadocia Herod had appeared gullible, but we can understand that the affair of Alexander had demented him. It is, however, even more difficult to understand Herod's gullibility in an almost incredible episode which took place in Jerusalem while Nicholas was in Rome. That episode concerned a man from Sparta named Caius Julius Eurycles (known to us also from mentions of him by a number of pagan writers). A wandering intellectual, devoid of moral sense or scruples, Eurycles had found the pickings in Greece rather shrunken, and he had come to wealthy Judea in the hopes of finding them better. The Jews had always had a warm affection for Sparta, for I Maccabees 12 relates that toward the end of the fourth century, shortly after the conquest by Alexander the Great, the king of the Spartans had written to the high priest in Jerusalem in the friendliest of vein, even asserting that they, like the Jews, were descendants of Abraham. Eurycles, on arriving in Jerusalem, was something kindred to the modern distinguished lecturer from abroad, to whom the homes of the best families are available, and for whose entertainment the best families vie. Among Eurycles' credentials was his report of the high esteem in which Archelaus of Cappadocia held him. Eurycles had had the foresight to invest some of his dwindling funds in suitable gifts for Herod, aware that he would receive greater ones in return. So this notable visitor, once he was welcomed in Jerusalem, gained access to Herod's entourage. He had frequent occasion to visit Herod, and to flatter him, and his warm reception at the court was such that he became the house guest of Antipater.

Eurycles quickly caught all the nuances of the relationships in the court. Though quartered with Antipater, he used his supposed relationship with Archelaus of Cappadocia to cultivate Glaphyra and Alexander, though in secret, lest Antipater be offended. In turn, Alexander brought him into relationship with his younger brother Aristobulus. Once Eurycles had the confidence of the brothers, he began to manipulate them. In close touch with Antipater, he endeared himself to the latter by his comment that it was an injustice to this oldest son of Herod that his half-brothers should be tolerated in their intrigues against him,

Antipater. To Alexander his comment was that it was unjust for a prince, married to a princess, to be below the
son of a mere commoner in the line of succession to the
throne. Both Alexander, and then Aristobulus, were indiscreet enough to confide to Eurycles all the grievances
which they felt, beginning with the death of Mariamne
and running through the hatred which Herod felt for
them, to the point that Herod had ceased to speak to them
at dinners or family gatherings. What the brothers confided, Eurycles promptly disclosed to Antipater; he added
the warning to Antipater that the deep emotion with
which Alexander and Aristobulus expressed their grievances reflected their willingness to resort to murder; and
hence Antipater and Herod faced a real danger. After
Antipater had listened to the reports and comments, he
offered Eurycles money in return for a favor which he
wanted of the Spartan, that Eurycles should tell Herod
what he had been telling Antipater. Eurycles accepted the
money.

Eurycles prefaced the purchased disclosures by repeatedly singing the praises of Antipater to Herod. In a place
where the habit was calumny, Herod found pleasure in
hearing words of praise. Eurycles then began to earn his
money. Having praised Antipater, he veered into an attack
on Alexander and Aristobulus. All the old calumnies were
revived, conveyed this time by a distinguished man, gifted
with a fluent tongue. He painted a portrait of Alexander
as an implacable enemy of Herod, ready to die himself if
thereby he could destroy his father; moreover, Alexander
was prepared to call on the assistance of his father-in-law
Archelaus against Herod, and even to call on Caesar. Alexander, according to Eurycles, could tell Caesar all about
the oppressions and unbearable taxes through which Herod
had grown wealthy, and had enriched his venal associates;
and Alexander could remind Caesar that Herod had mur-

dered his great-grandfather, his grandmother, his uncle, and his mother.

Having fulfilled the conditions of Antipater's bribe, Eurycles took his leave of Jerusalem and set forth for a new field, the court of Cappadocia.

The revival of the accusations against Alexander came at a juncture when matters between Herod and Alexander had appeared to have been settled favorably, through the intervention of Archelaus. Now the old suspicions were again alive, and they were vivid, and Herod believed implicitly the varnished tales which Eurycles had brought him.

The next move of Antipater was to suggest to Herod that Alexander and Aristobulus were moving from the mere contemplation of destroying Herod into a specific plan of action. Two of Herod's cavalry commanders had been degraded by Herod for some misdemeanors; Antipater reported that the brothers were holding clandestine meetings with these two officers. Herod brought the two officers to torture. He could obtain no confession from them, but in the midst of the torture there was produced a damning letter, cleverly forged by Herod's secretary. The letter was presumably written by Alexander, addressed to the commander of the fortress of Alexandreion, asking for refuge there after the brothers carried out the planned slaying of their father.

The commander of Alexandreion was brought before Herod and put to torture. He too abstained from any confession. Indeed, still another visitor to Jerusalem, Euarestus of Cos, a friend of Alexander, was closely questioned by Herod, but he insisted that he had heard no treasonable words from Alexander. But Herod persisted[6] in his torture of the two cavalry commanders; finally he got a confession that Alexander had bribed the two officers to kill Herod sometime when he was out hunting. The keeper of the

stable had supplied the officers with spears belonging to
Herod, so went the confession, with the plan in mind that
the death of Herod would appear to be a result of Herod's
fall from his horse rather than an assassination.

In this atmosphere of deepening suspicions and supposed
verifications, and as Herod's hatreds became indiscriminate,
Aristobulus now wrote a letter to his mother-in-law,
Salome, warning her that Herod was about to rake up an
old charge against her, namely, that when she had had her
affair with Syllaeus the Nabatean, she had revealed state
secrets to her lover. Whether the information in the letter
was true or false, the writing and sending of it amounted
to an act of disloyalty against Herod, and Aristobulus
thereby was most indiscreet in warning his mother-in-law.
When Salome received the letter, which was prompted by
her son-in-law's solicitude for her, she immediately ran to
Herod with it.

Now, at long last, through Eurycles, through forced
confessions, through Aristobulus' letter to Salome, all the
years of suspicion and hesitation came to a peak. Herod
had his two sons arrested, and imprisoned, separately,
preparatory to bringing them to trial. The confinement
seems to have taken place first in Jericho; Josephus fails
to make clear why the scene shifted from Jerusalem to the
other city, but perhaps Herod was fearful of stirring the
citizens of Jerusalem to revolt.[7]

Yet even in deciding to try his sons, Herod devoted
some time to indecision and delay. A minor official arrived
from Cappadocia. One wonders why the shrewd Archelaus
so misjudged the new situation as to offend Herod by not
coming himself. To the representations by this official
Herod replied by summoning Alexander before them for
questioning, especially about the aspect of the plot which
supposed that Alexander and Aristobulus would flee from
Judea. Where, demanded Herod, did they plan to flee to?

The reply from Alexander was, to Archelaus and then to Rome. Was not Herod justified, then, in attributing hostility to Archelaus himself? Next, and still in the presence of the Cappadocian and of the bound Alexander, Herod held an interrogation of Glaphyra. She, however, was so overcome by terror and grief that she could only beat her head, and groan loudly and piteously. One of Herod's counselors demanded that Alexander disclose whether or not Glaphyra was aware of his acts. Alexander's reply implied affirmation: "How could she not know of them, being dearer to me than life, and being the mother of my children?" Glaphyra then cried out that she knew nothing that he had done that was improper. If, however, she could save him by accusing herself, she was prepared to make a full confession. Alexander insisted that the only unfilial intention he and his brother were guilty of was the decision to go to Archelaus and then to Rome. Herod became convinced that Archelaus was his enemy. (Later Archelaus asserted that he was willing to receive the brothers as a means of preventing Herod from taking some action Herod would regret, and that at no time had he intended to send the young men to Rome.)

But the end result of the arrival of Archelaus' emissary was the confirmation of Herod's intention to put his sons to trial. Yet, before he could proceed, he needed the consent of Rome. He therefore wrote a petition to Caesar. Apparently at a time just before Herod's petition reached Caesar, the able emissary Nicholas of Damascus found his opportunity to carry out Herod's mandate in Rome. Since the Nabateans had already fallen out among themselves, with Aretas IV sending a mission to Rome to counter the efforts there of Syllaeus, those Nabateans opposed to Syllaeus were in possession of some documents, letters written by Syllaeus, which incriminated him. Nicholas managed to win the confidence of these Nabateans, and he learned about the documents. He determined not to seek a direct audience on Herod's behalf but to contrive, instead, to be present before Caesar when the rival Nabatean claimants would appear before him. When the two sides stood before the emperor, Nicholas was entrusted with presenting the charges by the one group of Nabateans against Syllaeus. Nicholas brought up the old accusations of Syllaeus' murder, by poison, of Obadas and of his adulteries in Nabatea; he added the accusations that Syllaeus had borrowed money for nefarious purposes and had engaged in adulteries in Rome comparable to those he had engaged in, in Nabatea. The climax, however, was the accusation by Nicholas that Syllaeus had deceived Augustus, especially in falsehoods relating to Herod. Caesar interrupted, asking how many Nabateans Herod had killed on his invasion of Nabatea, for Syllaeus had raised the figure from twenty-five to 2,500. Nicholas replied only indirectly, saying that he had a number of instructive things to say about the charges against Herod, and that few if any were true in the way in which they had been reported to Caesar. He then went on to mention the loan which Herod had made, and Syllaeus' failure to repay it, despite the promise made to Roman officials to do so. When Nicholas finished his statement, Caesar turned to Syllaeus with the renewed question, how many Nabateans had Herod slain. Syllaeus, caught in his falsehood about the numbers, contended that he had innocently transmitted misleading information which had been given him. But now the loan contract was read before Caesar, as were the letters from Roman officials and from the affected cities, which had complained of the forays by the rebellious natives of Trachonitis. Nicholas won the day; Syllaeus was condemned to pay his bills, and then to be punished. (The Romans put him to death in 4 B.C.) As to the throne of Nabatea, Caesar was still displeased that Aretas had not petitioned him for the right to the throne; he therefore contemplated ceding Nabatea to Herod, as a mark of a renewed favor which Herod found with the emperor.

But before Caesar could take this step, there came before him the petition from Herod to try Alexander and Aristobulus. Caesar concluded that Herod was too old and too overburdened with problems with his children to be able to undertake the responsibility of an additional kingdom.

Caesar granted Herod's petition to try his sons. He recommended that Herod should adopt the procedure of holding a full-scale investigation before the full assembly of Herod's relatives and the Roman tribunals. Unquestionably Caesar hoped that an open inquiry of this sort might dissuade Herod from extreme action, and, indeed, from any action at all.

The letter from Caesar sanctioning the trial expressed the emperor's distress at the need to try the sons; it added the hope that Herod might find that their guilt was not an intent to commit parricide, for which Herod would need to execute them, but only their intent to flee, and, in that case, a severe admonishment would suffice. But by the time of the trial Herod was beyond any capacity for pity or reason or temperance. The tragic events began to run their course in a farcical setting.

The trial of the two princes was set for Berytus (modern Beirut), well away from Jerusalem and the passions that could be aroused there. Not only did Roman officials preside, but the royalty of all Syria was present, with the exception of Archelaus—Cappadocia was at that time administratively a part of Syria. Salome and Pheroras are mentioned by name as present, and we are told that other relatives and highly placed friends were in attendance.

The people assembled were the most eminent of the area, but significantly absent were the two accused princes;

they were held at a seacoast village to the south of Berytus. Their presence might easily have led to an awakening of a renewed sympathy for them, on the part of the hundred and fifty people assembled; hence Herod deliberately kept them away.

Yet, despite the absence of the young men, when Herod arose to accuse them, it was with a ferocity that would not have been greater had he been charging them to their faces. He was violent, furious, unrestrainedly emotional. He rehearsed the various affronts, the many mockeries, the searing insults, all of which he said were more cruel than death itself. As if he were aware that the documents which he had gathered to read did not truly or adequately bear out his allegation that the princes had plotted to kill him, he took care that these documents not be examined by the nobility present; instead, he resorted to emphasizing those passages which were uncomplimentary to him, and these he read in a loud and exaggerating voice. Finally, he commiserated with himself in saying that if he won his case against his sons, his triumph would be a bitter one, for he would himself be the loser.

The first Roman to speak was Saturninus, the governor of Syria. He expressed himself as willing to condemn the princes, but not to death, for he himself had sons, and execution was too severe a penalty. But a second Roman official spoke, and he favored the death sentence. One by one the remaining persons who spoke advocated the execution of the sons. Finally the verdict of guilty was in. All that remained was for Herod to fix the time and manner of the execution.

Herod left Berytus for Tyre, taking his sons along with him. At Tyre he was met by Nicholas, who was returning from his sojourn in Rome. Asked for his opinion, Nicholas advised Herod that it was sufficient punishment to keep the young men imprisoned and in chains, and that it was neither necessary nor advantageous to execute them. Above all, advised Nicholas, Herod must so conduct himself, whether he executed the princes or not, as to make clear to everybody that he was not acting out of anger.

The party set sail for Caesarea. There they encountered a reflection of the terror that gripped all Judea, in the uncertainty whether or not Herod would indeed kill his sons. Broad as was the sympathy for the young princes, Judea was still a police state, and it was unsafe to risk expressing an opinion favorable to the princes and unfavorable to Herod. An old soldier, a man named Tiro, however, was moved by indignation beyond all prudence, and not only did he speak openly about justice being trampled, but he even presented himself to Herod, and accused him of being the tool of Salome, Pheroras, and Antipater, whose slanders Herod was believing. The army, Tiro added, was filled with officers indignant at the treatment of the princes, and some day the army would rise in revenge. Herod thereupon launched an investigation of the army and of the loyalty of its officers to him.

At that point one of Herod's barbers spoke to Herod, accusing Tiro of having appealed to him to slit Herod's throat when shaving him, for which the barber would be richly rewarded by Alexander. Tiro, and his son, and the barber were arrested and put to torture; the son offered to trade his safety and his father's for a confession which would give the names of the disloyal soldiers, and the offer was accepted. The confession by Tiro's son was a simple one, declaring that Tiro had some access to Herod, and had determined to kill the king. But promptly the populace lynched Tiro, the son, the barber, and some of the accused officers.

If there was some slight lingering chance that Herod might spare his sons, the revelation by Tiro of disaffection among his army officers destroyed the possibility. Herod now moved away from hesitation and delay, and he declined to listen to the advice that was offered him. He sent his sons to Sebaste, the city in which he had married their mother Mariamne, and there he had them strangled. Their bodies were buried at Alexandreion where Mariamne's father and most of her ancestors were buried.

For all his frequent condemnations of Herod, Josephus pauses to wonder whether or not some blame for the tragedy should not attach to the youths, who over a period of time drove their father to the extremes of hatred and managed to make him irreconcilably hostile. One wonders, moreover, that the princes, knowing that Herod could slay Mariamne, should have thought themselves immune. When Herod had slain Mariamne, she was his wife, but not his flesh and blood. Now having slain his own flesh and blood, he had created a precedent, to which there would be a sequel.

Notes

1. As noted above, p. 52, the name appears in modern writers in a variety of spellings: Nicolas, Nicolaus, and Nicholas.

2. The account in *The Jewish War*, which is much briefer, tells that Herod took only Alexander to Rome to appear before Augustus, and that the charge there was that Alexander had tried to poison Herod. On the principle that the account in *Antiquities* represents fuller research by Josephus, it is probably to be preferred.

3. At this juncture in *Antiquities*, Josephus provides a review of Herod's program of building. He mentions the completion at that time, 13 or 12, of the rebuilding of Samaria/Sebaste, and its dedication, and the magnificence of the accompanying events. The list of places includes a city, Antipatris, in the Plain of Sharon, named for Herod's father; a palace near Jericho, named for his mother, and a tower, as high as the famous tower of Pharos, which he named for his brother Phasael; he also built a city near Jericho named Phasaelis. On the island of Rhodes he had paid for

the building of a Pythian temple. Near Actium he helped in the construction of a town, founded by Caesar, called Nicopolis. He provided the broad, main street of Antioch in Syria with both polished pavement and colonnades. He gave gifts which enabled the Olympic games to regain a stature they had lost, so that he was recorded as permanent honorary president. Josephus next turns to the recording of decrees by Augustus and Agrippa, and by the proconsul Julius Antonius, which relate to the rights of the Jews in Asia Minor and Cyrene in North Africa. Josephus spends a paragraph explaining that he cites these documents so that his Gentile readers, for whom he has prepared his book, will know what the rights of the Jews are, and thereby be moved to "reconcile the other peoples to us, and to remove the bases for their hatred that takes root in thoughtless persons, both Jews and Gentiles." Josephus then turns to the matter of the Tomb of David.

4. Josephus digresses here to comment that Nicholas, whose history of Herod he regards as sycophantic, mentions the building of the memorial, but not the unfortunate entrance into the Tomb. Nicholas, he says, praises Herod excessively for his just acts, and zealously apologizes for the unjust ones; moreover, Nicholas was writing propaganda, not history.

5. Josephus presents us with some confusions. In *Antiquities* XVI, 228, Cypros is refused to Salome's son and married to Pheroras' son; in *Antiquities* XVIII, 130 ff. he tells us that Cypros was married to Salome's son, still another Antipater.

6. Josephus gives us an inconsistency in the sequence of events, and in the outcome. My word "persisted" is an effort to reconcile the difficulties in *The Jewish War* I, 527–528 and *Antiquities* XVI, 313–330.

7. To Jericho is also ascribed the questioning and torture of the cavalry officers and the commander of Alexandreion; there the populace stoned these accusers of Alexander and Aristobulus, and they needed to be forcibly restrained from lynching the brothers.

Part VI

瑞瑞瑞瑞瑞瑞瑞瑞瑞瑞瑞

The Final Horror

6-4 B.C.

6

The executions of Alexander and Aristobulus took place in 8 B.C., when Herod was about sixty-six. The cost to him of the decision and the action is beyond estimation, and the decline of both his mental and his physical capacities was hastened by the anguish caused by his fears and his anger, and now by his severity. He was unmistakably an old man. Yet he was still a resolute man, still the king by the grace of Rome, but in Judea disaffection had continued to grow.

Antipater's position was marked by uncertainties. The execution of his brothers might have benefited him, but did not; the populace did not share his father's opaqueness, but held Antipater to be the real culprit in the shameful end of his half-brothers. Even though he was his father's designated heir to the throne, Antipater understood that it was likely that the populace would reject him, and if to speak of the "populace" is to trespass into vagueness, then quite definitely there existed within the military establishment a marked aversion to him and to his hopes. Furthermore, his path to the throne, since he had no Maccabean blood, was possibly subject to obstruction by the two sons of Alexander, and the children of Aristobulus, three sons and two daughters. Glaphyra was no longer in Jerusalem, for Herod had sent her home, returning her dowry with her; but Bernice, the widow of Aristobulus, was around to exert her influence on behalf of her orphaned young princes.

To the accusation that he was responsible for the death

of his half-brothers, Antipater had the ready reply that all that he had sought was the safety of his father. In further pursuit of this safety, Antipater continued to denounce those people at the court whom he regarded as his enemies. Since his enemies were proliferating, he found it necessary also to win some friendships, especially of those who, in the event Herod continued to live for some time, might remember Antipater's plots and find opportunity to disavow him. Living on a generous allowance, Antipater used a large part of it for what he considered to be judicious gifts, designed to win such friends. Beyond the court and even beyond Judea, he carefully cultivated the Roman officials, especially the provincial rulers located in Syria. He sent munificent presents as far as to Rome. Within the court Antipater felt that he must win over Pheroras, and this he tried to do by ingratiating gifts and attentions. Also, he arranged for Bernice to marry an uncle, the brother of his mother, Doris, and he hoped thereby to win the affection of Bernice's mother, Salome. Somehow, it seems never to have occurred to Antipater that as the oldest son his cue was to do nothing but remain in the background and wait. Believing that he must bestir himself to some activity, he found that the more presents he bestowed, the more people disliked and distrusted him. Salome, however much she still yearned for Syllaeus, went through a third marriage, to a man named Alexis, and she was no more influenced to gratitude by Antipater's arrangement for the marriage of Bernice than she had been earlier to solicitude for Aristobulus; in neither case did her daughter's marriage impede Salome in her dislikes, or in her tendency to stir up family strife.

In addition to these marriages, which Antipater proposed and which Herod carried out, the failing king had his own ideas for betrothals calculated to ensure the welfare of his offspring. He planned for certain grandchildren to marry second cousins, and other grandchildren[1] to marry other near relatives. Antipater came to recognize that these marriages contemplated by Herod might well threaten his succession to the throne; if, for example, Archelaus of Cappadocia supported the cause of Alexander's son, then Pheroras might join with Archelaus in support for that son, betrothed to Pheroras' daughter. So Antipater began to manipulate a revision of the intended marriages, and in place of what Herod had originally proposed, Antipater himself married a daughter of the Antigonus whom Herod had ousted from the throne in 37; thereby Antipater could regard himself as strengthened by being married to a woman with Maccabean blood; his son married the daughter of Pheroras, whom Antipater could now reckon as a close ally.

These marriage arrangements, whether the original ones intended by Herod, or the revisions fostered by Antipater, marked Herod's awareness that he was in his declining years, and that he needed to settle his affairs before he passed on. His wives at this time numbered nine;[2] of his ten only one, Mariamne I, had died; the total number of his children is difficult to count accurately, but appears to be at least thirteen; his grandchildren defy counting, and, moreover, they often bore the names of the earlier generations and this circumstance adds to the confusion in distinguishing one from another.

On at least one occasion Herod assembled his entire family and the court, and spoke with deep emotion of his wish to provide for his grandchildren, even for those who through his own action were orphaned. Such concern for the third generation did not sit well with Antipater, the oldest child of the second generation, and hence his entry into the matter of the projected intra-family marriages.

Antipater's capacity to influence Herod in the matter of the marriages was a single symptom of the larger control that he had come to wield, for Herod had turned over more and more authority to him, and Josephus alludes to him as co-ruler with Herod. The people of the court had reason to be fearful of Antipater's malice, and they succumbed to his intimidation. Since Pheroras was persuaded that Herod's throne was already destined for Antipater, he found it useful to collaborate with his nephew, and Antipater found, reciprocally, that his uncle was a usable ally. The feminine maneuverings went on apace. Pheroras' despised wife, who had once been a slave, vented her spleen on her husband's relatives, and they on her; and Salome was around to witness all the maneuvers and hear all the slanders, and to give reports to Herod. So complex were these currents of female slander that in self-defense the women found it useful to seem to quarrel openly with their real allies, lest otherwise the incipient alliances come to the ears of Herod and alarm him.

All this feminine intrigue was disconcerting to Herod, and he needed a ready culprit. He found her, or rather he rediscovered her, in Pheroras' wife, whose marriage to Pheroras he had earlier opposed. Now a basis, or else a pretext, presented itself. Among the Pharisees there was a rising tide of opposition to Herod, occasioned by a reversal of a policy of Herod's. Previously Herod had exempted some Pharisees and the Essenes from a required oath of loyalty to Caesar and to him; now he required the oath at least of the Pharisees,[3] but many refused to take it. Herod imposed a fine on some group of them—Josephus counts this group as numbering over six thousand—but Pheroras' wife intervened and paid the fine. We are given no explanation about the circumstances or about the motivation for this intervention. The woman's beneficiaries repaid her kindness by informing her of the good tidings for the future, that Herod and his descendants would lose the throne, and the royal power would move to her and to her descendants. Since some employees of the court were Pharisees who gossiped about the prediction, and since privacy and secrecy were unknown, a version of the prophecy reached Salome. She reported to Herod that a Pharisaic plot was in the making, that it reached into the court, and that it was stimulated by Pheroras' wife. Promptly a round of executions took place,[4] and promptly Herod moved against Pheroras' wife. He summoned her to a trial, charging her with insulting his own daughters, with subsidizing the Pharisees to oppose him, and with alienating Pheroras from him through bewitching him with drugs. He ended his list of the woman's trespasses with the demand that Pheroras choose between him and divorcing the woman.

Pheroras did not hesitate; he replied that he would sooner die than be without either his brother or his wife, but that he would not divorce the woman.

Herod had made an empty threat—as Pheroras quite probably knew—since Herod was uniformly reluctant, even averse to punishing his family. So, all that ensued was that Herod forbade Antipater and Doris any contact with Pheroras and his wife. Antipater, however, continued to hold secret meetings with his uncle, but, fearful that Salome would learn about these and report them to Herod, he thought it wise to be away from the court for a time. He therefore wrote to his friends at Rome, and, at his request, they addressed a letter to him, urging him to visit Rome. If reason is sought for Antipater's sudden and surprising need to be away from the palace, it may lie in the rumors which arose that he and the wife of Pheroras were intimate, and that his mother, Doris, had helped to arrange the intimacy, and that Pheroras was aware of the rumors. The proposed trip to Rome by Antipater suited Herod completely, for it could be a means of strengthening Herod's weakened ties with Rome. Not only did he pro-

vide an expensive retinue for his son, but he sent on to
Rome his will, which named Antipater his successor to the
throne. Another son, the one named Herod, borne to him
by Mariamne II, was designated in the same will to be the
successor, in the event that Antipater predeceased the
father. We know little about Antipater's stay in Rome,
except that he encountered there the Nabatean Syllaeus,
who was still busy defending himself against allegations
made by King Aretas of Nabatea, and even busier with
new, but unsuccessful allegations against Herod.

With Antipater away in Rome, Herod found no domestic interference with his wish to persuade Pheroras to
divorce his wife, but Pheroras remained stubborn. In a
pique Herod sent him and his wife away from the palace,
ordering Pheroras to return to his tetrarchy in the Perea.
Pheroras went reluctantly, and angrily, vowing that he
would never return to Jerusalem so long as Herod lived.
This vow as apparently made in 5 B.C., at a time when
Herod took sick and was not expected to recover, and he
wanted to discuss affairs of state with his brother. But
recover Herod did and now it was Pheroras who took
sick. Herod, loyal as always to his family, journeyed to
Perea to wait on his brother personally. After a few days
Pheroras died; the report spread that Herod had poisoned
him, unquestionably a bit of malicious and untrue gossip.
Pheroras' body was brought to Jerusalem, and Herod there
proclaimed a period of national mourning, and he provided
a magnificent funeral.

The death of Pheroras, through a curious chain of circumstances, led to a tangle of events of consequence. After
the funeral, certain freedmen, that is, slaves whom Pheroras had set free, came to Herod with the tale that Pheroras had indeed died of poison. They said, furthermore,
that the day before Pheroras had fallen ill, he had dined
with his wife, and that his death had resulted from a drug

served to him in some unusual concoction. They had
learned, moreover, that two days earlier the drug had been
purchased from a Nabatean woman who was expert at
making aphrodisiacs, for which Pheroras' wife was a cus-
tomer, and wished to have the aphrodisiac for her aging
husband.

So a new set of suspicions arose for Herod, and he began
to inquire into the matter of the drug with utmost vigor,
and with his usual instrument, torture. He ordered the
slaves of Pheroras' wife and also the slaves of her sister
and mother to be brought before him. Among the slaves
were some who were unable to withstand the pain, and a
round of confessions began, in the midst of which one of
the slaves exclaimed, "May God, governor of earth and
heaven, punish the cause of our miseries, Antipater's
mother." It was a strange and surprising ejaculation, and
Herod needed now to extend his investigation to his wife
Doris. The information came to light that it was the custom
of Doris to visit with the women of Pheroras' household,
that is, the wife, her sister, and her mother; moreover,
quite often Antipater and Pheroras had spent the night
carousing with the three women. As Herod persisted in his
inquiry, he discovered that the slaves of Pheroras' household knew the substance of confidences which Herod had
entrusted only to Antipater. Quickly Herod suspected that
there was a plot against him in which Antipater and Pheroras had been united. He questioned the slaves even further. From them he learned that Antipater had spoken of
his hatred for his father, that Antipater had lamented to
Doris that Herod was stretching out his life so long that
Antipater would be an old man before he came to the
throne, that his half-brothers and their children were
being groomed for the throne along with him, so that he
had no secure hope to succeed to the royal power. Moreover, Antipater had said that Herod was necessarily fully

senile if he supposed that Antipater would let any of the family remain alive. As Herod analyzed matters, it was evident that Doris, a commoner, rejected by Herod when he had married Mariamne I, had the fixed intention that her son, and not the son of some other wife, should gain the throne. Moreover, it was she, according to the slaves of Pheroras, who was a central figure in all the wickedness. Herod threw her out of the court, penniless.

But there was more that came to light. The double departure, that of Antipater to Rome and Pheroras to Perea, was no accident, but an arrangement mutually agreed upon between them, to foil whatever evil designs Herod might have against them. Indeed, Pheroras was preparing to flee to Herod's enemies, the Nabateans.

But there was even more for Herod to learn: Antipater had secured, through a Samaritan agent, a drug which he had sent to Pheroras, and with which Pheroras could poison Herod. Pheroras had turned the drug over to his wife for safekeeping, and this was the drug that she had put into Pheroras' food. Pheroras' wife was sent for, and she was confronted with the accusation, the implication being that it was her affair with Antipater which had prompted her to murder her husband. The woman was tortured until she agreed to bring the remainder of the poison to Herod. On her way to fetch the poison she threw herself from the roof of one of the buildings. Unhappily for Antipater, the woman did not die. While she was recovering from her injuries, Herod offered her immunity from punishment in return for a full confession. She accepted the offer. Her confession confirmed what Herod had by now come to expect. She told Herod that Pheroras had confided in her before his death that he had been mistaken about Herod's true feelings for him; Pheroras had been led to believe by Antipater that Herod hated him, and that was why he had acquiesced in the plot to poison Herod. But when the king had solicitously visited him and had nursed him, Pheroras had seen the truth. He had told her to bring the poison to him and to burn it in his presence. This she had done, but she had kept a little of it, unburnt, to use on herself if, after her husband's death, the king might decide to put her to torture. At these words she brought out the poison in its box. The Samaritan agent was arrested and put to the torture, and his statement agreed with that of Pheroras' wife.

So Doris was involved in the plot, and Antipater was especially involved. In the course of the elaborate inquiry it turned out that Mariamne II was acquainted with the plots of Antipater, and that she had acquiesced in concealing them from Herod. The king promptly divorced her, cut the name of the son[5] she had borne him out of his will, and deposed her father from his office as high priest. It was as if all the family were plotting against him, their benefactor.

Antipater was, meanwhile, relatively safe in Rome, and uninformed of the sudden turn of events. He was busy plotting, but to his misfortune, two of his machinations came to light. The first was disclosed when a freedman of Antipater's, a certain Bathyllus, arrived in Jerusalem from Rome. Promptly arrested and put to the torture, Bathyllus confessed that he had brought with him a second drug which he was supposed to give to Doris and Pheroras (of whose death Bathyllus was not yet aware), this in case that the first poison designed for Herod did not do its work. Second, Bathyllus admitted that he had brought with him letters from Rome with accusations prompted by Antipater against two half-brothers, Archelaus the son by Malthake, and Philip the son by Cleopatra of Jerusalem, to the effect that these princes were continually slandering their father as the murderer of Alexander and Aristobulus. This was Antipater's way of being rid of his brothers.

But despite the way in which reports and rumors sped throughout the world of royalty, Antipater knew only one item of the many events of the seven months which elapsed since he had set forth for Rome, the ousting of his mother from the palace. We do not know why he chose at this time to return to Judea; perhaps it was to intercede on behalf of his mother. Or perhaps he simply wanted to be on hand to do whatever it would be judicious for him to do. Respecting Doris' banishment from court, he wrote to Herod from Rome that he was setting out soon. Herod feared that Antipater might learn something of what had gone on, and abstain from returning so as to escape apprehension; he replied to Antipater in warm and affectionate terms, even to the point of suggesting that by an early return, Antipater might possibly persuade him to drop the complaints against Doris. Antipater left Rome before Herod's letter reached him.

While at Tarentum, en route home, Antipater learned about the death of Pheroras. He became frightened that the matter of the poison might come to light, but in the midst of his anxiety the affectionate letter from Herod reached him, and it gave him the necessary reassurance. Yet he, as Herod's son, was, like his father, readily susceptible to suspicion, and as he neared Asia, he began to wonder what might lie ahead of him. With him were hangers-on who presumed to advise him, some that he stay away from Judea until he could learn exactly what was going on, and others that he return as promptly as possible and by his presence nullify anything untoward that might have arisen.

Antipater disembarked at the port of Caesarea. When he had sailed for Rome, he had been given a tumultuous and adoring send-off; on his return, there was no one to greet him. All Judea knew about the danger in which he stood; only Antipater was in ignorance.

If the ignominy of no reception at his disembarkation alerted him to some peril, he was no longer able to retreat, and he had no choice but to rely upon his proven tools of guile and brazenness. He made his way to Jerusalem, to the palace, and to the presence of Herod, hoping or even expecting to be embraced as the returning favorite son. Instead, Herod pushed him away, and denounced him to his face as a parricide, and announced to him that the next day he would stand trial before Varus, the Roman legate to Syria, then in Jerusalem at Herod's request so as to advise the king. Understandably agitated, Antipater sought out his wife[6] and his mother, and from them he learned what his situation was and what an ordeal he faced. He learned also of a letter, which had never reached him, prepared by Doris and sent on to him to Rome, with the advice not to return to Judea unless he had the support of Caesar.

The council was held the very next day, in the presence of Varus and of Herod's family, including Salome. Immediately on entering the council chamber, Antipater prostrated himself before Herod, begging not to be condemned until he could speak and establish his innocence. Herod was too full of hatred, too sick physically, too sick of his family, too despondent to be willing to listen. He embarked on a recital of the pitiable wrongs he had suffered, of the misery of having begotten sons who brought misfortune upon him, and of the bitterness of reaching his old age and needing to face the rascality of an Antipater. He heaped on the prince the real responsibility for the death of Alexander and Aristobulus; he reminded Antipater of having been on the verge of resigning the kingship a while before in Antipater's favor; he reminded those present that he had publicly nominated him in his will as his successor. To Varus he turned with the advice to beware of Antipater's hypocritical pleading, of his lamentations, and of his constant falseness in the face of Herod's full trust of him. Then emotion prevented Herod from speaking any further. Nicholas of Damascus was asked to complete Herod's unfinished denunciation, and it was he who set before the assembly the allegations and the evidence, with allusions to adulteries, carousings, and poisonous drugs.

Then it was the turn of Antipater. He spoke, first of all, of all the honors which Herod had heaped on him, honors which would never have come his way if he had not merited them through his virtuous obedience and honorable treatment of his father. Having received these honors, and having witnessed the fate of his two brothers who plotted against the king, he asked if it was credible that he would jeopardize the high status which he enjoyed, virtually as co-regent, to grasp what was already so nearly his. As for his conduct in Rome, he had with him, so he said, letters from Caesar commending his behavior in the capital, and these surely merited reliance, in place of the slanders which came out of the mouths of people put to torture. He admitted that he stood condemned before his father—he piously mentioned that he stood condemned before God too—but he nevertheless entreated for the privilege of undergoing torture and attendant interrogation. This speech of Antipater made an impact on everyone present, except Herod; the king alone remained dry eyed.[7]

Varus then begin to cross-examine Antipater, but the young man did little more than continue to invoke God's guidance. Varus thereupon ordered that the tiny remainder of the drug, once in the possession of Pheroras' wife, be brought in. There was present a prisoner under sentence of death; he was ordered to taste the drug. He did so, and promptly died. To Varus, this incident was the equivalent to definite proof of the allegations, so he arose and ended the session. He conferred briefly with Herod, and then departed for Syria; ultimately he sent from there a report to Caesar. After Varus had left, Herod ordered Antipater put in chains, and he prepared a report to Caesar, transmitted both by letter and by personal emissary.

Antipater stood convicted, and Herod had to determine the punishment. Delay was inescapable, for Herod needed to receive some word from Caesar, and, above all, he had to make up his own mind. Whatever mercy he might have shown Antipater became dissipated in the ensuing days, because of the interception of two letters written in Rome. The first letter was a brief note, purportedly by Antipater, addressed to his agent who had procured the poison; the point of this note was to advice this agent that still another letter was on the way. The servant of Antipater's agent who was openly carrying the first letter was searched, and the second letter was found sewn in the inside of his tunic. This second letter was from a woman named Acme, the maid of the Empress Livia (later known as Empress Julia), and was addressed to Antipater. It was brief and to the point, reporting that some assigned task had been accomplished. That task, it developed from questioning, was the forging of letters to incriminate Salome, charging her with transmission to Livia of accusations against Herod. That is to say, Acme's brief note assured Antipater that the letters[8] supposedly by Salome had been prepared.

Salome immediately began to importune Herod to do away with Antipater. The king, however, flirted with the notion of sending Antipater to Rome to undergo there a Roman trial; on second thought, he realized that to send Antipater away, even in chains, was to invite him to escape. He therefore continued to bide his time, and sent a new batch of letters to Rome, describing all that had happened. But Herod, already sickly, now took seriously ill, and

it was uncertain that he would survive. He therefore made
a new will; with all his distrust of Antipater, he nevertheless believed Antipater's calumnies against his two sons,
Archelaus and Philip, conveyed in the letters brought by
Bathyllus, p. 249, so that he designated Antipas, his son
by Malthake, as the heir to the throne. He also made pro-
vision for gifts to Caesar and to the empress, Livia. He
recorded an enormous sum of money to go to Salome, and
provided generously for other members of his family.

But, fearful of dying, he became uncontrolled in his
anger and unrestrained in his harshness, especially when the
rumors of the popular detestation of him spread through
the palace. His illness is well described by Josephus,[9] and
the report on both its repugnance and its acute pain
filtered through the land, leading to the conviction that
the king was undergoing a divine visitation for his misdeeds in general, and for the violation of Jewish laws in
particular.

The most prominent of these violations was a visible
one, the erection over the great gate of the Temple of a
huge golden eagle, this a clear trespass of the Jewish
aversion to the representation in the arts of a living being,
for such a representation was kindred to idolatry, and
especially so in view of the prominence of the eagle in
Roman temples and on the standards of Roman troops.
Since the report was widespread that Herod was dying,
the occasion was ripe for an uprising. The eagle, representing both the power of Herod and also, remotely, the god
Zeus, the chief of the Greek pantheon, served as the focus
for an insurrection. Two sages, Judas the son of Sep-
phoraeus (also spelled Sariphaeus), and Matthias son of
Margalus, used the occasion of their lectures on Scripture
to young men to denounce the presence of the eagle on the
Temple, and to stir the students to remove and destroy it.
Some young followers of the two sages chose a midday

for their purpose. First they climbed to the roof of the
Temple and then, letting themselves down by cords, they
began to chop away at the eagle. An army official, possibly one of those assigned to the Temple, heard what was
going on; he brought a group of soldiers with him, and
these arrested some forty young men and brought them
before Herod. The king asked, "Who ordered you to do
this?" The answer came, "The Law of our fathers." He
reminded them that they stood on the verge of death, and
that they were mistaken to be defiant and even exultant.
"We shall enjoy even greater happiness after death."

This open insurrection against him acted not further to
weaken the ailing Herod, but, to the contrary, the need
to defend his throne and retain his power enabled him to
find unexpected resources of strength. He ordered the
young men bound, but rather than court more uprisings in
Jerusalem, he sent them to Jericho, to try them there. He
himself went to Jericho, not only for the trial, but to seek
the relief provided by the natural baths in the vicinity, at
a place named Callirhoe, close to the northeast shore of the
Dead Sea. He almost perished during one of the baths,
when his physicians, to raise his body temperature, had
him lowered into a bath of heated oil.

The trial of the young men took place in the amphitheater
at Jericho. Herod appeared before the assembly lying on a
couch. Weakened as he was, he had enough strength to
boast of his adornment of the Temple, in contrast to its
neglect by the vaunted Maccabeans, and then to rage and
rail at the indignity to him of the young men in choosing
broad daylight to tear down the eagle he had had erected.
It was not only an insult, it was sacrilege. He then meted
out the punishments, mild in the case of the young men, but
death to the two sages; as for the incumbent high priest,
Herod held him partly responsible and deposed him, ap-
pointing instead a brother of Mariamne II.[10] That night

there was an eclipse of the moon; modern astronomy is thereby able to date the event in Jericho, as March 13, 4 B.C.

But the chief item still before Herod was the matter of Antipater. Now, at last, the word for which he had been waiting reached him, that Rome approved of whatever punishment, expulsion or execution, he chose for Antipater. On the one hand, this word from Rome, confirming his authority, strengthened Herod; on the other hand, the need to punish his son further dispirited him. Having asked for Rome's permission, however, he could scarcely now refrain from doing something. What Herod wanted most was to evade the responsibility of doing anything. Once before, on the occasion when he had fled Jerusalem in 40, he had thought of suicide; now, while paring an apple, he suddenly raised the sharp knife as if to stab himself. A relative who was there observed the act, rushed to Herod, seized the weakened right arm and prevented Herod's death. The news of the incident promptly made the rounds, and it even penetrated to where Antipater lay bound.

Again, the wise course for the young prince was to do nothing. But Antipater, on learning of Herod's suicide attempt, appealed to his jailer to release him, and he promised huge gifts, both then and in the future, when he would ascend the throne. But inevitably a report of Antipater's promises came from the head jailer to the dying king. Herod mustered enough strength to shout out that Antipater should be immediately executed. The sentence was quickly carried out; Antipater was buried without ceremony.

Once again Herod changed his will. Now he left the region of Galilee and Perea as a tetrarchy to his son Antipas; the regions east of the Sea of Galilee he left as a

stop

tetrarchy to his son Philip; he bequeathed money and three towns to Salome; and the throne of Judea he left to his son Archelaus.

He died five days after Antipater.

Archelaus provided a rich and extremely impressive funeral, and Herod was buried in full pomp at Herodeion.

Notes

1. Alexander's son was betrothed to the daughter of Pheroras; the son of Aristobulus was betrothed to a daughter of Antipater; a daughter of Aristobulus was betrothed to a son of Antipater; the other daughter of Antipater was betrothed to Herod's own son by Mariamne II, also named Herod.

2. Two are not known by name. These we know: Doris, Antipater's mother; Mariamne I; Malthake, a Samaritan woman, who had borne him two sons, Antipas and Archelaus, and a daughter, Olympia; Cleopatra, a Jerusalem woman, who had borne two sons, Herod and Philip; these four sons were all brought up in Rome. Still other wives were named Pallas, Phaedra, Elpis, and Mariamne II.

3. In context Josephus attributes the power of foreseeing the future to the Pharisees, a capacity he elsewhere attributes to the Essenes; some scholars, accordingly, see the word "Pharisees" here as a secretary's blunder and prefer to read "Essenes."

4. Among those executed was a eunuch named Bagoas, who somehow expected that he would usher in a king—possibly the Messiah—over all the people, and that the king would give Bagoas the ability to marry and to beget children of his own. The passage is most puzzling, especially to medically minded scholars. The motif of a eunuch begetting children may be derived from Isaiah, 56: 1–5.

5. This son is known in Josephus as Herod, but in Mark 6:17 the name is given as Philip. He was the first husband of Herodias who, improperly, went on to marry Herod Antipas. Salome, who danced for the head of John the Baptist on a tray, was the daughter of this disowned Herod-Philip and Herodias.

6. Her name is unknown; she was the daughter of the Mac-

cabean Antigonus who had reigned from 40–37 before Herod became king.

7. In *The Jewish War*, the sequence of events is given as Herod's accusation and then the signal to Nicholas to begin; then Antipater interrupts with his plea; and thereafter Nicholas gives the bill of particulars. I have followed the sequence given in *Antiquities*.

8. The two accounts in Josephus about the letters so diverge as to yield a general confusion from which, however, one can extract the point that Antipater was involved in forging letters designed to injure Salome.

9. His illness is described as an ulceration of the bowels, and intestinal pains of acute nature, and a moist suppuration of his feet; moreover, his scrotum had become gangrenous and maggoty; his breath was most unpleasant; and he underwent frequent convulsions in his limbs, and his whole body itched. Some modern medical men have diagnosed his illness as arteriosclerosis, accompanied by the deterioration of the heart and of the kidney functions, leading to dropsy. They explain that the bodily poisons remained unexcreted and accumulated in the blood; sharp and constant abdominal pains and even ulceration of the bowels and diarrhea set in; the scrotum became distended and gangrenous, and a lesion there could well become infested with maggots. Other medical men point to both paranoia and to a combination of cirrhosis of the liver and of portal hypertension, and diabetes.

10. In *Antiquities* XVII, 164–167, Josephus recounts a minor incident relating to the deposed high priest. On the eve of the Day of Atonement, this high priest had had an erotic dream and an accompanying seminal emission, thereby disqualifying him from the responsibilities of the sacred day and necessitating the temporary appointment of a substitute high priest. The incident is also mentioned in rabbinic literature (Tosefta Yoma I, 4; Yerushalmi: Yoma I, 1 p. 38d, Megillah I, 12, p. 72a; Babli: Yoma 12b, Horayot 12b). In itself relatively insignificant, it illustrates the way in which from time to time data in Josephus and in the rabbinic literature confirm each other.

Part VII

ⴰⴰⴰⴰⴰⴰⴰⴰⴰⴰⴰⴰ

In Lieu of Eulogy

7

Herod was hated, and he was cruel.

He was also maligned. Such was the case, for example, when there was attributed to him descent from an ancestor who was a male prostitute in a pagan temple of the Philistines at Ascalon. Such, too, is the case in the account of Josephus that just prior to his death, Herod assembled Jewish notables from all over the land, gathered them in the hippodrome at Jericho, and gave orders through Salome that at his death, his soldiers should slaughter all the important people assembled there, thereby to ensure that a period of mourning by the populace would follow his death.[1]

Such, too, is the case in the passage in rabbinic literature which tells us that Mariamne I preferred death to marrying Herod—as if the marriage did not take place!—and that after her death Herod preserved her body in honey for a period of seven years; the tale then diverges into two opinions, whether or not he committed necrophilia upon her.

Such, too, is the case in the Gospel according to Matthew, which attributes the birth of Jesus to the last year of the reign of Herod. It relates that Herod, informed that a child was born who was to become king of the Jews, gave orders to kill all male babies (just as Pharaoh had ordered the slaughter of Hebrew children in the time of Moses). Joseph, the father of Jesus, thereupon fled to Egypt with the infant Jesus, and escaped Herod's slaughter. Not a word of this is in Josephus.[2]

None of these motifs is historical; they are simply extensions of the animosity which the ancients felt for Herod, and which have prevented modern historians from a balanced appraisal.

That Herod was guilty of needless killing is beyond challenge. But, as scholars have pointed out, these killings were never without some direct relation to events and crises; there is no single incident recorded in Josephus which would represent mere wanton, unrelated, and unmotivated killing. To clarify this point is in no sense to exonerate Herod of cruelty or to condone his actions, but only to describe the framework of his actions so that the man Herod may be comprehensible.

Ambition led Herod to seek a throne not his, and he attained it. Having attained it, he needed to retain it; to retain it, he needed to be ruthless, merciless, and despotic.

The question, however, which arises is the matter of his disregard of all moral restraints. Clearly neither his almost psychotic toleration of the misdeeds of his family and his necessary obsequiousness to Rome are not to be classified as moral restraints. The question, rather, is that as a legatee of Scripture, and as a person born in and exposed to the high standards and imjunctions of the Jewish religion, why did neither of these enter into Herod's ken at all? The easy answer, of course, is that, like all despotic personalities, he simply disregarded what was inconvenient, and further, that he was more a Greek than a Jew.

But the question persists. Granted that Herod wished to be a power all to himself, like other client-kings, and granted that he was no different, but only more extreme than other minor Hellenistic kings, why did not the religious restraints exert a brake on him and inhibit him? The answer may possibly lie in the relative weakness at the time of these restraints, just as religious restraints in other ages have usually had little or no force against the will or the inner compulsion of the highly placed. But beyond all that, perhaps we should see in the acts of Herod the universal tendencies in men who both realize ambitions and are also victims of insecurities and suspicions. The particular age, and the consequences of overt actions, can result in different forms of sequels in such men. For example, even if we take with adequate grains of salt the "muckraking" accounts of business tycoons in the past century in the unfolding industrialism and capitalistic enterprises, we can see that what is different between a political dictator and an industrial dictator is the form of the self-preservation and the nullification of the rival, for what remains constant in those who have risen to great heights is their power, and their ceaseless and unallayable suspicion.

There is such a thing as the malaise of the great executive, whether he be a king, an industrial leader, or a powerful person in a progressive, socially approved endeavor. Executive power is never absolute, or at least never unremittingly absolute, for always some higher power is latent, and can come to be near at hand. In the case of Herod, the higher power was Augustus Caesar. In the case of a tycoon, it is a Board of Directors. In the case of a political leader, it is some sort of praesidium. The very same ambition which has brought one person to the executive position animates a dozen others who wish either to succeed to the executive's power or to supplant him. Executive insecurity may at times be stifled, or it may momentarily disappear, but it is an inevitable omnipresent factor in all levels and forms of society where some form of organization exists and one man or woman is the king, or the president, or the governor, or the mayor, or the chairman, or the general, or the admiral, or the dean, or the superintendent.

The restraints, whether of religion or of law, may obstruct the executive from particular action which he would like to take; he may sublimate his action in accordance with accepted social demands or with his knowledge of the direct consequences. These restraints may determine the form of what he adopts for self-protection and for retaliation, but the executive personality necessarily faces the moments in which he sees the fruits of his ambition and achievement challenged, and his power desired by others, and, hence, self-protection and retaliation become dispositions inherent in the executive personality.

In relatively civilized segments of society, especially in western countries where the slogan has been government by laws, not by men, the executive personality feels impelled to sublimate or to cover up the potential cruelty arising from the executive malaise; but the executive malaise is always present.

What is striking about Herod, in this light, is how primitive he was, and that he neither sublimated nor covered up the cruelties concomitant with his high position, his insecurities, and his need to protect himself. He did what in more civilized persons is done with genteelness and subtlety. Whereas others in roughly comparable settings ruined their foes either financially or in their social standing, Herod simply killed. He did not content himself with the dream of killing, or accept the disgracing of his foe as a requisite substitute for the killing; he simply proceeded to kill.

The veneer of civilization varies in its thickness in different ages. Sometimes it even defies stripping off. In the case of Herod, however, the veneer was a thin one, for thinness was the characteristic of the restraints of the "client-kings." The difference between Herod and other minor kings of his time was that of degree, not of kind. In the case of Herod, the slayings of Mariamne I, of Alexander and Aristobulus, and of Antipater, fraught as we have seen with hesitation and deferment and inner anguish, represent

only the extreme in punitiveness, and not a substantial difference. If one were to argue, as the cliché has it, that a
difference in degree can amount to a difference in kind,
then one needs to weigh Herod in the light of a Mark
Antony, a Cleopatra, a Brutus, to discern the pattern of
the times and to conclude that in only one respect was
Herod different. It was not in his slaying of Hyrcanus or
of Mariamne; the chief point of difference was in his slaying of his three children.

Let it be conceded that these children merited some punishment. We saw the counsel of Nicholas of Damascus to
Herod to use some clemency, to reduce the punishments.
We saw, too, the possibility that paranoia on Herod's part
rather than simple and unmistakable guilt blurs the consideration of the misdeeds of the children. The question
might therefore be put in this way: Granted that Herod
had to punish, did the punishment have to be slaughter?

The reluctant answer needs to be that for a human being
like Herod the slaughter was a necessity. It was the price
a primitive man like Herod had to pay for rising to the
heights to which he ascended and for remaining at those
heights. Someone else might have had a choice of alternatives, but Herod had no such choice simply for the reason
that he was Herod. He acted as he did because, being
Herod, he had to. It was this kind of compulsiveness in him
which his children misunderstood, for unless we understand them as misunderstanding him, we need to attribute
a colossal stupidity to their acts of defiance and their resort to plots. Herod was as excessively permissive with his
family as he was tyrannical with the populace, but his
family confused excessive permissiveness with the total
absence of limits, and they crossed the limits.

Even the maligners of Herod attribute great abilities to
him. One need not admire the particular abilities he dis-

played. One need only recall that, dependent on Rome, detested by the populace, and harassed by intrigue in the palace, he managed to retain his throne for thirty-three years, and to bequeath it to his children. They had neither his abilities, nor his skill in retaining the throne, and some grandchildren were virtually degenerates.[3]

Yet it must be clear that for all the pathos that one might possibly recurrently associate with Herod, he was a thoroughly wicked man. His special eminence in wickedness is, to be sure, accidental, namely, the circumstance that the Gospel according to Matthew brings him into relationship with Jesus, and as a consequence Herod receives more attention in the western world than he really deserves. Thoroughly wicked, he is only a minor name in a list of the men of wickedness who have dotted the history of Europe from the ascendancy of Rome until our own days.

Herod is the recurrent figure who, in the guise of a Napoleon, or a Mussolini, periodically arises. We hold such people properly in scorn, but we are often tempted to ridicule the diabolic abilities that they possess and put to use. All too often a powerless or complacent populace consents to the seizure of power by such men, as if they are impossible to resist. It is only in extremely civilized states that the mores or the laws manage to impede the rise of such persons to power, but even high civilizations, such as that of Germany, have succumbed to such a person.

One wonders if mankind will ever manage to forge the machinery through which emergence of a Herod can be prevented. There are reasons to suppose that humanity will always experience some new Herod, that it is inevitable that as Herods arose in the past, so they will arise in the future.

Yet, on the other hand, unchanged as man is and apparently is destined to remain, mankind is susceptible of

learning by bitter experience. There is something of Herod
in almost all of us, and if we are intelligent enough to
recognize the universality of the lust for power among men
and man's inherent capacities for cruelty, perhaps we may
progressively learn the means by which to prevent dictators
from seizing power.

To Lord Acton is credited the statement that power
corrupts, and absolute power corrupts absolutely. If Herod
teaches us anything, it is that the fear of the loss of power
is the mightiest corrupter of all.

Notes

1. The rabbinic work Megillat Ta'anit (in *Hebrew Union
College Annual*, VIII–IX, p. 343; see also pp. 271–272) tells that
Herod died on Shebat 1, and therefore that date is a holiday, and
fasting prohibited.

2. See, as a typical judgment of modern scholars, Walter E.
Bundy, *Jesus and the First Three Gospels* (Harvard Press, Cam-
bridge, 1955), p. 34, opinion that the matter is "a literary fabrica-
tion based on his [Herod's] known cruelty and barbarism."

3. After Herod's death, Archelaus, Antipas, and Philip went to
Rome to await Augustus's confirmation of the details of Herod's
will, and there to counter a Jewish deputation which petitioned
that none of the children be given royal authority. Augustus
nevertheless confirmed the will, so that Archelaus became "ethnarch," rather than king, of Judea. Herod Antipas became the
tetrarch of Galilee and the Perea, and Philip the tetrarch of
Batanea, Trachonitis, and Auranitis.

Philip, a just and relatively mild ruler, reigned until A.D. 34.

Archelaus, at one time married to still another Mariamne,
divorced her in order to marry Glaphyra of Cappadocia, the
widow of his executed brother Alexander; in between, she had
married King Juda of Mauretania. Like Herod, Archelaus was a
great builder, and a ruthlessly cruel ruler. In A.D. 6, a deputation
from Judea appeared at Rome to lay charges of misrule against

Archelaus, and as a result Archelaus was deposed. Judea thereafter was ruled by a succession of Roman officials, "procurators," among whom was Pontius Pilate, whose term encompassed 26–36.

Antipas, called in the Gospels "Herod," and alluded to as "that fox" in Luke 13:32, is the Herod who beheaded John the Baptist. He ultimately lost his tetrarchy, possibly through the ambitions of his second wife, Herodias. She was a daughter of the executed Aristobulus. She nagged Antipater into demanding a title higher than tetrarch, and the Romans replied by deposing him, in 39.

The emperor, Caligula, replaced the procurators of Judea with Herod Agrippa, the son of Aristobulus, as king of Judea in 38; he died in 44, leaving three daughters and a son, also named Agrippa. Roman procurators again ruled Judea, until 66. With one of his sisters, Bernice, Agrippa II seems to have had incestuous relations, this in intervals between her marriages; a second sister, Drusilla, divorced her Gentile husband, King Azizus of Emesa, and married the Roman procurator Felix. Agrippa II rose to the Judean throne in a somewhat unclear way; in the Jewish revolt against Rome in 66–70, he remained loyal to Rome, to the extent of keeping close company with Titus, who conquered Jerusalem in 70. His sister Bernice became the mistress of Titus in Judea; in 75, she went to Rome with Agrippa, and for a while resumed her relations with Titus. Agrippa faded from the scene in the ensuing years, and with his death, perhaps in 100 or shortly thereafter, the dynasty of Herod came to an end.

To the Scholar

The field of my chief interest is the first Christian century, both in Judaism and in Christianity but, of course, the antecedents and the sequels necessarily demand attention and possess a relevancy. My primary preoccupation is the history of religious ideas, as these are found in intertestamental literature, the New Testament, and rabbinic writings, and only secondarily in the political history, but the political and social history cannot be brushed aside. Like many a professional scholar I plan some day to bring together the various threads of my research, and toward that end have been accumulating notes for a work with the tentative title, *The First Christian Century in Judaism and Christianity: Certainties, Uncertainties, and Obscurities*.

My focus on Herod became particular when the editors of the *Interpreter's Dictionary of the Bible* invited me to prepare a number of articles, including one on the dynasty of Herod. Toward the latter end, I prepared a manuscript which, as is the case in such endeavors, was much too long for the available space. The excisions necessary to reduce the manuscript to the appropriate size prompted me to think of preparing a book on Herod, and the present manuscript is indirectly the result.

The interpretation offered here differs in some essential elements from those available elsewhere, but most essentially in what the subtitle, "Profile of a Tyrant," implies. Three usual formulations have seemed to me inappropriate. The first such is typified in Joseph Klausner, *Historia Yisre'elit*, which is marked by so emotional a hatred of Herod as a usurping alien that the author does no justice to Herod, and he is blind to the misdeeds of the Maccabeans. A second is found in Hugo Willrich, *Das Haus des Herodes zwischen Jerusalem und Rom*, which is pro-Herod in the sense of ascribing Herod's difficulties to his futile efforts to bring the recalcitrant Jews to conform to the needs and benefits of the Roman empire. The third is the understandable but extravagant aspersion of Herod in Christian lore.

One might possibly add a fourth, the role of Herod in imaginative works such as the drama by Stephen Philip, *Herod* (1900), or Jacob S. Minkin, *Herod, King of the Jews* (1936), or William J. Gross, *Herod the Great* (1962). There are virtues in these writings, even though literary creativity rather than reliability characterizes them.

A full-scale study of Herod was in my judgment a great desideratum at the time I prepared the article on the dynasty, and I contemplated such a work. At that time the two chief tools were Walter Otto, *Herodes* (1913), a book which appeared originally as articles in Pauly-Wissowa-Kroll, *Realency-clopädie der klassischen Altertumswissenschaft,* and the relevant portions of Emil Schuerer, *A History of the Jewish People in the Time of Jesus Christ,* which predates Otto, but the later revisions of which will postdate him. There appeared in 1960 a work in Hebrew which has magnificently met the need for a full-scale study—Abraham Schalit, *Hordos Ha-Melech: Ha-Ish u-Fo'alo* ("Herod the King: The Man and his Work"). This book, scheduled soon to appear in German, ought to be translated into more western tongues, particularly English, for it is by far the best book on Herod yet produced. Admirable as is Stewart Perowne, *The Life and Times of Herod the Great* (1956), it has neither the completeness nor the penetration of Schalit's masterly study. With the appearance of Schalit's book, and in 1960 the publication of Volume I of Otto Michel and Otto Bauernfeind, *De Bello Judaica,* and in 1965 of Louis Feldman's superb completion of the translation of Josephus *Antiquities* in the Loeb Classical Library, the resources for studying the period have moved far beyond what was available to F. De Saulcy, *Histoire d'Herode Roi des Juifs* (1867), and the French editions of Josephus, *Oeuvres complètes de Flavius Josephe,* completed in 1929. With the appearance of Schalit's book, a new full-scale study is no longer needed. My effort is different, more restricted.

An unsolvable problem for any researcher is how to handle Josephus. The dual accounts of Herod (*The Jewish War* I, 204–673; *Antiquities* XIV, 158–XVII, 192) bristle with contradictions, inconsistencies, and instances of possible tendentiousness. The theory of Richard Laqueur, *Der Jüdische Historiker Flavius Josephus* (1920), that the latter is permeated with an animosity toward Herod not discernible in the former, appears to me, as it did to Ralph Marcus in his volumes of the Loeb Classical Library, to be either misstated or overstated. Yet portions of Josephus are marked by variations in the attitude to Herod, so that the modern scholar, though apprehensive of Laqueur's theory, is faced by the challenge to peer through the pages of Josephus and then to imagine that he is able to arrive either at the truth or at some judicious sense of balance. I sense that I have been helped by H. St. John Thackeray, "Josephus and Hellenism: His Greek Assistants," in *Josephus, the Man and the Historian* (1929). There are on the record judgments of Josephus which convict him either of gross carelessness or, in his partisanship for Rome, of actual fraud, and these judgments are not reckless or inappropriate. Without Josephus we should know virtually nothing; possessing him, we know what is in some instances palpably untrue and in other instances doubtful. No one ever satisfactorily handles these problems in Josephus. I have been greatly assisted by Ben Zion Wacholder, *Nicolaus of Damascus*, an excellent research into Josephus' primary source for the age of Herod, for Wacholder helps one achieve an approach to judiciousness.

Moreover, Dr. Wacholder's critical reading of my manuscript, in the light of his vast and precise knowledge of rabbinic literature, has helped me inordinately. I am grateful, too, to a very old friend, Professor Morton Enslin, who did me the kindness of reading the manuscript and who made welcome suggestions.

Dr. Nelson Glueck, President of the Hebrew Union College-Jewish Institute of Religion, made secretarial help available to me. I express my thanks to Mrs. Rissa Alex and Mrs. Helen Lederer for their gracious assistance. I am especially indebted

to my secretary, Mrs. Miriam November, for her solicitude
and her help, these beyond all call of duty, and also for her
unique skills. A professor writes in moments in between recurrent obligations, and these can obstruct the single-mindedness which an unfolding book requires. Mrs. November supplied much of the single-mindedness.

As to this book, beyond the natural interest I have had as a
professional scholar in the age of Herod, the man Herod has
exercised a great fascination for me. The present volume is a
distillation of my effort to understand the man for myself.
I have dutifully made mention of his building program, but I
have not felt impelled to reproduce this data in detail, not even
in connection with the Temple at Jerusalem. I have used foot-
notes to clarify some issues that seemed relevant to my immediate purpose; other matters, however, must await another
occasion. My study is expository, but it is also interpretive for
I have tried to see beyond the simple facts. In pursuit of the
latter, I have perhaps moved from the position where the evidence supplies support, and have gone in the direction to
which the evidence points, but does not quite reach.

When the Hellenism of Greece and the Tradition of Judaism
encountered each other, various responses ensued, on various
levels, and in various forms. One such was the quasi-philosophi-
cal mysticism of Philo of Alexandria and a second was Christianity. Herod represents still another response of Judaism to
Hellenism, not in the realm of religion, but in the realm of
politics, and especially kingship.

Passages Cited

References to Josephus are as
follows:

PART I
The Jewish War I, 19–203
Antiquities XII, 1—XIV, 157

HEROD

Index

INDEX